MW01001003

UNCLEAN HANDS

JAMES ROSENBERG

Copyright © 2021 by James Rosenberg

All rights reserved.

No part of this book may be reproduced in any form or by any electronic or mechanical means, including information storage and retrieval systems, without written permission from the author.

This book is dedicated to those who work with passion to right injustices and inequities everywhere.

CHAPTER ONE

THE LANKY MAN, clad only in black jockey shorts, squinted at the sun squeezing through the bent metal blinds he neglected to adjust before falling into bed the previous night. The sheets, unchanged for weeks, reeked of sweat and lay strewn at the foot of the bed.

Rick Waterston scratched at his face and the first conscious image to enter his mind was of a firm glass, two hefty cubes of ice and a healthy dose of whiskey. *How ironic,* he thought, *two years since my last drink and still it's the first thing that comes into my head each morning.*

The news, on all night, blurted out from the flat screen not yet mounted to the wall.

The effort of getting to a seated position made him want to drop his head back onto the pillow. He dragged his heavy legs over the edge of the bed. Small flecks fell into the air as his hands swiped at his eyes. His head bobbed from weariness, and despite the lack of brain activity, his schedule for the day popped into his head. It didn't take much energy to remember his one appointment today—an eleven o'clock court hearing, where he would present his motion to withdraw as counsel.

Waterston raked off his stubbly growth in the shower and pulled a suit out of his closet after patting his body dry. *At least I still own some stylish threads,* he thought, as he ran a hand over the delicate fabric.

"Thank you, Wilson, O'Malley and Sanders for the fine memories and the expensive wardrobe," he mumbled as he yanked up his pants. He made short work of tying his red tie allowing the front tip to rest on his belt buckle, exactly how his dad had taught him, and exactly how he had worn it at his dad's funeral when he was thirteen.

His wavy, brown hair, combed straight back, glistened with moisture from his shower. A quick inspection of his hairline revealed it hadn't receded in the past day. He pointed double gun barrels at the mirror amazed he still could present the cocky guy image, despite the pangs of regret and doubt swirling in his gut.

Rick pulled on his suit jacket and grabbed his keys ready to trek to what passed for his office energized with the daily hope that new clients and additional work would appear in his waiting room. He pushed away the nagging fear that, like most days, when he returned in the evening, his future prospects would remain the same.

The latest iPhone lay on the table next to his bed, always the last item he gathered before his exit from the apartment. Three text alerts registered on the screen. "Damn, this can only be . . . ," he whispered, while unlocking the device.

His head nodded as he read them with his lips squeezed together. 12:30 a.m., marked the time the first arrived. *"Are you up?"*

Ten minutes later came the next one. *"We need to talk."*

The third showed up at 2:10 a.m., causing him to think, *I*

was awake when you texted. I'm real sorry I didn't see it. His inward sarcasm made him grin.

The text read, "*She's having a hard time. I need some assistance. Can you help? Will you? By the way, you still owe me for the last three months.*"

He placed the phone in his suit pocket. "Crap, Molly. Every night, you send me another missive to ruin my morning," he said, closing the door of his unit behind him.

CHAPTER TWO

JERRY HAWKINS SAT across the small, wooden dinette from his wife who stared at him without a shred of facial movement. He possessed no idea what might be pinging around in her head, but didn't put much effort into figuring out her thoughts either.

She looked nice though. Still trim, with brown hair highlighting her blue eyes. She sported a tank top and shorts which showed a lot of leg. He liked that other men always turned their heads to catch a second glimpse of her.

He still loved her. Not for the sex, which happened with scheduled spontaneity the third Friday of each month. It wasn't her sense of humor, because she didn't have one and on the off chance she found something funny, her laugh echoed off the walls like a donkey's bray. Her family made his stomach churn— she was the only one among them who wasn't an abhorrent human being.

Rather, the bond keeping them together was their consensus on most important subjects–politics, money management and that he understood the ways of the world to a deeper degree than she and thus was in a superior position to make the major decisions in their lives.

Brown spots littered the small parcel of grass outside of their kitchen. Two wooden Adirondack chairs purchased at a garage sale sat in the middle of the small lot. A scattering of beer cans surrounded them.

They shoveled spoonful after spoonful of oatmeal into their mouths, having uttered less than ten sentences between them since sitting in the warped, metal chairs. The brand-new, too-large, television projected an image of a police car with flashing lights as the news anchor droned on about a series of petty thefts hitting the local commercial area.

Jerry didn't need much conversing. In fact, most of the time when his wife spoke her voice messed with the thoughts in his head. Every time she began to speak, he blinked rapidly, attempting to focus on her words, but would inevitably lower his head and return his attention to his cereal. He demanded near silence when they ate, no longer needing to yell at her when her rambling interrupted his solitude, confident she understood her babbling was unnecessary.

She stared at him as he lapped up the last morsels. He readied for her to spout about something he didn't want to discuss, so he grabbed his bowl to take it to the sink.

Before he stood, she said, with no emotion in her voice, "Anything planned for today?"

He placed his dish back on the table and took in a huge gulp of air. "Darling, I'm not sure what I will be doing, but don't you fret, my day will be productive."

Emily wiped her hands on a towel laying on the Formica counter. She glanced in the direction of her husband, but not quite into his eyes and waited a moment before replying, "Honey. I think your day will be so much more than you think it might be. It will be life changing."

Jerry rolled his eyes towards the ceiling. His wife's optimism often clashed with the reality of their lives.

The neck of his white t-shirt extended when he grabbed it. He snatched the bowl again and attempted to stand.

Emily reached across the table and put a firm hand on his arm. She cocked her head to the side. "What about the computer programming company?"

He pulled away. "What about it?"

She frowned, and he realized their conversation would extend further. "You promised you would give those people a call and sign up for an interview," she said.

"I don't remember saying that. I think I said, 'I would consider it,' which is, what I've done."

"And . . . . ?"

"It's not for me. Too much geeky technology. Do I seem like a programmer to you?"

"I don't know. You seem like someone who's not holding up his end of our bargain. We need the money and you promised you would be bringing more to the table by now."

"Did I?" Jerry flashed a smile, which melted into a frown. "We've discussed this. We're doing fine. Look at everything we got." He reached out with both hands. "You're familiar with my plan."

She stepped forward and allowed him to put his arms around her, her faint scent of dish soap rising into his nostrils. He squeezed her because she was less likely to talk when cocooned. After a few moments, he released his hold.

"I'm leaving to do some shopping," he announced.

"Fine. Don't forget we need some other things for the house.

He looked at the three empty boxes by the back door and winked at her. "I know exactly what you want."

"How long will you be out?"

"At least a few hours."

"Good. That'll give me some free time." She said, almost under her breath.

He sidestepped his wife and grabbed his lucky windbreaker, throwing it over his shoulder as he yanked the handle to the back door, which closed with a dull thud. He gazed up to the sky and heaved a huge, cleansing sigh.

CHAPTER THREE

"SIT UP STRAIGHT, son, you're slouching."

Morgan Askew looked up at his mother and raised his eyebrows. He had little interest in his posture while relaxing on the couch. *I'm twenty seven. I can sit any way I want.*

His mom's voice sent his thoughts back to the series of detentions and poor grades in High School. Her scoffing sounds triggered his recollection of his two semesters at Lakehurst Community College.

He pushed the series of failing grades out of his head, but images of his drug and alcohol dominated life after college flooded his mind. He shook his head, like he had learned to in AA classes, to clear his thoughts.

He took in his mom's squat frame and chuckled.

During the months after he dropped out, when he had loads of unscheduled free time, he hung out with a delinquent high school buddy, who espoused the brilliant idea to spend an afternoon throwing rocks at the windows at the rundown factory down by the river. Monica Askew didn't shame her son when the cops came to the house. She paid his fine and restitution, informing him he could reimburse her when there was something in his bank account.

Taking care of him was her responsibility, so she has cooked dinner for him every night since, including the two years when he didn't have any job. He still hasn't paid back the money for the windows.

Morgan adjusted his six-foot-two-inch body to square his shoulders and align his spine. He flashed a smile. At least she cared more about him than the disheveled mutt she brought into the house last year. He regretted how often he failed to meet her expectations, but believed, despite his prior poor decisions, she loved him. For every past disappointment, she responded with over-compensating bursts of support.

"How's your day looking, sweetie?" Monica asked while tossing some dishes in the dishwasher.

"The same as every other." Morgan took another bite of his cereal. "Got a huge shipment of laundry detergent coming into the store."

"Sound's nice," she responded without thought.

Morgan pushed away from the table and walked over to her give her a kiss. She blushed when he commented about how attractive she was.

Her cajoling had made him consider AA meetings, and he now respected her judgment despite sometimes resenting her intrusiveness. He was in a better place living under her roof and complying with her rules than having his own apartment, following his instincts. Plus, she didn't charge him any rent, so he had a few dollars saved.

The job at B & D wasn't glamorous and when he told women about what he did, their eyes glazed over. Being Assistant Store Director didn't cause them fall into his arms, but it was better than telling them he didn't have a job. Working an eight-hour shift, five days a week, helped to keep some of his demons at bay. If asked, he would admit he was almost happy.

A blue, plastic, grocery sack containing a turkey sandwich, celery sticks, three Oreos and a napkin appeared three inches in front of Morgan's eyes.

"Here's something to eat during your shift," she said.

"Dammit mom, I don't like to take my lunch to work." He glared at her and smacked the bag out of her hands. The meal landed on the carpet four feet away. She shuffled backward, her eyes widened.

"I can take care of myself." The shrillness of Morgan's tone and his volume rose with every word. She stood motionless as he lunged towards her. She tensed, but kept her eyes locked with her son's.

Morgan stopped a step away while she turned her head away exposing the left side of her face. Pausing for effect, he leaned over and placed his lips on her cheek. He erupted in laughter while bending over to pick up the grocery bag. "I like when you take care of me. You know how much I need you."

His mom allowed a scarcely audible breath to escape and let him hug her. She grimaced when he pulled away. "I love you, son. Have an amazing day at work."

Morgan grabbed his coat and headed towards the door. He smiled, confident his mom would always adore him.

CHAPTER FOUR

RICK WATERSTON SAT ALONE in the first row of seats in the spectator section of the courtroom. The only other person present was a short, overweight, middle-aged man who threw fleeting glances in his direction. Despite a lack of coverage on top of the man's head, a ponytail draped down his neck and gyrated like a pendulum each time he moved.

Entranced with the swinging braid, Rick remained somewhat amused at the circumstances which had brought them into court.

The diminutive man, at least for the moment, was Rick's client. He had come into his office a year earlier spewing wild accusations against his business partner. They ran a wildlife zoo trading in exotic animals, opening their "reserve" to the public for the chance to pet a baby tiger in exchange for eighty-five bucks. Better yet, those willing to fork over a greater share of their money received the opportunity to party in a room with a wild cat or slimy reptile.

The short guy turned again and raised his hand to chest level and waved.

The inevitability of interacting with his client stared Rick in the face, so he trudged across the room and extended his hand.

"Billy, how're you doing?"

Rick wiped his hand against his pants and grimaced after receiving a mealy handshake.

As they were about to engage in meaningless banter, the door in the front of the courtroom opened and the tipstaff appeared. The time was precisely 9:00 a.m.

"All rise," the woman yelled, standing near the witness box. "The Court of Common Pleas of Mahoney County is now in session. The Honorable Judge Raymond Markum presiding. All those with business before this tribunal may proceed."

The Judge, stocky with a full head of dark hair with hints of gray at the edges, strode in from the front of the courtroom with his black robe askew and walked up the three steps to his perch above the proceedings while carrying a single manila folder. He sat in his high-backed chair and muttered, "You can sit." He waved his right hand in the air without looking up.

Judge Markum raised his eyes to his almost empty courtroom.

"Apparently, most lawyers were able to resolve their motions without the court's involvement. Which leaves you, Mr. Waterston. Welcome."

He leaned over to his tipstaff demanding a cup of coffee while Rick placed his papers on the lectern.

After a few moments of additional private discussion about getting muffins, the judge turned his head. "Go ahead Mr. Waterston, please."

"Your Honor, this is my motion to withdraw as counsel for Mr. Blevins. I represent him in a series of lawsuits against his business partner. He's trying to regain control of the company and filed a lawsuit claiming breach of contract. His partner filed suit against him for tortious interference. I'm seeking an injunction on behalf of Mr. Blevins and he's also pursuing a federal court claim."

"Your hands are full, Mr. Waterston, what's the problem? Is Mr. Blevins stiffing you?"

Rick shuffled his feet. "No, sir, Mr. Blevins always settles my bills timely."

The judge cocked his head up to the ceiling and then back at Rick. "So you're getting paid. There's got to be some basis for your motion. Why do you need to withdraw?"

"We have some issues with communication," Rick said with a bit of a stammer. He paused and turned to his client. "We don't view the world the same way and this interferes with me representing him to the best of my capabilities."

The judge stared down with bemusement. "I'm not sure what you're saying, but so far I haven't heard any legitimate reason to let you withdraw."

At counsel table three feet behind him, Billy Blevins stood and halfway raised his hand. "Mr. Judge, I think I can explain some of what my attorney is trying to say."

"Go ahead, I think I will find your explanation rather elucidating."

Blevins moved next to Rick and placed a stubby hand on his back. He was at least six inches shorter and tilted his head up at him as he spoke.

"The problem is, we get along really well. He's a talented attorney and he's winning all the cases he's handling for me. I love talking with him and I'm confident he'll obtain the best results possible for me."

"So, what's the issue?"

"I'm getting there." Blevins removed his arm and placed it on the lectern.

Rick rolled his eyes.

"Unfortunately, the last time we were together, I told Rick I thought I was in love with him."

The judge held up his hand and Blevins stopped talking. "You told him you loved him. What was his response?"

"Mr. Waterston made clear he did not share the same feelings."

The judge leaned back in his high leather seat with his hands behind his head, gazing at the cracks running along the ceiling of his courtroom. After pondering the situation, he returned to an upright position, directing his gaze at Rick. "Did you give any indication you shared your client's feelings?"

Rick let out a deliberate huff of air. "No, Your Honor, I did not."

"Did you do anything to suggest to him at any time you might want a different type of relationship?"

"No." He let the word drag out a little too long, and he knew it sounded a bit too defensive.

"Counsel, was there any intimate physical contact between you and your client?"

He shook his head. "Of course not."

Judge Markum scanned his papers, attempting to cover any looming snicker.

Rick had appeared before him many times in the past three years since opening his own practice. Markum was the only sitting judge in their small county forcing all lawyers to try to figure out a way not to offend him. All civil and criminal matters came before him. Indifferent facial expressions hid the deep well of feelings Markum held for many of the attorneys and litigants. Rick had always maintained a professional demeanor, but still had managed to irk the judge. Having him sweat a little might make him act with a bit more humility the next time he appeared in his courtroom.

Markum turned his attention back to Rick.

"You appear to maintain a positive working relationship. Nobody's stepped over any lines. Mr. Blevins, do you want to hire a different attorney?"

"No, sir, Mr. Waterston is a fantastic lawyer. I'm sorry I made him uncomfortable. I won't act like that again.

"Counselor, what are your thoughts?"

Images of his desolate office and infrequent calendar appointments popped into Rick's head. It's not as if he was swimming in clients, and this one paid his bills. More so, the tiger litigation was a respite from the red car/blue car cases he typically handled. Plus, the thought of playing with exotic cats was alluring.

"Your Honor," Rick began, "Mr. Blevins understands I am his lawyer which will be the only relationship we will ever have. He also knows if he attempts to cross the line again, I will renew my motion to withdraw as counsel and I suspect the court will grant it."

"You assume correctly," Markum interjected.

"If Mr. Blevins affirmatively agrees my only role is acting as his attorney, I will be happy to represent him and use my legal skills to the best of my abilities to assist him."

"Mr. Blevins, do you understand the parameters of Mr. Waterston's relationship with you?"

"I do."

"Glad you see the big picture. I will deny counsel's motion with the understanding he can present it again if circumstances change. Is there anything else I can assist you with, gentlemen?"

"No," both men said at the same time.

They turned to shake hands and Rick said, "Let's meet next week to discuss strategy. Get in touch with Audrey and she will set something up."

They parted to leave out the back of the courtroom.

As Rick reached the hallway, his phone buzzed. He smiled seeing the name on the caller ID.

"Arnie McBride. Why do you grace me with a call?"

"Rickie boy. We haven't talked for a long time," came the raspy voice on the other end. "I wanted to work something through with you. Can you get lunch?"

Rick glanced at the time. "Sure. How about we talk at Tusk's? I'm right across the street. I can be there in five minutes."

"Perfect. I will meet you there."

Rick placed his cell phone back in the pocket of his suit. He hadn't talked to his former best friend for months. He hoped this would go better than the last time they had seen each other.

CHAPTER FIVE

THE STEADY DIN of the few patrons in the soon-to-be crowded restaurant hovered in the air. The thin woman with ultra-sheened, blonde hair and a form fitting white blouse, led Rick to a booth at the back of the eating area. As they walked past the bar, he snuck a wistful glance at the people sipping from their rocks glasses.

Alone at the table, he played for a few minutes with the salt shaker before a smack on the shoulder drew his attention to the white-tooth grin of Arnie McBride hovering above him.

McBride slid into the opposite side of the booth and gave Rick a playful whack on the arm with the menu.

"Dude, what's new? It's been a while. Thanks for taking my call."

Rick waved his hand in the air. "I'm glad you called. How's life at WOMS?"

"Give me a minute. Tell me how you're doing. How's being a solo practitioner been treating you?"

Rick wanted to lie and say everything was awesome–how his practice was overflowing with clients, and he was getting along in his personal life. He also realized he could never pull it off because Arnie was one of few people who would call out his BS.

"It's been the same since Molly walked out. I'm on my own personally and professionally. Not like when we roamed the hallways at Wilson, O'Malley and Sanders. I miss those days."

The left side of McBride's mouth curled up. "So long ago. We thought we were so cool when we started at WOMS. It was hard work, but we learned how to blow off steam."

"Come to think about it–that might have been what got me into trouble." Rick raised his eyebrows.

"They railroaded you. Nothing fair about what happened to you."

Rick pursed his lips, remembering how a security guard had perp-walked him out of the swanky suite, not allowing him to say goodbye. Most people avoided his gaze as he slunk away. It felt like the elevator doors took five minutes to open. The whole time his co-workers stared bullets into his back.

The waiter interrupted to take their order. Both requested a sandwich, more concerned with speed than quality.

Rick turned his attention back to his companion. "I try not to think about what happened much. The day they cut me loose, I thought it would be the worst of my life. I'd dedicated years to the firm and without any notice, they booted me out."

Arnie laughed. "They gave you some warning. How many times did the partners talk to you about your drinking?"

Rick nodded. "A few I guess, but I never let my boozing affect my work, and they accepted it. Weekends were rough, and we participated in our share of late night partying after work, but I was at my desk the next day. Every time."

"You were a competent lawyer. The firm lost an asset."

"Thanks, man. Unlike my other buddies, you supported me."

A few minutes later their food arrived. They dove in. As Rick took another bite, he recognized a hint of forlorn in his friend's eyes. "How are things going for you?"

Arnie bit his lower lip. "Funny you should ask. It's why I wanted to talk."

Rick directed his attention squarely on Arnie. "Go ahead."

"Let me tell you–I've been with the firm nine years. We started together and I've lasted four years since you left. I'm working like a dog every day. My billings are ridiculous. They're making boatloads off of me."

"So what's the problem?"

"You remember Spencer and Crotec?"

"Of course. Three years ahead of us. Joined at the hip. Thought their shit didn't stink. A couple of douche bags. I never trusted them–always more concerned about moving up than being part of a team."

"Your memory is perfect. About three years ago after an unrelenting campaign of ass kissing the partners and undermining the associates, they made partner early. A year later, while continuing to destroy the careers of those in their path, they took over as co-managing directors of the firm."

Rick leaned forward in his chair. "Not surprising. So how are they handling being in charge?"

"They suck. Everybody is running scared. People are billing more hours, yet bonuses shrunk this year. I keep my head down and service my clients."

"Sounds noble," Rick said with a note of sarcasm.

"It's not. I'm trying to protect my hide, but it's not working. Those two ass clowns gave me my review last week. They should've made me a partner last time, but they put me off with promises for this year. I didn't complain, at least not to them, and given my billables and productivity, they should hand me the keys to the partners' restroom."

"Is there really such a place?"

"No, but not the point. Instead of becoming a partner, Frick and Frack removed me from the partnership track. I can stay as an associate, but with no chance of sharing in the profits. Bastards."

Rick shook his head. "Damn, that sucks. At least they had an excuse when they got rid of me. You're much better at keeping your partying under wraps. It's all a pretense not offering you partnership. They don't want to split the pie any more than necessary. What are you planning to do?"

Arnie examined his hands and rubbed his fingers together. "I'm not sure. This hit me like a load of bricks. I spent the weekend feeling bad for myself, but now I'm trying to develop an action plan. I can't stay at the firm. No way. If they don't think I'm skilled enough to be their partner, screw them. It's why I got a hold of you. I'm putting out feelers to find out if anybody is hiring. I don't want to put you on the spot, but can you tell me of anyone looking for an experienced litigator?"

Rick pulled back in his seat and placed his hands in his lap. He sighed. "I wish I could. Openings at most firms don't exist. It's tight everywhere, so not a lot of jobs are available. The kids graduating from law school are having no luck. My firm? I'm lucky I can keep paying my secretary."

"I understand, man." Arnie shook his head. "I'm talking to as many people as I can. No pressure, but let me know if you find out about any open positions. I'm still getting a paycheck, so I'm not handing in my resignation until I get something on the other end. There's no way they get twenty-four-hundred hours out of me like last year. I'm putting in enough time to keep up with my cases, but nothing extra."

The waiter approached with the bill. Arnie grabbed it before Rick had a chance to protest. He handed over a credit card. Arnie smirked and pointed. "Firm account. I'm billing our meeting to 'client development.'"

Rick chuckled at the irony. "Fine by me. Thanks for the meal. Let's make sure we keep in touch and I will let you know if I hear anything."

Arnie rose from the booth and smacked Rick on the shoulder. "I love hanging with you. I'll call you." He walked away leaving Rick alone, trying to figure out how bad things were for Arnie at his old firm.

CHAPTER SIX

EMILY HAWKINS CLOSED the front door of the house and threw the mail on the small wooden table. Nothing in her cursory review of the five items grabbed her attention. The electric bill would join the others in the unpaid pile.

She sighed.

Her vision of how her life would play out did not line up with the reality of her marriage with Jerry. Her thoughts often drifted to changes she would impose if only he could alter his view of what they could accomplish. Unfortunately, he didn't have enough imagination to dream of interesting friends or exotic travels, or of new ways to satisfy his wife.

The dishes in the sink and the food remaining on the counter from lunch grabbed her attention. She needed to straighten up before Jerry returned from shopping or risk another prolonged lecture on their division of labor The drudgery of the tasks she needed to complete before his return overwhelmed any lingering enjoyment from the past few hours.

She grabbed a toothpick from the drawer and began digging it into the crevices around the warped, wooden cabinets and drawers to wedge out any accumulated grime. An immaculate kitchen was beyond hope, but each time she nabbed a small hunk of grease it provided her with a modicum of satisfaction. She pushed any thoughts of Jerry taking her for a lavish meal at a fancy restaurant out of her head, latching onto each victory achieved with the toothpick.

She got off her knees and thought about fixing dinner, but realized she needed Jerry to return from shopping before she made any decisions because the fridge was nearly empty.

With her hands on her hips, she sauntered over to the refrigerator. The dirt sports on the shelves and produce bin could stand a good wiping down. The ancient white appliance towered above her 5′ 1″ frame, but she remained undaunted. She grabbed the rag on the counter and reached under the sink to find the new bottle of Spic-and-Span purchased two days earlier at the dollar store.

The front doorbell buzzed as she was about to spray some solution on the shelf. She shook her head, wiped her hands on a paper towel and headed down the small hallway.

Through the peephole she spied a muscular cop with his hat in his hands. His face bore no expression. The door squeaked as she yanked it open and pushed the screen door away.

"Hello, officer," she said in a pleasant tone.

"Ma'am, Peter Mitinger from the seventh avenue station," he said with a raspy voice. "Are you the wife of Jerry Hawkins?"

"I am." Emily rubbed her hands together.

The officer looked at his feet. "Sometimes we have to inform people of difficult news. I guess this is one of those times." He paused for a moment. "I'm sorry to report your husband has died."

Emily's hand involuntarily rose to cover her lips. She tried to respond, but nothing came out of her mouth.

He continued, "He was in the parking lot of the B & D store. The paramedics came, but weren't able to revive him."

Emily took a deep breath. Her entire body quivered. "Was it a heart attack?"

"No, ma'am."

"Oh my god, what the hell happened?"

The officer swiped at his brow. "We're not sure, but we arrested an assistant manager at the store and are beginning a murder investigation."

The suddenness of receiving this information made her stomach ache. The bitterness of bile rose in her throat, leaving her needing to vomit. She dropped to her knees and placed her head on the ground.

CHAPTER SEVEN

THE LAWN WAS SMALL, but maintained with extreme care. The hue of the shutters offered a perfect contrast to the trim colors of the windows. Two peach trees out front were budding, offering a promise of renewal. They cast long shadows on the grass as the early evening sun dropped in the sky.

Rick was not feeling the seasonal vibe and stared at Molly's house in a detached wonderment. The house morphed in his imagination to the tiny bungalow they lived in after getting married. It was small, but it was their home, until she threw him to the curb. "Get your damn drinking under control," Molly had said, pushing their small daughter back into the house as Rick left.

Ultimately, he found an apartment while Molly moved into the smaller house in which she now lived. How did she make everything look so easy? She moved in here a year ago and somehow it's like she'd been overseeing the maintenance of her place for years. Mentally he compared it to his apartment. He had done little to make his place more livable, or in any way inviting. He didn't care much because most visitors were after hours hook-ups where his décor choices weren't a significant issue.

An hour earlier, Rick had texted Molly *"I'm free to talk. Can you?"*

She responded within seconds, *"Yes, but you're going to have to come here."* Surprising given he almost never got invited in the house, usually only standing on the stoop waiting to pick up Sammie for his scheduled visitation. He couldn't remember the last time she allowed him past the front door, but this time Molly grabbed his arm and led him to the sofa in the living room.

"Thanks for getting back to me," she began without giving Rick a chance to acclimate. He sensed an anxious pitch to her tone.

"No problem. Your texts last night disturbed me."

She paced for a moment before plopping into the oversized reading chair across from the couch. "Sorry. Rough night. Not for you to worry."

His eyes narrowed and he squeezed his knees together. "She's our kid. Of course, I'm worried. Where is she?"

"My mom's watching her. She's staying for dinner so you'll miss her."

Again, no surprise. He presumed she called her mom to take Sammie once he told her he was coming over. Perhaps not manipulative, but an attempt to keep their conversation short and focused.

"Tell me what's going on," he said. The aroma of barley soup wafted in from the kitchen.

Molly grabbed a pillow and placed it on her lap while she twisted to sit on her feet. She wore no makeup, making no attempt to hide the small, purplish bags underneath her eyes. Despite this, she retained the girl next store aura that Rick had responded to when they first met.

"She's not right. Her mood changes come on without warning. Sometimes her kindergarten teacher calls me to pick her up. She's not acting right at school, and they can't settle her down. Last night she, once again, couldn't get herself under control and couldn't fall asleep. I'm a mess."

Rick felt an odd detachment. This was his daughter, and he cared, but he wasn't around and Molly was in charge, for the most part. There'd been similar conversations in the past few weeks over the phone, but each time he thought she was just venting and didn't want his input.

"What can I do?"

She shrugged. "It's nobody's fault—you're not in her life much. I mean, it's kind of what I want and you don't fight it much."

Shards of nagging anxiety crawled up Rick's spine, and the familiar urge to withdraw crept into his brain. "Do we need to go over this again? I want to be involved. I'm trying to figure out our situation. Can we talk about her and leave *us* out of the conversation?"

Molly bit her lower lip and waited an extra moment before responding. "Yes, you're right. I'm at a loss for what to do."

Rick leaned forward. "You're much closer to what's happening. I'm trying to throw out some ideas, but do you think you should talk to her pediatrician?"

"Of course. She's scheduled to see her at the end of the week."

He took in a long breath. "When? Should I come?"

"It's during the day. I figured you would be too busy."

"You didn't check with me. I can rearrange."

"No, I got it covered."

He smacked both of his legs with his hands. "Dammit, Mol. Don't you think we should talk before you start making these decisions?"

"If I thought you would put some effort into helping I would've called you."

Rick stood. "Apparently you don't need my input. That's been clear for a long time."

Molly didn't respond and he assumed she wanted him to lose his temper. He took a deep breath. "I'm here for her. I would love to work together on this to find the best solution. Call me if you want my help."

Rick walked out the room towards the front door and Molly didn't say a word to try to stop him.

CHAPTER EIGHT

Monica Askew shook her head, attempting to regain her equilibrium. The jarring ring of her cell phone had interrupted a well-deserved nap. The cobwebs in her head interfered with her comprehension of the monotone voice on the other end.

"Ma'am, this is the Mahoney County jail. Will you accept a call from a Mr. Morgan Askew?" The operator's emphasis on the second syllable of her last name caused Monica to focus on the pronunciation of the name, rather than the substance of the question.

"Morgan Askew," she said, enunciating the surname the proper way. "Yes, he's my son."

"Ma'am, may I repeat? This is the Mahoney County jail, will you accept a phone call from Mr. Askew?" She pronounced the name without error.

"Oh my, of course, yes." Monica, now awake, rose to pace around her couch. She waited for a beep and yelled, "Morgan. Morgan. Are you alright?"

A slight hissing and some distortion pinged in her ear, but

her son responded. "Mom, yes, I'm okay. I'm in the County lockup. Can you get me out?"

"Of course. Please, tell me what to do." Monica's voice screeched on the last part of the sentence. She continued without pause, "Oh my god, why are you in jail? Did you pilfer something? You know I taught you better."

"Mom, stop. I didn't steal anything."

"So why in the Lord's name are you locked up? I'm so worried." Monica plopped on the polyester couch and fanned herself with a magazine.

"It all happened so fast. I shouldn't talk about this with you, but I need you to get me out of here."

The desperation in her son's voice rang in her ears. She leaned back and collapsed into the cushions. "Honey, I have no idea what to do. Should I find some money to bail you out?"

Askew sighed. "There's a preliminary hearing in a few days. I'm not sure what I should do. I need help."

"I still don't understand. Why are you in jail?"

Morgan paused and the silence ran up Monica's spine. The chills spreading across her back made her shudder.

"Something bad happened. A man died, and they're charging me with murder."

She swallowed the undeniable urge to retch and sucked in a breath to regain a bit of control. "Oh my Lord. Don't you worry. I'll figure this out. I love you son."

"You, too, mom."

The line clicked. She imagined an overbearing guard leading him back to a grungy cell. She pulled the browser up on her phone hoping a picture of the city's best lawyer would pop up because she didn't have any idea where she should begin.

CHAPTER NINE

THREE DAYS after the death of her husband, Emily Hawkins stood on a patch of manicured grass, shaking her head at his freshly dug grave.

The ceremony was short and to the point. The minister, who Jerry never met, as he hadn't been to church for twenty years, made pleasant sounding, generalized comments about the deceased, which could've applied to almost anyone.

Long estranged from most of their family, only her sister and his uncle attended the funeral. They threw dirt on his coffin, and then hugged Emily, before making their departures.

Once sure she was alone, she smirked at the hole in the ground. "You sure must've done something stupid," she said kicking a couple of stones into the gap. "This wasn't our plan. How did you get yourself killed? I promise you I will find out. Someone's going to pay for what they did to you and where it's left me."

The flowers she held in her hand fell to the ground as she turned to walk away from his plot. She closed her eyes, trying to picture what took place in the parking lot of B & D, but she couldn't imagine the scene. What happened to him? Why was someone from the store charged with murder? The need to answer these questions replaced the feeling of helplessness which had taken over since the cop knocked on her door.

She didn't know where to turn for help, but the outlines of a plan to give her answers about her husband's untimely death began to form as she walked through the mowed grass away from his final resting place. She didn't glance back as she realized where she would go first.

CHAPTER TEN

STILL DRESSED in the dark pants suit she wore to the funeral, Emily pulled into the B & D parking lot. The late model pickup truck in the space next to hers towered over her sputtering sedan. She walked towards the cement outer wall typical of many big box retailers. Adorned on the façade was the name of the store in commanding bold letters and in script writing below, the company's tagline: "Your Products . . . at *Amazing Prices*."

The lot teemed with customers headed to the sliding glass doors at the entrance while others pushed over-sized shopping carts filled with bags of purchased wares back to their cars. Emily shopped here often as it was one of three places in their small town which sold groceries Its competitive advantage was that it also offered the convenience of selling clothes, outdoor supplies, and other items they needed.

The thought of her husband dying, or rather, someone killing him, in this location filled her head. She examined the landmarks differently than the other times she had been here, trying to picture where and how he came to his demise. The painted hash-lines of the crosswalk, the flimsy metal frames of the cart corral and even the towering light standards were always present, but somehow they now took on a different significance as Emily wondered if any, in some small way, contributed to her husband's death.

In the time since Jerry died, the store hadn't contacted her. The police would not give her any details, only putting her off by informing her she had to wait until they completed their report. The local coroner had, at least, contacted her, but failed to provide her with any semblance of a story of what had happened. He told her he called in the medical examiner from the largest county in the state because, "Under the circumstances, this was beyond the capacity of his office."

She stood in the parking lot with her fist clenched, realizing she had almost no information about how or why someone killed her husband. Emily swiped at her eyes and dabbed her nose with a semi-used tissue, gathering her resolve to walk into the store. Unsure of what she wanted to accomplish, she reminded herself to be assertive.

The customer service desk sat to the right of the entrance doors, and she waited in the queue of three customers for the two women offering assistance. It took a couple of minutes before the shorter, older employee waved her to approach.

"May I help you?" the woman asked.

She nodded while looking at the floor. "My name is Emily Hawkins. My husband died here a few days ago. I would like to talk to somebody."

The service clerk creased her forehead. "Of course, honey. Let me find Mr. Oliver. He's the Store Director." She picked up the phone and held up one finger.

Five minutes later, a middle-aged, African-American man, wearing glasses and sporting a deep baritone approached. He stood eight inches taller than her and carried himself like a former athlete. "Mrs. Hawkins, my name is Wayne Oliver. I'm the Store Director. We are so sorry for your loss." He grasped Emily's right hand with both of his. "Can we talk?"

She followed him to a small office near to the registers. "It's not much, but I don't spend a lot of time in here," He grabbed a chair and placed it in front of his desk. He sat on the other side and clasped his hands.

Locking eyes with her, he said, "Please Ms. Hawkins, tell me what I can do for you."

Emily dropped her eyes and pondered how to ask why someone killed her husband in this store. Finally, she said, "Mr. Oliver, nobody will tell me what happened to my husband. I hope you would help me figure out how he died here."

"Yes, ma'am. I agree you're entitled to find out how he came to pass away."

Emily interrupted. "Sir, not to be rude, but he didn't pass away. He was murdered."

Oliver shook his head and bit his lip. "I don't want to quibble with you, Ms. Hawkins, but 'murdered' is such a strong word for what occurred."

"Well, why don't you tell me what happened, and then we can decide what to call it?"

"I want to give you as much information as possible. The problem is I was on my day off, so I have no direct knowledge of the circumstances of his demise."

Oliver's avoidance of providing her with any details was now beginning to irk Emily, who sat forward in her chair. "I understand you didn't witness what happened, but I assume as Store Director–that's what you called yourself, isn't it?–you would try to figure out how someone is killed on your property."

"Of course. Our corporate office is in the midst of conducting a thorough investigation. They are speaking with everyone present. I'm not involved. It's out of my hands." He turned his palms up.

"Is there any video of what happened?"

Oliver paused, appearing to formulate his words with care before responding. "My understanding is some exists."

"What's on it?"

"Oh, Ms. Hawkins, I'm not at liberty to provide those details."

Emily's eyes narrowed, and she forced herself to slow down. "I would like to watch the video. Please show it to me."

"I wish I could, but I can't."

"Why not?" Her voice almost cracked.

"I'm under instructions not to allow anyone to view it. I made a copy and sent it over to corporate."

"Who told you not to let me watch the video?"

"Our legal department."

"Are you kidding? So far you haven't told me anything. You won't tell me what happened, who was involved or what's on the video."

Oliver's face lost all expression. "Ms. Hawkins, I assume you can appreciate this is a delicate situation. I've been given certain instructions to not talk about this until our investigation is complete. You can understand, can't you?"

Emily's cheeks flushed crimson and her jaw clenched. "No, I don't understand this at all. I have no idea what happened to my husband or why, but I'm getting much more suspicious every moment I'm with you. Is there anything you want to tell me?"

"One detail about the evening was odd and I think triggered everything. I shouldn't tell you this," he said as he leaned forward, "but it all started right after your husband was caught shoplifting."

Emily's heart thumped in her chest. "You act like this is a

joke. Jerry was killed on your property and now you accuse him of stealing. You're not being forthcoming with me, Mr. Oliver. Something's odd about how you're treating me and I'm going to figure out why." Emily stood and extended her hand. "The next person you will hear from is my lawyer. Good day."

She felt the sweat on Oliver's hand when they shook. "*At least he doesn't know I've never spoken with any attorneys.*" she thought. "*All I have to do is find myself the right one.*"

She walked out of the store with her head held high and the contours of a plan solidifying.

CHAPTER ELEVEN

B & D sat in the commercial area of town. Fast food joints, a couple of diners, hardware stores and strip malls lined the roads. A few small, almost dilapidated, office buildings squeezed in between the retail locations, not garnering much attention from the people who came here to shop.

The small car pulled out of the parking lot. Emily Hawkins gripped the steering wheel, cursing Wayne Oliver's unwillingness to provide any substantive information.

She wasn't sure where she should drive or how to find an attorney, but knew she wanted to find someone who would give her some advice and shine on a light on the path to solving the mystery of Jerry's death.

She considered yanking out her phone and googling, "personal injury lawyer," but saw a placard on a small building to her right–"Waterston law: *We're in it for you.*"

"*Maybe god's sending me a sign,*" She thought. She lifted the paddle for her blinker and made the turn into the dusty parking lot.

As she entered the darkly lit office, a tall, woman behind

the desk with a bored expression who forced a smile when she looked up said, "May I help you?"

"Yes, I think I would like to discuss a potential case with a lawyer."

"You've come to the right place. Mr. Waterston is in his office. Let me find out if he's available or would you rather schedule an appointment for another day?"

"I would like to speak with him now, if possible," Emily said as she gazed around the lobby area. A weathered, leather couch with a couple of tiny holes in the legs rested near to the restroom. Legal diplomas in mahogany frames hung on the wall, lending an air of legitimacy to the operation.

"I'll be back in a minute." The woman ducked away towards the hallway.

Emily leaned on the desk and noted how tidy the area was. The only sounds she could hear were the hum of an air conditioning unit jammed in the window and the faint ticking of a grandfather clock in the corner.

Within moments, the woman returned trailed by an angular man in jeans and striped button-down shirt. "This is Rick Waterston," she said, reaching behind to point at her boss. "I'm Audrey, by the way."

Emily grabbed Rick's hand when he offered it, and she appreciated his firm grasp without the mealy handshake some men defaulted to when greeting a woman. His glassy eyes and mussed hair caused her to wonder if he had just woken from a nap.

"I was working on an appellate brief," Rick said, "but I'm glad you showed up. I'd rather have a conversation than focus on the law of restitution. Come, let's go back to my office."

She followed him down the narrow hallway, until he turned into the first doorway. He gestured towards a curved, leather chair while taking a seat behind the wooden desk.

Spreading out his arms, he said, "What brings you here today?"

Emily glanced around not ready to answer. A tear formed at the corner of her eye before she spoke. She pushed her mouth to the side and tried to formulate her words.

Rick handed her a tissue, "Take your time."

"I live not far from here, in Westdale. I come over this way sometimes to shop, but I never noticed your office before. I was driving by and thought you might be able to help me." More tears flowed and Emily dabbed at her eyes. "I'm not making any sense."

Rick's lips arched into a smile. "I'm sure I can assist, but you're going to have to tell me your problem. Take a breath and just say what's bothering you." He reached across the desk and patted her sleeve. "Also, remember everything you tell me–at this meeting, or any other conversation we ever have–is private. The law calls it 'privileged.' I can't tell anyone anything you tell me because it's confidential."

"Privileged." Emily repeated. "I like the sound of that." She smiled.

The computer on Rick's desk emitted a slight electronic hum and for a moment was the only noise in the room.

Emily nodded. "A few nights ago, my husband died. Well, from what I understand, he was killed. The police won't tell me what happened. I'm trying to figure out how he died."

Rick leaned forward. "Start at the beginning."

She twisted the tissue between her fingers. "He said he was going shopping, and he went to the B & D. He was late, but I wasn't worried. Then the cop showed up and tells me he had been killed. I went to talk to the manager, but all he did was accuse Jerry of being a thief. He died in the parking lot, but I don't know anything more."

"Let me interrupt you and ask you a few questions and tell me if I have this straight. Your husband went shopping?"

"Yes."

"He never came home?"

"Correct."

"He died, or was killed, in the parking lot of the store?"

"I believe so, yes."

"You still don't know why or how he died?"

Emily kept nodding her head as Rick jotted down notes on a legal pad he grabbed from a drawer in his desk.

"You went to the store and the manager told you your husband was a shoplifter?"

"Yes."

"Did he tell you your husband died because they thought he had stolen something?"

"Not in those words, but I suspect it's true because of one more thing I forgot to tell you."

"Which is?"

"One of the other managers is in jail on murder charges."

Rick glanced up with his eyebrows raised. "You left out an important detail."

"Sorry," Emily said, blushing. "It's because I'm not thinking straight."

Rick continued to write notes on his pad. "Take a breath. Did you ask to watch any video at the store?"

"I did, but the manager said I couldn't."

"Interesting." Rick sat back in his chair and put his hands behind his head.

Emily also leaned back and sucked in a gulp of air.

After a few moments of contemplation, Rick assumed his original position. "Here's what I think. You're entitled to find out what happened. I can't decide if we should assert a claim because so many of the facts are unknown. So this is what I propose. Let me do a little digging. I want to review the video and maybe I can scare them into letting us view it without resorting to filing a lawsuit. Once we determine what's on the video and obtain a copy of the police report, we can figure out what to do next."

"I like it. This sucks. My life is upside down. I want to dump this in your lap and let you deal with figuring it out."

"Which is why I'm here. I'll have a letter to B & D tomorrow. With some luck, we'll watch the video next week."

Rick stood to signal their meeting was over.

Emily stared into his eyes and gave a quick grin.

Rick broke eye contact and walked to the other side of the desk to lead her out of the office.

As she got into her car, Emily realized she couldn't wait to see the video and find out what had happened to her husband. She said a little prayer that her new lawyer would be able to get it for them soon.

CHAPTER TWELVE

FOUR DAYS in the dank cell with the subtle smell of stale piss lingering in the air was enough to convince Morgan Askew he was in way over his head. What little control he had previously exercised over his life was now gone.

Dressed in standard prison coveralls, his hands cuffed in front of him and his feet shackled, he shuffled down the hallway, each step causing the heavy chain to clank on the dingy, tile floor of the basement level of the courthouse.

Two armed sheriffs escorted him until they reached the door marked "attorney conference room." "We'll take off the handcuffs if you promise there won't be any problems." The bigger guard leered.

Morgan grunted his assent realizing he was incapable of causing much trouble for the physically imposing guards. Once the shackles were off, the guards gave Morgan a small shove into the conference room. As he composed himself, he spotted two men seated at the long table who chuckled and made no effort to assist him.

The taller man in the impeccable gray suit greeted Morgan

as he rose and moved towards him to direct him to a cheap metal chair.

"I'm Virgil Spencer." He gestured to the squatter gentleman with the thick bush of curly brown hair still seated. "This is my partner, Seb Crotec."

Crotec glanced up, nodded and returned his attention to the stack of documents.

"Thanks for your help. But who are you?" The early morning hour and his unexpected meeting with lawyers clouded his thinking.

Spencer tilted his head at Crotec and then back at Morgan. "We're your attorneys here to represent you in your criminal proceedings."

"I don't have any lawyers as far as I know. What happened?"

"You can thank your mom. From what I understand, after you were arrested she contacted the company and insisted they hire you a lawyer. I guess it's only fair because you were working when this went down. Our firm does the legal work for your employer, so here we are."

"How much trouble am I in?"

"We'll answer your questions—in time." Crotec responded. "Let's talk about your schedule. Your preliminary hearing is in thirty minutes, so let me tell you what will happen. You're about to be taken into court. The purpose today is to decide whether to hold you over for trial. It's not a high standard. Based on my review of the file so far, it may be difficult to convince the judge to dismiss the case right now, but at worst we can find out some information which will help us out in our defense. There will be other opportunities to work on the judge to drop the charges."

Morgan dropped his head. "Damn, this sucks. I'm not sure why they have me behind bars. I didn't do anything."

"I understand your frustration," Crotec continued. "You need to wrap your head around the concept that this will be a long, drawn out process. We will do what we can, but we aren't miracle workers. Let's head over to court."

Crotec walked over to the door and gave it a quick knock. The two guards entered and placed the handcuffs back on Askew. They helped him to his feet and led him out of the room.

Crotec and Spencer gathered their papers and followed their newest client out the door to meet him in the courthouse where he would be taken through the underground passage shackled in chains.

CHAPTER THIRTEEN

AFTER THE BAILIFF called the court to order, Judge Markum took his seat and announced the first case, "*The State v. Morgan Askew*. This is the preliminary hearing to determine if the defendant should be held over for trial. Is the State prepared to proceed?"

"Yes, Your Honor," a voice from the back of the courtroom called out. A young prosecutor with closely trimmed, brown hair and round glasses, moved to the front of the room and placed his folder on the table next to Spencer and Crotec. "Simon Tokles for the State."

"Go ahead, Mr. Tokles. Call your first witness."

"Thank you, Your Honor. The State calls Officer Peter Mitinger."

From the side of the courtroom a uniform police officer approached the witness stand and raised his hand in the air.

The court reporter stood and mirrored the witness by also lifting her right hand. She muttered, "Do you swear to tell the truth, the whole truth and nothing but the truth, so help you god?"

"I do." Mitinger slid into the witness chair.

Tokles waited behind his counsel table. "Officer, please give the court your job history as a police officer."

Mitinger turned his lanky frame towards the judge. "I've been a police officer since graduating from the Academy fifteen years ago. I started as a patrolman in Dexter County in the southern portion of the state. Six years ago, I was hired by Mahoney County. I still patrol the streets."

"On May third, were you summoned to the B & D on Beaver Avenue?"

"Yes. We received a dispatch indicating a Caucasian male in his early thirties was being detained. We proceeded to investigate a possible retail theft. We arrived seven minutes later to the parking lot of the B & D. Four individuals had placed themselves on top of another person. We instructed them to move off the suspect. When they did, the guy didn't respond. We called for an ambulance."

"Please continue, officer. What happened next?"

"My partner began resuscitation protocols. Paramedics arrived less than five minutes later. We allowed them to take over. The man was unconscious lying on the blacktop. They attempted to resuscitate the man, working hard for fifteen minutes, but were unable to detect a heartbeat. While continuing their efforts to revive the man, they got him on a gurney and into the ambulance. Mr. Hawkins was pronounced dead at Memorial General after they arrived."

Tokles moved from behind the table and into the center of the courtroom. "Did you begin an investigation?"

"We did. A man had died on the scene, and we needed to speak with the witnesses to try to determine what happened."

"With whom did you speak?"

"We spoke to all the witnesses, but much of the information we received came from the defendant."

"You're referring to Morgan Askew?"

"Yes, sir. He identified himself as the manager in charge at the time of the incident. He approached me and told me the unconscious man shoplifted from the store. Mr. Askew indicated he witnessed the man stealing and followed him into the parking lot."

Tokles squinted at the witness. "Officer, did you read Mr. Askew his rights?"

Mitinger shook his head. "Not right away. We did not believe Mr. Askew was a suspect in a murder investigation. Like I said, Mr. Askew approached us and voluntarily provided us with the information. Once we believed he might be a suspect, we read him his *Miranda* rights, but he just kept on talking."

Tokles smirked. "What did he tell you?"

The officer paused. "May I refer to my notes?"

"Of course."

Mitinger pulled out his pad and flipped to the proper page. "I was writing this down as he spoke to me." He waved the papers in the air. "The defendant said he followed the gentleman into the parking lot and wanted to recover the stolen items. The deceased was pushing a shopping cart, but was too far away from Mr. Askew, so he yelled to a kid shagging carts to stop him. The deceased shoved the kid away when he got in front of him, so Mr. Askew began to run after him."

"What did he tell you happened next?"

"He said he caught him quick. He jumped on his back to drag the alleged shoplifter to the ground. The man continued to resist so Mr. Askew held him down. Mr. Hawkins struggled, so Mr. Askew received assistance from two other shoppers and the kid he called to assist, who helped restrain the man. They sat on him until we arrived, at which time, as I noted, the man was unresponsive."

"Did Mr. Askew indicate to you whether the man expressed difficulty breathing?"

"He did. He said the man claimed he was having trouble breathing, but according to Mr. Askew, continued to struggle for at least five minutes before stopping."

"Thank you, officer. I have no more questions. Mr. Askew's lawyers now have a chance to question you."

Spencer eased into a standing position and held his yellow pad in front of him. "Officer, Virgil Spencer representing the defendant. Sir, how many witnesses did you interview?"

"Five. Four holding down the deceased and one other person."

"Did all confirm Mr. Hawkins struggled after being detained?"

"Yes."

Spencer asked open-ended questions and didn't lead the witness as he would if this was the trial of his client. Questioning a witness at a preliminary hearing was like being at a deposition–an opportunity to gain information, not the time to try to put words into the witness's mouth.

"Did you verify Mr. Hawkins took product without paying?"

"Yes. I reviewed the video of the incident and it appeared like Mr. Hawkins left some items on the bottom of his cart he had not purchased. I also compared his receipt to the items in his cart and extra items remained in his cart, which did not appear on his receipt."

"Tell me, officer, do you have an understanding as to the State's Retail Theft Act?"

"Yes, I often deal with people accused of violating the statute."

"Does the Act authorize merchants and their employees to stop people suspected of stealing?"

"It does–under certain circumstances."

"So if Mr. Askew had a reasonable belief Mr. Hawkins had stolen, he would be privileged to stop him."

Officer Mitinger shifted in his seat. "Sir, I am familiar with the Retail Theft Act, but wouldn't say I am an expert on every situation which can arise. The Act gives store owners and its employees the right to detain shoplifters, but I wouldn't want to comment on when or under what circumstances they can."

"Let me ask it this way, wouldn't you agree it was reasonable for Mr. Askew to stop a shoplifter if he witnessed the person stealing from the store?"

"I can't agree. Like I said, there's a lot of gray area–He was outside, he forcibly detained Mr. Hawkins, and Mr. Hawkins was killed in the process. Sounds like there may be some issues here." Mitinger offered a weak, somewhat condescending smile which Spencer did not return."

"Sir," Spencer continued, "did the witnesses agree Mr. Hawkins continued to struggle after he was on the ground and was attempting to flee the scene?"

"The witnesses indicated Hawkins struggled for approximately six minutes. He was yelling, but was quiet for many minutes until we arrived. Mr. Askew and the two customers continued to sit on top of Mr. Hawkins. He died at some point before we arrived."

"Thank you, officer, I have no more questions for you."

Officer Mitinger left the stand and before he was out of the witness stand Tokles informed the court the prosecution would call no more witnesses.

Spencer jumped to his feet. "Your honor, on behalf of Mr. Askew, I move to dismiss the charges against him. The prosecution has failed to produce sufficient evidence at this hearing to prove the defendant should be held over for trial. Accordingly, the charges should be dismissed."

Once Spencer completed his argument, Tokles stood again and spoke in calm, measured tones. "Mr. Askew chased the deceased into and through the parking lot of the store before jumping on his back and dragging him to the ground. He became the judge and jury and ordered two shoppers to assist him in keeping Mr. Hawkins pinned to the pavement. Despite Mr. Hawkins screaming he couldn't breathe, Mr. Askew and his deputies continued to use excessive force to detain him. This tragic decision led to his death. More than sufficient evidence exists to hold Mr. Askew over for trial. A jury should decide his criminal culpability."

Judge Markum jotted notes on a yellow pad while occasionally making eye contact with the lawyers. After the courtroom quieted, he said, "I have listened to the evidence presented and the arguments of counsel. I believe the prosecution has presented sufficient evidence that Mr. Askew should be held over for trial on the charge of manslaughter in the second degree. We will set a scheduling order at a later date." Markum banged his gavel and turned to leave the courtroom.

Spencer and Crotec leaned into their client. Crotec spoke in a whisper. "The guards will take you back to your cell. We will work to gather evidence to assist in your defense and will be in contact with you soon."

The sheriff deputies approached from behind and yanked Askew from his chair.

As the courtroom emptied, Morgan Askew shuffled between the armed law enforcement personnel toward the door leading to the holding cells with terror etched on his face.

Monica Askew reached out to touch her son as he passed by her.

CHAPTER FOURTEEN

THE AIR of calm evaporated with the boisterous, "I got the papers you told me to bring." The words reached Rick Waterson while he reviewed a set of interrogatories almost causing him to throw his cup coffee over his shoulder. Billy Blevins' sudden appearance dressed in a purple top and tight-fitting, white, flared pants, would take precedence over whatever Rick was working on—not the first time Billy had shown up without scheduling an appointment. Rick hid any sign of irritation and flashed a smile.

Rick waved Billy into the office who plopped into the leather chair in front of Rick's desk. His head rotated from left to right. "I like what you've done in here. Anything new since the last time?"

Rick shook his head and picked up a small stack of documents next to three brown file folders. "Same old crap that's always here."

With little interest in engaging in more small talk, Rick changed the subject. "I went through the papers we got in discovery from the other side. I want to talk about one in particular." He thumbed through the pile while Billy hummed an off-key rendition of "When the Saints go Marching In." After a minute, Rick pulled out a set of stapled documents, waving them. "What do you think about these contracts?"

"They're a bunch of fakes and forgeries. I don't remember seeing any of them before. These contracts are crap because they ain't real. I wouldn't have signed them." Billy's face turned a dark cherry hue and his voice hit an octave ordinarily reserved for the falsetto portion of his favorite country tunes.

"Are those your signatures on the contracts?"

"They resemble my signature, but I never would have signed these. Did you read them? They suggest he has a claim to my zoos. The bastard's going to steal both of them and all the cats. I would never agree to those terms."

The contracts were part of a document dump Rick had received last week in the discovery responses served by counsel for Billy's partner, Jerry Dale. Billy was correct about one thing–if they were legitimate, he stood to lose his business. Rick shook his head. "These contracts may be one-sided, but they're well-crafted. Why didn't you send them to me when I asked you for everything you had?"

"I sent you all my files. Like I said, I've never seen these before."

"Billy, we'll get to the bottom of this. We're getting close to the end of discovery and now I'm hit with this. Let me review these more closely and figure this out." Rick rubbed his temples and stood.

Billy got to his feet at the same time. "I trust you, man. My life is in your hands."

Rick walked around the desk and Billy moved forward to offer a hug. Rick stepped to the side. "Let's skip that and call it a day."

Billy nodded and strutted out of the office.

Rick picked up the stack of documents and shook his head knowing the hours which lay ahead pouring over every sub-paragraph. This was not the glamorous side of the law, but he recognized the grunt work was a necessary part of saving Billy Blevins' business interests. He melted back into his chair. *At least Billy's good for paying his next bill.*

CHAPTER FIFTEEN

THREE DAYS LATER, Rick paced around his office desk four times before walking into the hallway where he noticed no changes in the five minutes since he last walked out of his office.

His client still hadn't arrived.

Most lawyers waiting for a wayward appointment would read emails, call an attorney on a case or answer some outstanding discovery. Unfortunately, Rick didn't have a huge backlog of work, nor a stack of papers on his desk to address, so while he waited for Emily Hawkins to arrive, pretty much all there was to do, was to wait for her arrival.

After she left his office days earlier, Rick drafted a letter to the company's president, store manager and director of loss prevention demanding a copy of "all video in the store's possession of the incident wherein the husband of his client died as a result of the acts or omissions of the store's employees."

Rick didn't know whether the employees played any role in Jerry's death, but wanted to put a bit of a scare in whoever read the letter hoping they would respond quickly.

He included the typical threats that failing to preserve all the video related to the claim would result in a jury charge informing the jurors the defendant "willfully destroyed relevant evidence and the jurors should presume the evidence, had it been retained, would be damaging to the defendant's case."

Such pressures, far from idle, allowed plaintiffs to review evidence prior to initiating a lawsuit, or at a minimum, made sure a defendant didn't destroy anything potentially relevant. He was rather proud of the forceful, yet not over the top, tone of his threats.

Three days later he received correspondence and a disc from Blaze Rondowsky, the titular head of Theft, Diversion and Loss Prevention for B & D. *Sounds like a bit of a douche*, Rick thought when he took in the title and the name of the person holding it. The letter read, "Pursuant to your request and in compliance with applicable law, enclosed is video of the relevant events you requested."

He shoved the disc into his computer and discovered twenty-four hours of moving images from every conceivable angle in the store. By experimenting with the program which ran the video, Rick discovered the company stationed thirty-six cameras throughout the premises which recorded pictures whenever the camera detected movement.

"This is a boatload of information," he screamed when the program displayed each camera view in a six-by-six grid revealing random shoppers acting like busy ants walking through aisles, or employees working in backrooms.

Watching all the cameras at the same time overloaded his senses making him unable to focus on one angle at a time. Rick figured out how to coax the program to display the images from only one camera which made it easier to interpret the events, but increased the amount of time ten-fold he would need to figure out what happened to Emily's husband.

After trying to find her husband among the hundreds of shoppers in the store, Rick realized it would be easiest to start at the end and work his way backwards. Finding the ambulance in the parking lot was simple and then tracking backwards, he documented Jerry Hawkins' path from the time he parked his car, until his demise. His present understanding of the timeline was far from perfect, pieced together from a variety of camera angles, some of which barely captured the events and none of which contained any audio. He hoped reviewing the images would enhance Emily's ability to interpret Jerry's actions.

After viewing and rewinding the images for hours while jotting notes of the relevant times and cameras, Rick called the owner of a service he utilized for recording depositions and court replay of testimony. Within a day, he received back a new disc of edited video tracking Jerry Hawkins from the moment his car entered the B & D parking lot, until the ambulance pulled out with his lifeless body, futilely transporting him to the hospital.

With the edited version in his possession, Rick couldn't wait to review it with Emily, now confident she had a viable, and perhaps lucrative, lawsuit against B & D.

CHAPTER SIXTEEN

THE CELL WALLS hadn't moved, Morgan Askew was confident, but he wanted a tape measure to check, to make sure they weren't any closer than before. Incarcerated for two weeks while facing a significant amount of time in jail was taking a toll. The coveralls hung on him and his eyes sank back into their sockets. Each night, awake on the filthy mattress hoping sleep would come, he tried to avoid thoughts of the afternoon which led to his arrest, but the muffled screams of the man lying face down on the pavement saying he couldn't breathe prevented him from escaping into unconsciousness.

Boredom permeated his cell. Under the rules of the prison, his murder charge prevented him from receiving much time outside and aside from a couple of books, he didn't have anything to occupy his mind. His lawyers, to their credit, kept him updated about his progress through the legal system. He was about to speak with them again, but had little reason for hope. He waited anxiously for their arrival. His level of concern elevated because they were five minutes tardy.

The lawyers informed him at their last meeting of their

confidence the judge would finally set bail because of Morgan's clean criminal record and that he didn't appear to be a flight risk. The seriousness of his alleged crime gave them some concern, but they claimed the judge would not force him to stay locked up until his trial which might be months away. Bail would likely be high. Morgan informed them he didn't own assets he could use for collateral. They told him a family member should help to raise the necessary funds. Morgan seethed at the thought of getting his mom involved in bailing him out, but he couldn't think of anybody else who would help him.

Monica Askew offered to pay for the bond the second Morgan broached the subject. He had no idea how she would raise the necessary funds, but recognized her involvement would mean major sacrifice. He promised he would pay her back and both understood the chances of this happening were slim. The thought of his mom having to to pay for his mistakes sent him into a deeper spiral.

Morgan paced his small cell nearing hyperventilation, until a guard announced his lawyers' arrival. The guards had to restrain him to transport him and then removed his shackles once they arrived at the meeting room.

Spencer and Crotec waited in the same seats as the last time. His life was repetitive, each day a near replica of the day before.

Morgan stared at his counsel gaped mouth as they showcased ear-to-ear grins ordinarily reserved for receiving a raise or hearing an original off-color joke. He assumed they had reason for appearing to be so jovial.

"What's going on?" Morgan asked as the lawyers remained quiet, yet continuing to display unbridled happiness.

"Oh nothing," Crotec said, turning to Spencer and shrugging his shoulders.

"C'mon guys. We got to discuss my bail. I'm sick thinking about having to hit up my mom for the money."

"You may think so," Spencer interrupted, "but you wouldn't be correct."

Morgan stared at his lawyers, not sure what game they were playing.

Crotec put a hand on Spencer's arm. "Let me tell him." Spencer nodded his assent, allowing Crotec to continue, "We have news."

Morgan leaned forward. "I'm all ears."

"So, the company you work for," Crotec said, "employs a bunch of politically well-connected people. We would like to take credit for this, but we can't. We've been working with the police and the DA's trying to convince them to dismiss the charges because they couldn't make them stick, but they didn't listen to us. At the same time, some exec at your company talked to someone higher up and convinced them that if they charged you with a crime, they would also have to charge the two shoppers with the same offense. Given one is a minister and the other a sweet, law-abiding woman, they realized they had quite a dilemma. Long and short . . . ,"

Crotec turned to Spencer, who completed the sentence, ". . . the DA dismissed the charges against you."

"What?" Morgan felt the blood release in his body with the thought he might be walking out of this hell-hole.

"You heard us. Your worries are over. You'll be skipping out of here this afternoon."

"Oh my god, thanks. This is the best news anyone has given me in a long time." Morgan reached forward with his hand. "What's the catch?"

Crotec took a hold of Morgan's outstretched hand. "You have nothing to worry about, but let me give you some instructions. The criminal charges are being dropped, which is awesome, but your employer expects a civil suit. Nothing yet, but lots of time remains for a lawsuit to be filed. When it happens, we will be the lawyers, and you will be the key witness. Don't talk to anybody about what happened. You understand? Nobody! The company will take care of you, if you protect the company. Any questions?" Crotec raised an eyebrow while staring at Morgan, who sat dumbfounded.

He expected bail would be set so high his mom wouldn't have the means to pay it, and he would spend months in jail waiting for his trial with the potential of spending a significant portion of his young adulthood behind bars. Now, he was about to walk out of prison with the possibility of jail time in the rearview mirror. His concerns about being locked up withering in the wind.

"I just want out of here. Please." Morgan grabbed Spencer's arm who placed a hand on top. "The paperwork is being drafted as we speak. You'll be having dinner with mom tonight. Make sure to toast your newest, best friends." Spencer pointed back and forth between himself and his partner.

Morgan lowered his head praying this wasn't a joke. He made a silent promise he would be the best employee ever going forward.

Crotec stood and knocked on the door. The guards returned and placed Askew in chains for the last time.

CHAPTER SEVENTEEN

THE BREEZE HIT Rick in the face when he opened the door to his office to welcome in Emily Hawkins. Dressed low-key in a pair of jeans and a loose sweater, she avoided prolonged niceties and zipped past Rick to head to his office.

Emily plopped into the leather chair and picked at imaginary lint on her clothes.

Rick stood by the recently mounted sixty-five-inch television. "The large screen will help you pick out details, but the video is only so good. Don't think this will give you answers to every question you may have." Rick noticed no movement on Emily's face. "This won't be easy. It gets a little gruesome at the end." His voice trailed off.

Rick grabbed the remote control before dropping it to his side. He walked towards his client and put a hand on her shoulder. "I think this may be rough for you. Are you sure you want to do this?"

Emily nodded. "Yes, I'm going to see it at some point. No time like the present." She forced a smile.

"Like I told you, my AV guy edited this together, so we

could get a continuous view of Jerry. It's a little choppy, but the time-line has become a little more straightforward."

Rick pushed some buttons on his keyboard and the flat screen jumped to life. The grid with the 36 moving images popped up. "He started with this so you could see every angle. The company sent me video from all thirty-six cameras for twenty-four hours before and two hours after your husband came to the store. The camera ID number is in the upper right of the picture and the time is stamped in the upper left."

Emily leaned forward in her seat. Rick wondered whether he should have popcorn available, but realized they weren't watching a Star Wars movie–far from it. They were taking in a snuff film and the victim's loved one would be one of the people watching.

The video cut to a single image which filled the entire screen. The digital clock denoted 15:10:45.

"So you understand," Rick explained, "the time notation is military time, which means it was three-ten and forty-five seconds p.m. The number four in the upper left corner means you're watching Camera four."

The image displayed an overview of the store's parking lot with a multitude of cars parked and others searching for a space or leaving the lot.

Holding a laser pointer, Rick directed a red dot on the screen.

"Here's Jerry pulling into the parking lot," Rick said, while circling the blue Honda Civic with the red light beam. The beam followed the car as it made a right-hand turn into an available parking space. The passenger door opened and Jerry, wearing a red windbreaker, exited the car and walked towards the entrance of the store. "Nothing unusual so far, right?"

Emily shook her head, not removing her gaze from the screen. "Nope, not yet. He's wearing his 'lucky' jacket."

The video cut to an image of customers entering the store through the sliding front door. Camera 6 showed a straight on view from the front door into the parking lot getting a view of the faces of customers walking into the store. Jerry walked by the camera with his head pointed down twenty-six seconds after closing his car door.

On camera 8, Jerry grabbed a cart from a row in the vestibule inside the first entrance door. He stepped back a couple of steps, turned to his right and headed inside the store through the second entrance door leading into the store.

Rick knew from being in the store grocery items were to the shoppers' right and the video showed Jerry first entering the produce section. The video cut from camera to camera depicting the entire path Jerry took through the store.

"I didn't detect anything unusual about what Jerry was doing," Emily said as the video showed Jerry completing the shopping portion of his trip and walking in the main aisle appearing as if he was having trouble picking a checkout lane.

"I didn't either," Rick said, "but he's looking unable to decide whether to go into this lane with the Hispanic cashier, but choosing not to."

"True. He started to go into the one with the black lady cashier also, but didn't."

"I noticed that, but he moves to the line for the self-check-outs, which is near to the exit from the store." Rick tapped his keyboard and the image on the screen froze with Jerry waiting for the next available self-checkout register of the six clustered in the area.

Emily squinted and pursed her lips. "I can't believe this is the last thing he did in his life."

Rick leaned over and offered her a tissue.

She nodded her thank you and dabbed at the corner of her eye.

"I stopped here to remind you these edits are only focused on your husband, but we put together another video which focuses on Mr. Askew, the assistant manager. We will watch it another time, but let me tell you watching Askew is interesting.

"By the time Jerry got up to the register, Askew was talking to a cashier and giving him instructions. It's clear something caught his eye which turns out was your husband." Rick reached down and touched Emily's shoulder. "You ready?"

Rick took a breath before re-starting the video. *She's a gritty woman. I wouldn't be able to witness the last minutes of my spouse's life like this.*

She bobbed her head in assent and the video continued with Jerry taking items out of his shopping cart with care and scanning them before placing them in the white plastic bags at the packing station.

"Jerry started with the smaller items," Rick offered, "including the canned goods and some small hardware products he selected like screws and nails."

"Nothing wrong with that. He's a little OCD, so he did things in a certain order."

Jerry placed one or two products in a plastic bag and put the bag into his cart. He moved with excessive deliberation unlike most shoppers who check out with alacrity to speed their exit from the store. As the number of unscanned items dwindled, the amount of plastic bags in his cart multiplied. After scanning for almost eleven minutes, Jerry pulled two bills from his wallet and slid them into the cash slot. He collected his change and his receipt, and pushed his cart toward the exit.

"The company didn't give me a copy of his receipt yet, so I did my best to calculate what he purchased," Rick said. "It appears he scanned twenty-eight items and I'm estimating, but the cost totaled about thirty-eight dollars. By my count, he put fifteen bags into his cart." Rick turned again to Emily. "This is where things get interesting."

On the video, Jerry headed to the exit and as he neared the exit door, a person wearing a yellow button-down shirt and tie jogged over and placed a hand on the cart. Jerry stopped, glancing sideways in the direction of the man.

Rick said, "Boy, I wish there was audio, so we could hear what they're saying, but it's only video."

Emily didn't respond or appear to blink.

"He thinks about stopping," Rick said, "but shoves the manager's hand off his cart and moves towards the exit."

On the screen, Jerry pushed the cart out the door without looking back.

The video cut back to camera six, the one which showed Jerry entering the store, but now had him pushing the cart away from the store with greater energy than he displayed bagging his groceries. Jerry juked around two cars moving in opposite directions as he made a turn to the right in the general direction of where he parked his car.

Morgan Askew sprinted out of the store, his tie flipping over his shoulder and stopped, unsure where Jerry turned, as other shoppers impeded his direct vision into the lot.

Rick placed the red dot on Jerry at the edge of the screen and moved it to Askew standing in front of the door looking side-to-side.

"He has 30 yards at this point on the manager."

Emily nodded and offered a guttural grunt as assent.

"But now the manager sees him and begins to chase," Rick said.

On screen, the view switched to a higher-up angle from a camera mounted on the top of the outside wall. Rick directed Emily's attention to Jerry pushing his cart on the right of the screen and Askew moving fast on the other side trying to catch up.

"He's getting close to a group of parked cars, but there's a kid shagging carts near a cart return corral."

As Jerry got closer to the corral, Askew stopped and cupped his hands over his mouth. The clerk reacted and turned toward Jerry who was coming in his direction.

"This is where all hell breaks loose," Rick said more in the direction of the video screen than Emily.

Responding to Askew, the kid getting the carts moved to stand in the path of Jerry's cart. Jerry swerved around the kid, who reached and grabbed him by the back of his windbreaker, slowing him for a moment. The clerk maintained his hold of Jerry's collar as Jerry turned and punched his face. Jerry had him by three inches, and clocked the kid sending him flying. The kid ended tumbling back towards the line of carts, landing in a heap on the ground.

"Oh my Lord." Emily recoiled at the sight of her husband belting the boy.

Rick turned. "Should we keep going?"

"Absolutely."

"The video again showed Jerry moving towards his car, but the clerk slowed him down enough that Askew had almost caught him."

On the screen, her husband now closed in on their car and pulled his keys from the pocket of his jacket. The trunk of the car popped open, but before Jerry got to his vehicle, Askew leaped and tackled him from behind.

Before he first watched the video, Rick presumed Jerry died as a result of a head wound suffered because Askew slammed his head into the ground, but realized his assumption was incorrect when he saw both men landing on the ground. At this point, Jerry rolled on top of Askew and slammed his fist into his face, causing Emily to smirk a bit.

The video continued with Jerry grappling with Askew when an older man rushed into the scene and pulled Jerry onto the ground. Another woman came and jumped on Jerry. Askew rolled over to assist, joined by the cart boy. The four sat on top of Jerry, now in control.

"It's hard to tell what's happening here as the video is grainy. I think the camera is rather far from where this is occurring. It's doesn't appear like much from this distance and four of them sit on top of Jerry waiting. It's almost fifteen minutes later when the police car pulls into the lot. They order everyone off of Jerry and the officer radios for help. Three minutes later, an ambulance arrives and the paramedics run over to assist. They got him in the ambulance while still attempting to resuscitate him."

Rick stopped, realizing he was giving a soliloquy. He turned back to Emily and saw her with her face buried in her hands. He walked over and put his arms around her allowing her to bury her head on his shoulder.

CHAPTER EIGHTEEN

THE OFFICE WAS in its typical state—quiet—which was the way Rick liked it. More clients would likely add buzz, but would prevent him from doing some of his favorite things like imagining skiing down a mountain in a place he likely would never go to or fantasizing about women he likely would never talk to. He recognized his dreams should be more grounded in reality, but whenever he tried to think through issues tangentially affecting his life, like the behavioral issues of his daughter, this led to a maelstrom of self-reflection which alternated between painful and embarrassing. He had trained himself, when he had the time, to let his mind drift in a direction far away from his reality, or any reasonable, conceivable extension of his life allowing him to ignore his own problems, at least for a few minutes.

The fake chimes of the cheap doorbell disrupted Rick's mental ride down a steep, powdery western trail. He pulled his feet off his desk and yelled, "I'll be there in a second." A second wave from the bell interrupted his request for patience. He had no appointments for the afternoon, so whoever, or whatever, greeted him would be a surprise.

Emily Hawkins pushed her way through the door once Rick opened it a creak. Her hair was messy from the wind and fell unevenly over her eyes.

"Ms. Hawkins," Rick said, happy for the intrusion, "I haven't seen you since yesterday. I'm glad you're here."

Emily considered for a moment whether she was disturbing him and then the words spewed out as she pulled at the sleeves of her cream sweatshirt. "I should have called. I thought about texting, but decided to drive over. So, here I am."

Rick smiled. He barely knew Emily, but the seeds of respect for her were growing.. She had suffered a horrible tragedy, yet her resolve to find out what happened to her husband was evident. As a lawyer, he analyzed fact scenarios with an eye towards determining if anyone was at fault. Not everyone understood this concept and thought because a loved one got hurt, someone should pay. In his world, the first question he asked always was whether he could find someone legally responsible for an accident. He hadn't pushed Emily down the path towards litigation. Now, he assumed, he was about to find out if she wanted to invest the emotional energy necessary to proceed.

"Come in," he said, making a sweeping gesture towards the inside of his office.

She stepped in, her sweatshirt hugged her hips as she stepped from the sunlight outside to the relative darkness in the office. They walked to Rick's office, but she grabbed his arm, making him stop in the small hallway.

"I couldn't sleep all night after watching the video. It left me with more questions than before. Why would they sit on Jerry without ever checking on him? Why would two strangers get involved? Did Jerry do something wrong? I have so many questions, but you aren't able to answer them. I need to find out what happened."

She tilted her head up at Rick, who said, "I understand. Not knowing must be so agonizing for you." Rick glanced into Emily's piercing blue eyes, but she dropped her gaze.

"I never sued anyone. We would never have thought about litigation before this. I think I owe Jerry to find out. This won't be fun, but I want B & D to answer these questions. Will you do this for us?" She placed her hand on Rick's arm and raised her head so their eyes met.

"Of course, I will. I want to remind you that being a part of a lawsuit is serious work. It will drain you of all your energy. They will search your past to dredge up anything they can use against you." Rick paused and grinned. "Anything illicit I should worry about?"

Emily giggled. "Me? No way. We're too ordinary. We should be fine."

"Perfect. I will draft a complaint outlining your claims and send it to you for your review."

Emily smiled and extended her hand. "Awesome, I can't wait to read what my lawyer comes up with."

After Emily left, Rick pulled his chair up to the computer to research any potential legal challenge. His daydreams would have to wait for a few hours.

CHAPTER NINETEEN

MOST OF THE TIME, drafting a complaint for one of his clients didn't cause Rick much trouble. Identify the parties, set forth the facts and conclude with why the defendant owed his client money. Other aspects of practicing law were more glamorous, but compiling the necessary facts and supporting law was necessary to begin litigation. He walked a delicate tightrope trying to find the right balance between facts to include and those to exclude, only needing enough to put the defendant on notice of his client's claims.

He reworked every paragraph over and over, typing a sentence before backspacing over it because it failed to articulate what he wanted with sufficient precision. It was common not to have a complete picture of all events before filing a complaint–that's why discovery existed–to find out what witnesses knew and to fill in gaps. Drafting Emily Hawkins' complaint against B & D, however, forced Rick to reach deep to find the appropriate description of the harm caused to her life.

The day before, Emily had left Rick's office sobbing. They

didn't say much after watching Jerry die–she just got up and left. Later in the evening, he called her at her home to check on her. Her spirits and resolve sounded better. Rick tried to focus on her mental well-being, but Emily put off his overtures of concern and insisted she was fine. She kept repeating she didn't want to relive his death over and over. He told her to take whatever time she needed. Emily expressed her gratitude and blurted out that if she sued, she didn't want anyone else to represent her. He hoped to hear from her in a few weeks and so her swift return to the office surprised him.

Rick spent much of the afternoon researching potential causes of action against the company. He recognized her claims centered on a wrongful detention claim leading to Jerry's death. What concerned Rick was the assertion Jerry stole product from the store. If so, did the store employee retain any privilege to detain Jerry?

From watching the video, Rick couldn't ascertain whether Jerry shoplifted. The video raised so many extraneous questions. To calm himself, he kept mumbling, "No shoplifter should die because of stealing something."

As he typed new allegations into the complaint, he avoided pleading any facts which later might prove to be inaccurate. Jerry was dead, so Rick would never have the opportunity to question him about what happened in the parking lot. This was not the place to guess, so he described what happened to Jerry with no embellishment.

His head ached as he tried to categorize Emily's claims. He divided her causes of action into two buckets: The first for what are known as survivor claims–those asserted by a survivor on behalf of a person who died. These claims are for what happened to Jerry before he died. For these, Rick included battery, false imprisonment, and assault.

The second bucket included claims for wrongful death.

These were claims for Jerry's death, but more for what he would have offered if still alive–his earnings and the services he provided to the family. In the right case, these could be massive if a jury chooses to award a lifetime of earnings all at once. Emily also had a significant claim of her own–for loss of consortium–the injury she suffered for losing Jerry's companionship as a result of his death.

Finally, Rick pondered the concept of punitive damages, the type a jury awards to punish a wrongdoer. Only recoverable in a case where a defendant has exhibited conduct worthy of being punished and designed not only to make the defendant change its ways, but also as a deterrent to others to warn them against acting egregiously in the future. Rick still didn't have a complete grasp on what happened to Jerry, but made a few suppositions which, if true, might lead a jury to award punitive damages. He understood little at this point about how B & D operated or how it treated its employees, but wondered what policies, if any, the company might have to deal with shoplifters.

Most stores faced an onslaught of shoplifting and developed policies to confront it. Some companies deployed substantial resources to train its employees how to detain a person suspected of stealing, while other cut corners. Rick didn't comprehend where B & D fell on this continuum.

He pictured Jerry lying lifeless on the pavement. Only a complete failure to train would lead to this. He alleged, in lawyer talk, "Based upon information and belief, B & D failed to implement a training program to teach its employees how to approach suspected shoplifters. Its failure was willful and led to, and caused, the unnecessary death of the decedent."

His last decision was to decide which individuals he should name as defendants. The primary defendant would be B & D.

As a corporation, any negligent acts of its employees would be imputed to the company. If its workers were responsible, B & D would have to pay the judgment.

Blaze Rondowsky's letter had identified Morgan Askew as the manager in charge when Jerry died. Rick pondered whether he should also name him as a defendant. For purposes of paying a judgment, the company would foot the bill and had sufficient reserves, or insurance, to satisfy a judgment, even an excessive one.

After significant deliberation, Rick elected to name Askew as a defendant because it sent a message. Plus, Askew might be so upset about being a named defendant in a wrongful death lawsuit he would pressure the company to settle. Doubtful, because the company would be controlling the litigation, but he could dream of an easy resolution.

Rick also had to decide whether to name the other two customers who joined in the fray and sat on Jerry until he died. After further contemplation, he decided to forego naming them because he hoped to stay in their good graces and obtain testimony from them beneficial to his side.

Rick pushed his chair back and stretched his arms over his head, finally satisfied after seven solid hours hunched over a keyboard.

He had read and reread Emily's complaint at least seven times until comfortable it was a polished product. He didn't want to wait any longer, so he emailed Emily, attaching it for her final review.

He glanced up to the ceiling, hoping she would sign the necessary verification without requesting significant changes. Once she did, he would file the complaint and deliver it to the Sheriff to serve the defendants. Then the cat and mouse game would begin.

Two hours later, Rick received an email from Emily which said, *"No changes. I'm ready to start the lawsuit. Get the bastards."*

CHAPTER TWENTY

THIS TIME when the phone rang, Rick was trying to put the finishing touches on answers to interrogatories in a dog bite case he had been putting off for days. The alarming jangle of the incoming call caused him to jerk back in his chair and almost fall over. He didn't want to answer, but Audrey was not in the office to deflect unnecessary intrusions. *Better deal with this now,* he thought, as he grabbed the landline and avoided having to get the message later from voicemail.

"Waterston," he said as he tried to multitask and review his draft response to the last interrogatory.

"Hey, Rick, It's your old friend, Virgil Spencer."

At first, Rick couldn't place the name, nor the irksome tone, but tried to fake his way with a grunt which did little to further the conversation.

The voice on the other end cracked a bit. "Virgil Spencer, from Wilson, O'Malley. You remember us, don't you?"

Now Rick understood the cold chill which had traveled from the base of his spine up to his neck when he answered the call.

"Ah, Spencer. What can I do for you?" *You ball of head lice. We haven't talked since you and your buddy Crotec giggled as the security guard led me out of the building.*

"How's life in private practice, buddy?"

Rick flinched at the word 'buddy,' not believing in any residual kinship from their days working together.

"It's awesome. Not as glamorous as life at the big firm, but we keep ourselves busy."

Rick gazed around at his office, noting the four files sitting on his three-shelf bookcase. The incongruity between his words and his reality made him chuckle to himself.

"I'm happy you're doing well, but I wanted to talk about a new file we're working up."

Without further prompting, Rick understood which file he was referring to because there weren't many options from his end. "You mean the one where some psycho store manager killed my client's husband."

"Funny," Spencer said. "I was referring to the one where the store tried to stop a shoplifter who went crazy in the parking lot."

"At least now you've informed me of how you intend to defend this. What can I do for you?" Rick said, attempting to hide his suspicion all Spencer wanted was to shake him down for some pre-discovery information.

Spencer cleared his throat before speaking. "I thought it would be helpful to touch base before we answered the complaint. I hoped for a short extension, but also wanted to talk about where this case is going."

Without hesitation, Rick agreed to provide Spencer an extension to answer the complaint not caring if they delayed another thirty days before slamming each other with discovery requests. He waited for Spencer to identify the true purpose of the call.

"My client thinks the manager was justified in what he did?" Rick didn't respond, so Spencer kept talking. "Your client's husband, Jerry, that's his name, right? My people tell me he's not the smartest tool in the shed and got busted running from the store. The law's clear–reasonable detention for shoplifters– that's what happened here."

Rick still didn't respond, confident to let the silence force Spencer to continue the conversation.

Spencer blinked first.

"Our firm–you know how we work. There's going to be lots of discovery. I mean lots. You're a small shop. I doubt you can handle what we will be sending your way."

Spencer's insult compelled Rick to respond, "Don't worry about my little practice. We can handle it. What are you proposing?"

"Here the deal."

The words caused Rick to flashback to his termination meeting with Spencer sitting across the table from him while deploying the same phrase, *"Here's the deal,"* before telling him he would be leaving the firm without severance, notice, or references.

"My clients," Spencer continued, "want to explore settlement if your client is willing to mediate this case and possibly get to a quick resolution. What do you think?"

Rick wanted to tell him to take his suggestion and shove it up his ass, but only because it was Spencer's idea. At the same time, early mediation might be beneficial if they reached a reasonable settlement without incurring a lot of effort or expense. This was a plaintiff's lawyer's dream–get a hefty fee early before doing most of the hard work and the risk of losing the case became more apparent. He didn't trust Spencer or his motives, but for now, had little to lose other than some time and the mediator's fee.

He didn't jump at the offer.

"I'm not sure," Rick said. "Mediation before we've done any discovery doesn't seem like a recipe for success."

"It's mandatory in Federal Court. I've settled a bunch of cases early there. Not always, but it can be helpful to narrow down issues."

Rick didn't spend much time in Federal court, which wasn't relevant at the moment.

"I will talk to my client and get back to you."

"You can be convincing when you want to be. Call me with some dates after she agrees. I got another call. I'll talk with you soon."

Rick turned the phone to his face realizing nobody was talking anymore. He dropped it in his pocket and sensed the inner jitteriness marking the return of a level of anxiety he hadn't experienced since his last day working at WOMS.

He realized he didn't miss it.

CHAPTER TWENTY-ONE

"DAMN IT." Rick leaned back in his chair and locked his hands behind his head. "This doesn't help our case." The three-page report flew out of his hand and landed on his desk. He wanted someone else's input to gauge if his reaction was appropriate–if what he read in the police report wounded his case against B & D.

Not having anyone to bounce ideas off of was one of the many downsides of being a sole practitioner. He handled the lunches by himself and did the grunt work on every file, but sometimes it wouldn't hurt to be able to talk to someone with some insight into how to handle a case or provide a different point of view on how to respond in a difficult situation.

An hour earlier Rick received an email from an old friend who worked at the same station as Peter Mitinger, the investigating officer of Jerry Hawkins' death. Ordinarily, Rick waited weeks after sending a subpoena to receive a copy of the police report. This time, he called in a favor from a cop he helped defend two years earlier on a charge of police brutality. *He owes me*, Rick thought when he placed the call. Without much cajoling, his cop buddy agreed to provide him a copy of the report without delay.

Rick slammed the report onto his desk and pulled out his phone. He clicked the number for the cop.

"Parker," the voice called out. Rick pulled the phone away from his ear. "Hey, it's Rick Waterston, you got a minute to talk about the report you sent over?"

"Sure buddy. What about?"

"That ridiculous write-up–did you read it?"

"I glanced over it, but it's not my report. Not my rodeo, so it's none of my business."

"I hear you. What I don't understand is, how he can write, 'Justified detention. Suspect caught shoplifting and then attacked store employee legally attempting to detain him. Suspect struggled after detention causing the employee to request assistance. Shoplifter died by the time officers arrived. Appears to be justifiable actions of the store employee?'"

"I read it. I guess he thought the guy should have cooperated."

"Cooperated? He was slammed to the ground, and they sat on him until he died. Your cop friend used the word 'shoplifter' eighteen times in the report. A bit of overkill, don't you think?"

"I guess. Like I said, he was the investigating officer, not me. Mitinger took a while to write this up. Most of the time, we shoot these out in two to three days. It took him a couple of weeks. Another cop told me he talked to some people from the company before he finished. When he testified at the preliminary hearing, he played it down the middle. Maybe he's being pushed to one side now. Find a copy of the testimony from the prelim. I bet it'll give you a better picture of what he thought."

"That's helpful. I don't like this report. To me, he's gratuitously slamming the dead guy. No reason for it."

"Call me if you need anything else."

"I will." Rick tossed his phone at the end of the conversation. He wondered why a cop wanted to screw over a dead man.

CHAPTER TWENTY-TWO

THE TIDY HOME with red siding sat next to the church in a tiny plot, almost in the middle of nowhere. *Welcome to the boonies,* Rick thought, as he eased his truck in front of the house.

The police report identified the two individuals who assisted the store manager with "detaining" Jerry Hawkins—one man and one woman. Rick wanted to get their stories before the store talked with them. In Rick's experience, even witnesses who wanted to tell their story as honestly as possible, imperceptibly shaded their testimony towards the side which contacted them first. He wanted any potential witness who might slant their testimony to tilt it in his direction.

Michael McGarrity greeted Rick with an engaging smile and introduced himself as 'Mick,' the part-time pastor at the Church of the Redeemer, the small brick building less than thirty yards from his front door. Rick's first reaction to the gregarious man in his sixties built like a linebacker was a *jury will love this guy.*

Rick called McGarrity after reading the police report asking to talk about the incident in the parking lot. His next stop would be with the woman who also assisted in killing the husband of his client.

The man he most wanted to talk to was the assistant manager, Morgan Askew. He brought suit against him, so ethically he couldn't talk to him without the company's approval, which wasn't happening. He would have to wait until he took his deposition before sizing him up.

"Come in," McGarrity said, leading Rick into the home. "You want coffee, or a beer?"

Rick declined. "I don't want to take up too much of your time, so I'll jump right in. I wanted to hear from you about how you got involved in the situation at the B & D."

The pastor glanced downward at his clasped hands as leaned forward on the edge of the dark gray couch. "Mr. Masterson, my wife died too early. We were in our thirties, and after she passed, I decided to become a man of the cloth. I needed to move closer to the Lord and since, well, this is where I spend my time." He spread his arms.

Rick sat silent, wondering where this was heading, not wanting to interject, not even to make sure the pastor remembered his name.

"I have learned the Lord is mysterious and why He brings us to where He chooses is His business." He paused, making sure Rick maintained eye contact. "That afternoon, He brought me to that parking lot because it was His plan–a plan where I would help Him ease suffering and root out problems infecting our society."

Despite about fourteen more questions pinging in his head, Rick kept quiet, letting the pastor continue. Rick ignored the man's aftershave which hung over the room.

"I was walking towards the store and a voice rang out, 'I need help. I need help.' I didn't recognize where it came from, but it spoke to me. In my bones, I knew it was my responsibility to assist. This is what the Lord teaches." The pastor sat up straight continuing to stare at Rick. "I witnessed the man, the one who the Lord took, punching the manager from the store—hitting him hard. The manager needed my help."

Rick nodded and took some notes on his yellow pad.

"I ran over, and the manager got on top of the thief. I pinned the man's arms on the ground, and we waited for the police to arrive." He bowed and shook his head. "When they showed up, the man had passed. It was the Lord's decision."

Rick jotted a couple of notes. "Sir, thank you for telling me your story, but I have additional questions to try to fill in the gaps."

McGarrity squinted his eyes and leaned back. "Fill in the gaps?" he huffed. "I believe I told you everything about what occurred. I can still see it as if it's happening right now." The pastor stood. "There is nothing more to add. I'm sorry you find 'gaps' in my recollection."

Rick stood dumbfounded, but understood the pastor wouldn't expound on what he had said, but still wanted to give it a try. "Sir, do you remember anyone else with you while you waited for the police?"

The pastor straightened. "All I remember is the Lord's presence the whole time. He wanted me to assist, yet His plan was to take the young man into His realm. I cannot think of anything else to say."

McGarrity grabbed Rick's arm and led him to the front door. "Thank you so much for coming today," McGarrity said as he gave Rick a nudge forward. "I hope this helped."

Rick turned as the door closed. He stood on the stoop shaking his head.

This has only been weird. Time to go talk to the other witness and find out if the strangeness continues.

86

CHAPTER TWENTY-THREE

THE CAFÉ TEEMED with activity with so many people crammed at the various tables and booths it made finding the one person Rick wanted to spot difficult. He stood in the middle of the chaos turning in a circle when he spotted a waving hand from the booth at the back.

"I'm Rick," he said, extending his hand as he approached, "I hope you're Deandra."

The short, beefy woman half-stood and took Rick's hand. "Guilty as charged," she said in a husky voice.

Rick slid into the booth and placed his yellow pad on the table. He flipped to a clean sheet, but wanted to engage in a little small talk, unlike his previous encounter with the pastor. "Can I buy you some coffee?"

Deandra nodded and Rick flagged down a waitress.

"I'm sorry I made you come here," she said. "I sounded a little freaky on the phone, but I live alone and I never met you."

"Understood." Rick threw his hand forward and laughed. "I wouldn't want some strange man coming to my place to interview me. Don't worry. This is perfect."

She sat back in the booth so the server could place a cup of coffee on the Formica table-top. The clanking of dishes reverberated as all booths were occupied. Rick picked up his pen to signal he wanted to begin. "What happened in the parking lot, not what you were expecting, was it?"

"Never. Not in a million years." She blew out a huff of air and her shoulders eased down.

"Tell me your last name again."

"It's Bortz. Deandra Bortz. It's my married name, but I got divorced three years ago. No kids. Simply a forty-two-year old woman living by herself—except for my golden and princess, the stray cat I found last year."

Rick flinched at the deluge of information received from just asking for her name. *She's going to have a lot of work to do if she's wants to be a strong witness.* He put the thought aside. "Tell me what happened when you got to B & D."

Deandra raised her eyes and tried to formulate her words. It took a few moments before the thoughts gushed out. "I'll never forget how quickly the events unfolded. How scared I got and how concerned I was for everyone in the parking lot with so much commotion. So much screaming. I didn't have any idea what to do. I did like I was told until the police showed up. Then the guy didn't respond. Never thought that might happen."

Rick tried to put together Bortz's word salad, but couldn't make much sense out of it. "Let's take this a little slower. Did this happen before you went into the store or after you finished your shopping?"

"Oh, I didn't get a chance to do my shopping. I didn't know what I wanted, but I love the store. They sell everything. I think I needed to buy some underwear and some shoes, but I never got to go into the store."

"Other things got in your way." Rick smiled. He dealt with

many types of witnesses, and realized you don't pick them, you deal with whoever happens to witness an event. Some are able to tell their stories. Some have more difficulties, but ultimately, he only wanted people who told the truth as best they could.

"So what happened after you got out of your car?"

"Turns out, I parked close to where the fight broke out. I was in my car putting on some lipstick, but I didn't observe anything. I got out and saw the manager holding down this man. I didn't want to be involved, but he yelled he needed help and this guy was going to hurt him."

"So what did you do?"

"I went over. I kind of stood frozen. He told me to help pin him down."

"Did you?"

"Of course. He screamed at me to help, so I didn't think I had much choice. I sat on his arm. Then this older gentleman came over and held down his other arm. The manager kept telling the guy not to struggle and saying to us not to let go because he was trying to get up. I listened to the manager. He was in charge."

"Was the guy struggling?"

"I guess. He kept jerking around."

"Did he say anything?"

"Once or twice he said he couldn't breathe, but the manager kept saying he wanted to escape and for us not to let go. So we didn't. Finally, the police came and the man didn't respond. I can't tell you how horrible this is."

Rick shook his head and tried to picture the scene at the parking lot. He had only talked to two witnesses so far, and already everyone was giving conflicting stories. They said enough for him to piece together a credible story for his client, but a lot would depend on what these witnesses testified to during the litigation.

Deandra went through her story with Rick three times who noticed some significant detail alterations in each version. This wasn't unusual, but he couldn't evaluate whether she would make a believable witness or one who might sink his case. At least by the end he thought he had a better understanding of the events which led to Jerry Hawkins' death.

He wanted her to sign a witness statement, but also realized drafting one she agreed to might prove difficult. After broaching the concept of signing a statement, Bortz's discomfort returned, and she indicated she didn't want to sign anything, obviating any concern about what language to include.

They talked about their respective neighborhoods and jobs, leaving Rick confident of her likability – a person with real problems who happened to be in the wrong place at the wrong time.

As Rick left the diner, he couldn't evaluate how meeting with the two witnesses today had affected his case. One was a crazy pastor summoned by god and, the other, a sweet woman who had difficulty giving her name in less than one hundred words. Whatever he thought of them, they were the only identified independent witnesses of the death of Jerry Hawkins.

CHAPTER TWENTY-FOUR

THE STACK of papers dropped onto Rick's desk as if it was Manna from heaven– which it wasn't.

"You're going to love these," Audrey said as she leaned on the desk using her arms to support her body and inching her head over the papers.

Rick, who was looking out the window at passing traffic, turned to face six inches of documents with Audrey's eyes hovering just above. "What fun did you bring me this morning?" Rick reached a cautious hand towards the pile, but avoided touching it.

"They came in the mail today from your two favorite cases: 'Tiger vs. Tiger' and 'Death in the parking lot.'"

Though his assistant's nomenclature for his cases often amused him, today he wasn't in the mood for her hijinks. He waved her away, and she turned with a dramatic huff to leave.

She said over her shoulder as she headed to the door, "You got lots of work in both cases. I'll need some overtime if you want me to work on them."

Rather than responding, Rick heaved a pencil in her

general direction, which fell at her feet. She left with a satisfied expression etched on her face.

Rick scooped up the daunting stack of papers and placed it in front of him. The top grouping was from the Billy Blevins litigation. First, a set of interrogatories–written questions which Billy would answer with Rick's assistance.

Next a series of requests for production of documents. Rick thought Thomas Rohrspot, the attorney for Billy's partner, Frank Francisco, was "sweet" to limit his requests to *only* forty-five. These would compel Billy to spend hours compiling contracts, emails and anything else he conceivably might possess. Rick would have to review the documents and remove any containing privileged information before drafting legal responses to the interrogatories and requests for documents.

Lastly, there was a set of requests for admissions–fifty-two of them which Rick and Billy would answer either admitting to some fact, or denying its truth, while supplying an explanation why the alleged fact was in dispute. Under the court's rules, he must complete this chunk of work in the next thirty days.

The second set of papers was similar to the first. Under the signature of Virgil Spencer, the defendants in Emily Hawkins' case served a set of interrogatories, requests for production of documents and requests for admissions.

They would not have to gather as many documents because Emily was an individual and not a business like Billy Blevins' animal park. Emily had no prior experience with litigation and this would prove to be a difficult undertaking for her—one would involve Rick's active participation throughout the process.

"Damn, no more computer games. I got a lot of work to do in a short amount of time," Rick said in a whisper, turning to face the window. Considering the amount of work both sides would need to complete the Tigerland cases, Rick continued to think out loud. "With all of this discovery flying between the parties, perhaps Francisco would be interested in talking settlement also."

He jerked and yanked his phone off his desk. He grabbed the front page of the document from Blevins' case to find the phone number of his opponent's lawyer.

"Thomas Rohrspot, just the man I want to talk to," he said once they connected. He identified himself and *thanked* him for the mounds of discovery which had just dropped on his desk.

After a few pleasantries, he shifted to the purpose of the call.

"Tom, I got a call on another case where the defendant's attorney suggested mediation. He reminded me there's always a chance to resolve a case if the parties are in the same room. Once I got your papers, I was thinking now might be the right time for us to discuss settlement. I talked to a couple of mediators, and we might save some money if we use the same one for both cases. Take a half day for each and I'm sure we can negotiate a reasonable fee. Any interest?"

Ten minutes of a mixture of flattery and arm twisting convinced Rohrspot of the benefit for their clients to be in the same room trying to talk out their differences. The parties hadn't spoken for weeks and with three separate pieces of litigation, perhaps a smart mediator would help them sort out their differences. Rohrspot agreed they both had odd clients and sitting through trial with either of them would be unpredictable. He played coy for a few minutes prattling on about how early mediation was a recipe for failure, not to mention the wasted costs. With a modicum of prodding, he agreed, pending his client's approval, that mediation might bear fruit.

He wouldn't commit, however, unless Rick promised to provide responses to all the discovery requests before the mediation took place. Rick reluctantly agreed to provide responses, and agreed to mediate the case in the next month.

Once the call ended, Rick stared down at the stack of documents and opened up to first interrogatory to begin drafting responses. He bit down hard on his lip as he typed on the computer, aware he would be working on these late into the evening, but not despairing because he had no plans to do anything else.

CHAPTER TWENTY-FIVE

RICK THREW OPEN the door to Tusk's. The restaurant's clientele appeared almost identical to the last time he met Arnie McBride there. A similar din hung in the air and a gathering of lunch drinkers crowded the bar trying to put down a couple before lunchtime was over.

Arnie waited in the same booth they ate in for their last encounter, so a sliver of *deja vu* zipped through Rick's head when he slid in opposite to Arnie. He shook his head as Arnie wore the same suit and tie combination as the last time they met.

They stashed their menus next to their plates, a sense of anticipation swirling for their impending discussion. For the past two years, Rick never worried about having too much work. In a few hours, with the receipt of a some discovery and an increase in activity in a couple of previously dormant matters, his anxiety level over whether he had enough time to handle the influx of work had risen to a point where his chest felt tight every time he took a breath.

"I was thinking about when we started at WOMS," Rick

said. "Newly minted lawyers, fresh out of law school, and we thought life was going to be so easy. We got to work at a major law firm and make serious money with the assurance fancy restaurants, fat clients, and unlimited hot women would all be waiting for us."

Arnie shook his head. "We were young and naïve. What's your point?"

"None of it turned out to be true. They sold us a bill of goods, a dream which had no opportunity of becoming reality. We worked hard and never had a chance of succeeding. I understand my drinking was a significant factor in my downfall, but I don't think I ever was going to be accepted. The partying was only an excuse they latched onto to dump me."

"You're still bitter about how they treated you, aren't you?"

Rick shook his head.

"They screwed me up when they walked me out the door. I had no expectation they were about to throw me out, so it was a real gut punch when they did. So yes, I had a lot of rancor which sent me into a bit of a downward spiral. My marriage was breaking up, but getting canned didn't help. I drank a lot more after I left the firm. My wife walked out on me and my relationship with my daughter isn't the same."

"How they got rid of you really sucked. They never offered you any help."

"I don't look at my firing the same way. I think they did me a favor. We all have lawyer friends who can't cope and end up drinking themselves out of the profession, or worse. All this crap happening around the same time—losing my job, wife, my kid, and my dignity—probably was the best thing for me. It's taken a while, but I'm getting my life back together somewhat. I maintain a practice, if that's what you want to call my sad group of clients. My ex still talks to me and my daughter hugs me when I show up. It's a lot better than it might have been. Plus, I'm not drinking anymore."

Arnie smiled. "Dude, from all outward signs, you're doing great. Nobody could tell anything adverse has happened to you. Keep doing whatever you're doing."

Rick patted him on the arm. "I miss hanging out with you. The best part of working at the firm was spending time with the guys. Before I got married, we would work hard, party hard and start over again the next week. We had fun, back then."

"Yes," Arnie said, "but none of it was real. We were kids and being used. We had no concept of the overall picture, and weren't players like Spencer and Crotec. You remember how they would ingratiate themselves with the power brokers. Only three years ahead of us, but they acted like they owned the firm even as young associates–and people responded. You would always say, 'Perception is more important than reality.' They acted like pricks, but they schmoozed the right partners, joined the proper clubs and got accepted as leaders in the firm while we only cared about going out and raising hell. We were kind of stupid."

Arnie made grunting noises while banging his chest.

Rick chuckled. "I probably was the stupidest of all of us. It's amazing I lasted as long as I did. I hurt a lot after they fired me, but it's helped me find my way to a better place, I think. Remember the last time we talked about a year ago?"

Arnie nodded. "I was pretty rough on you."

"No, you were being honest. It was hard to hear someone tell me I was drinking my life away. Other people had told me similar things before, but coming from you, it resonated." Rick looked down at his lap. "I was pissed, but I took what you said to heart. I think I'm in a better place now, because you were so honest with me. So, thanks."

Arnie smiled. "I had a hard time telling you what I thought, but you needed to hear it. I thought you were pissed."

"I'm over it. Water under the bridge. I took some time to figure out what's important. Still working on it, but I know holding onto friendships is essential. Which leads me to my next question: How are you doing?"

Arnie grabbed his water and twirled the ice like the glass was filled with bourbon.

"My career is going down the toilet. I told you last time they kindly informed me I wouldn't make partner, ever. So now I'm dead man walking. Everybody gives me a little more room in the hallways like I'm carrying the plague, and they don't want to catch it."

"You got a plan?"

"Sort of. I'm talking to everyone I've ever met. Legal jobs are in short supply. Firms would rather hire someone right out of law school. They think they'll work even more for less money. Just like when we graduated." Arnie grimaced at the realization.

"Ironic, isn't it?" Rick added.

Arnie nodded. "If I had a book of portables, I could write my ticket to any firm, but I don't. I developed some business over the years, but the firm took over those clients. Last year, Spencer and Crotec received distributions on two clients I had brought in. I didn't receive anything." Arnie paused. "My only option is to keep working at the firm for as long as they will let me. I'm not in much of a position to bargain."

"Let me throw something out." Rick leaned forward. "All of a sudden, my practice is getting a little busier. I can handle the influx, I think, but that's the problem with running your own shop—it's your responsibility to manage every crisis. I was thinking that finding a release valve would help. I got these two cases heating up and thought you might want to jump ship and help me out."

Arnie stared at Rick with his mouth ajar. "You're joking right? You don't want to be working with this outcast. You're offering me some charity."

Rick shook his head. "No, you're wrong. You're a talented lawyer. I remember when you argued two summary judgment motions first year and you convinced the judge to grant both. Few lawyers would have got him to rule in their favor. You understood the facts. You massaged the law and you tied them together compellingly. I read depositions you've taken. You're able to manage witnesses and force them to lean their testimony in your direction. Your skills are top rate–and you're a friend."

"I'm not sure. Since my first year in law school, my image of me is as a big firm lawyer. I haven't thought about working for any of the mid-sized firms in town, let alone a firm like yours. No offense."

"Oh, none taken. This may not be a dream job for you, but we would make a helluva team. I'm not offering you charity, but I also realize I'm not bidding against anyone."

"So, you're saying I would be taking a cut in salary."

Rick snorted. "I can't compete with the blue bloods. I want you to think about what I said, and if you're interested, we can figure out the details.

"I didn't think this lunch was a job interview, but you got my attention. Maybe it's because you're the only girl at the dance who has talked to me, but I'm listening. Let me think about what moving across town would be like, and then we can talk some more."

For the rest of lunch they reminisced about assorted escapades from their time at the firm and argued over whether Spencer or Crotec was the bigger ass. They couldn't come to a consensus, but when the check came, Rick grabbed and paid it. They walked out together, neither sure of Arnie's next move.

CHAPTER TWENTY-SIX

THE CELL PHONE rested on the desk, but Rick had no difficulty hearing the voice screaming from it.

"Those ass wipes. I got back to my office, and they acted like I was a rookie. I worked in my office for the last four years, but all that remained was the desk, the credenza and the two chairs."

Rick had returned from lunch after running a couple of errands and picked up the call from Arnie, who offered no pleasantries and no idle conversation. Instead, launching into grievances with Rick unable to interject to slow the expletive laden tirade.

Rather than forcing himself into the conversation, Rick put the call on speaker, rested the phone on the desk, and leaned back to listen.

"I thought they would fire me, but no, that would have left me with some dignity. Instead, they lead me down the stairs to the bottom floor—the one where the messengers hang out and extra support staff gets thrown before they are assigned a station. There's no carpet on the floors, nothing hanging on the walls. In fact, the walls haven't been painted for twenty years."

Arnie took a moment to suck in a gulp of air before continuing.

"So they walk me past all the partners on the floor where my office was, down the stairs and then past everyone who works on the bottom floor. Then they lead me to the far end and point to a door next to the bathroom. Crotec leans against the wall beaming and says, 'Here's where we're putting you. Some new Ivy League recruits start soon, and we need the office space. Don't be glum. I'm sure we can move you back upstairs soon.'"

A banging on the other side of the call erupted from the phone, which Rick assumed was Arnie slamming his hand against the top of his desk.

"I took a step inside the office and audibly gasped. This little desk sat against the side of the office with a tiny wooden chair I'm supposed to sit on. The office is devoid of shelving or bookcases, so I have nowhere to put my files. It's so small I don't think anything else would fit, even if I wanted. I stared at Crotec and Spencer like they were playing a joke, but they gave me their pitiful, paternalistic smiles and then left. The whole way down the hallway they were giggling and backslapping each other."

Arnie lapsed into silence and Rick realized now was his turn to speak. "That's rough. You won't enjoy working on the lower level after spending so much time upstairs."

Rick pictured Arnie's former floor with a row of opulent offices overlooking the river. Each of the partners spent thousands of dollars selecting coordinated office furniture and even more on the art hung on the walls and the knickknacks scattered on tables and shelves. Even the assistants' and paralegals' cubicles were decked out–much more so than any space on the bottom floor.

The sound of a loud car horn honking came through the phone.

"Where are you, man?" Rick asked.

"I'm walking in town. I couldn't sit in that office, so I left."

Arnie paused for a moment. "I remember when they kicked you out of the firm. I was so mad because they tried to shred your dignity by having you do the walk of shame. Now they're doing the same thing to me, but it's worse, because they won't fire me. They want me to crawl past everyone in the firm every day–just for their enjoyment."

"Can you take it?"

"I could, but I don't want to. I'm not groveling to those bastards anymore. The next call I make is to Crotec to tell him to shove my little office up his ass. I'm quitting–which is why I called you. I might like to talk to you about the job you sort of offered me at lunch."

"What job are you talking about?" Rick teased.

"The one with the small salary and no benefits."

"Oh, that one. I think it's still open."

"Good, because I don't have any other options at this point."

Rick leaned forward and grabbed a pen. "Hey, buddy, why don't you keep walking to my side of town? The one with the strip malls and gravel parking lots. You big firm lawyers don't come over here very often, but I think you might find the change of scenery welcoming. Come over, and we can talk about the terms of our new partnership."

"I'll be at your door in fifteen minutes."

Rick detected a different tone in Arnie's voice and told him he would be waiting for him no matter how long he took.

CHAPTER TWENTY-SEVEN

A LONG FRIDAY night was winding down. Rick's shirt hung untucked over his butt, and he had dirt caked on his face. A weariness coursed through his back and up into his head. If he placed his head on a pillow he would be asleep in ten seconds, but rest would not be coming to him until he dealt with the little dynamo running in circles from his dining room, through the family room and then into his small kitchen.

The dervish stopped in the hallway and snuck a peek behind her, detecting nothing. She glanced in front and still, only silence. She slowly turned her head back behind her and saw her dad, army crawling on his belly, slithering towards her.

He snatched her leg and yelled, "You are captured–finally. Now is time for Princess Sammie to return to the castle for her beauty rest. Not that she needs any, because she is rather beautiful, but because all princesses must sleep, or they will be cranky in the morning."

Dressed in a flowing pink gown and bedazzled in necklaces and earrings, Sammie locked her arms across her chest. "It's too early, plus we're having fun." She lowered her head, stuck out her lower lip, and batted her eyes at her dad.

Rick mimicked Sammie by crossing his arms, but did not give in. "It's past your bedtime and if you don't fall asleep soon, your mom will not be happy with me. Let's go brush some teeth."

Sammie pondered her options for a moment, but turned towards the bathroom. "Can I sleep in my princess outfit?"

"Of course, but no jewelry in bed."

She again paused, but grabbed the earrings and necklaces, and dropped them on the floor. Rick considered making an issue of her transgression, but bent over and picked up the mislaid items and tossed them on the small table in the hall. Five minutes later, Sammie plopped into the small bed in the tiny bedroom at the end of the hall.

"Thanks for the new pictures on the wall," she said, pointing to the two posters of kittens and flowers Rick put up earlier in the week."

"You're welcome. Now what does this little five-year-old girl need to fall asleep?"

"Can you tell me a story?"

Rick reached over and grabbed a kid's book off the pile on the nightstand, but Sammie protested. "How about a made up story?"

Rick rolled his eyes. "Whatever the little princess wants."

He then launched into a whirlwind of a tale about a young girl on a magic horse who travels to a faraway land and gets lost. She visits many houses to ask how to return to home, but nobody can help her. She finds a magic tomato and befriends a gigantic cat, but ultimately gets into a speeding car that turns into an airplane which drops her into her bed, safe, secure, and very tired.

The story was a bit of a mess, with perhaps a few too many

adult undertones, but Sammie didn't pick up on them. Rick nodded his head with pride as her eyes drooped, and she fought falling asleep for the climatic ending. As he whispered the final line, he pushed away her blonde curls and kissed her forehead.

"I love you, daddy," she mumbled as the last vestiges of being awake drifted away.

"I love you, too. We can play more in the morning." Rick eased off the bed and tiptoed out of the room.

Once planted on the couch, Rick realized he had promised Molly an update after Sammie went to sleep.

He texted her, "*Princess in bed. We had a fun evening. Pizza, carrots, and milk for dinner. Not too many treats after. We played for a while and then got ready for bed. No issues. Thanks for letting me pick her up a little early.*"

Five minutes later his phone dinged with Molly's response: "*Thanks. Be here by ten. The princess and I have plans, so don't screw them up. Please have her here on time.*"

Slow down on the passion. Don't want me getting the wrong idea. He chuckled and remembered the mixed-martial fight which would be much more entertaining than the home improvement show, which popped on when he turned on the TV. He would avoid getting any fix-up clues for his place, which would remain in its usual state of chaos, and would watch two muscular men try to beat the crap out of each other

The sixth round of a welterweight battle played on while Rick scarfed down a final piece of pizza. He occasionally threw a jab or sidekick to assist the fighter in the yellow shorts who was beginning to wear down his larger opponent, except doing so caused the remnants of his food to fly towards the action and nestle in the green area rug in front of the couch.

He bent down to pick up the crumbs when an ear-piercing scream came roaring in from the back part of the hallway. He flung himself erect and sprinted to the second bedroom. As he entered, Sammie sat straight upward, stiff, yanking on her sheets.

"Sweetie, are you okay?" Rick asked as he sat next to her and tried to put an arm around her.

Sammie smacked his arm away and continued to scream. Her eyes were open, darting side-to-side, but she didn't recognize anything. Rick presumed she was still sleeping, having a nightmare. This continued for five minutes until she lied down and rested her head on the pillow, still asleep.

Rick got no response when he asked if she was awake. He sat next to her with his hand on her back, her top covered in sweat.

The fight continued as Rick slumped onto the couch distressed at his daughter's outburst, yet before he had a chance to contemplate its significance, the screams returned with even greater fervor. He ran to Sammie's room and, again, after about three minutes she returned to sleep.

By the time midnight rolled around, he had been back in the bedroom three more times in a futile attempt to alleviate the cause of the terror. In his own bed with his phone in his hand wondering if he would be able to get some uninterrupted sleep, Rick sent a text to Molly. "*Oh my god, she's been up screaming five times. What am I doing wrong?*"

Molly wrote back: "*That's what it's been like for the past six weeks. Every night. She's terrified of something, but she won't remember anything in the morning.*"

"*My nerves are standing on end,*" Rick texted. "*I'm fried. No way I'm getting to sleep anytime soon.*"

"*Welcome to my world.*"

The conversation had come to an end.

CHAPTER TWENTY-EIGHT

THE SMALL OFFICE, though far from immaculate, was in better shape than a few days earlier. It still retained the remnants of months of non-use with a few boxes piled in the corner and a broken desk lamp sitting on the floor.

Rick kicked a rolled up magazine behind the desk. "The mess was worse before I spent a few hours over the weekend throwing away the crap piled in here."

"I can only imagine," Arnie said as he bit down on his lower lip. "I got a few boxes of my stuff in my car. I grabbed my diplomas and the few files I managed to lay my hands on my last day. Once I bring those up, I can take a shot at fixing up this space." He placed a hand on Rick's shoulder. "I'm not worried about the office. My blood pressure is returning to normal now that I'm out of that place."

Ten minutes later, while Rick wiped down a window, Arnie returned lugging a box through the door. He said, "Stop.. I told you I would fix this place up."

Rick lowered the rag to his side. "I'm thrilled you're here. I don't want to think you might regret the move."

"I haven't been here more than fifteen minutes. I'm not regretting anything—yet."

The box he brought in contained an assortment of brown file folders. He pulled out one and placed it on the shelving unit behind the desk.

"They let me take some crap I brought in, but fought me on the better cases. Spencer called some of my clients right after I quit and told them they fired me—suggested I stole from the firm, so those clients would stay at the firm. They got to my clients before I contacted them. I lost the best ones. I managed to save a couple of smaller files, but that's all I'm bringing over."

Rick frowned at the thought of paying two attorneys on his caseload. "I started some marketing, but we'll improve how we find new contacts. I'm assuming prospective clients won't be able to resist the charm of two dashing attorneys."

"Hopefully we'll have more to sell than our good looks."

"We're funny, too."

"It's looking like we're in trouble."

They spent the next twenty minutes straightening the office, hanging diplomas, and placing some files on shelves. Rick sat in the faux leather chair he placed in the office.

"Now that you're close to being set up, let's talk about the work we have and how we can split the tasks."

Arnie pointed to the files behind him. "I got some work to do on those cases. A few depos and discovery responses, but I'm going to be a bit lean for a while." He frowned.

"Not to worry," Rick said. "Like I told you, a couple of my cases are heating up and they're why I asked you to come aboard. Both have a lot of outstanding discovery and are scheduled for mediation in two weeks before Ken Nisken. We have a lot of work to do to prepare for the mediations and if we can resolve either one of them, that might go a long way to getting some bills paid."

"I also wanted to let you know that when I went back to retrieve my belongings from the firm, Crotec and Spencer didn't leave my side, making sure I didn't cause any trouble. As I was leaving, they mocked me for coming to work with you. They called both of us losers, and said they would make you look stupid in your case with them. They promised to use all the big firm tactics we were taught and bury us under paper."

Rick waved his hand. "Screw them. Like I told you, I'm more than ready to handle anything they throw our way. So let's open up these files and learn them inside and out, so when we are face-to-face with them we can demonstrate our superiority."

Rick's voice got louder as he emphasized the last couple of words. He reached his fist in front of him and Arnie tapped it with his. "I got your back, brother."

Rick pictured two movie heroes standing back-to-back fending off the zombie mob, fighting until hope was almost extinguished and then figuring out a narrow escape route. He wondered in their newly formed tandem, if they would find redemption or get devoured before finding their path to safety.

CHAPTER TWENTY-NINE

DRESSED IN A PRIM, green, summery dress with delicate, long sleeves, Emily Hawkins entered the office and in a small voice announced her presence. "Hello, Rick, it's me, Emily. Are you here?"

She examined the framed picture of a smoky city, its buildings silhouetted by the dusky sunlight. Surprised hearing an unrecognized voice approaching her from behind, she spun and was greeted by a tall, dark haired man extending his hand.

"Arnie McBride. I'm new here. Hoping to help out on your case–if that's okay with you."

"Sure," Emily said with a lurch. "Is Rick still meeting with me?"

"Of course. We figured two for the price of one is an excellent deal."

Emily grinned and let go of Arnie's hand. "I don't know much about mediation, or what I need to do."

"Don't worry," Arnie said, "It's our job to answer your questions."

He led her to the conference room and before they took

seats, Rick arrived carrying a pile of papers with his yellow legal pad sitting on top.

"You ready to start?"

She pulled a chair from the table and sat. "Fire away."

For the next hour, they took turns explaining the dynamics of a mediation and trying to set her expectations at a reasonable level so there was, at least, a chance of getting the case resolved. The two lawyers explained how, unlike a judge, a mediator wields no real power, his purpose to allow the parties to find common ground to reach a settlement.

"He will start with everyone in the same room," Rick explained, "but will separate the parties and then move back and forth trying to convince Emily to lower her demand and getting the defendants to offer more money. If successful, they will meet somewhere in the middle and, poof, the case is resolved."

Arnie stood and walked to the window. "It's never that easy," he said, "B & D will come up with all sorts of reasons why they will win the case or how we're asking for too much money. We will try to convince the mediator why your monetary demands are more than reasonable.

Emily lifted her eyebrows and nearly raised her hand wanting to interject. "Will I speak at the mediation?"

Rick laughed. "Doubtful. Lawyers like to maintain control of their clients. We understand what you want and it's better if we do the talking. Sometimes people act testy. We're trained to maintain our composure."

"Which we can do, most of the time," Arnie said, smacking Rick on the back. He turned towards Emily, "I won't tell you about the time at a deposition where Rick got in a shouting match over whether he could confer with the witness–that's ancient history."

Rick pushed Arnie away with a subtle elbow and addressed

Emily. "I told you before, I worked with the attorneys representing the store. Arnie did also and truth be told, neither one of us likes them. I don't think they're trustworthy, but that's not your problem—it's ours. I doubt our relationship with them will be a factor at the mediation, so no need to worry."

The two lawyers sat opposite Emily and explained how the facts of the case are important at the beginning of the mediation, but predicted how the mediator would move away from what happened to Jerry in the parking lot because he didn't want the parties to bog down in arguing over whose side was right. Rather, he would focus on the money and as long as the parties continued to compromise, the mediator would be happy—and the likelihood of a settlement would increase.

"What's my role, if you guys are doing all the talking?"

"Fair question," Rick said. "Your role is important. You're supposed to scare them. Not by being an ogre, but by being someone they wouldn't want in front of a jury. We want you to be calm and appear reasonable. Not someone who would fall apart if they got a chance to cross-examine you. We want you to be sympathetic—which won't be too hard because you are now a widow as a result of what they did."

Rick explained how other clients had torpedoed possible settlements by being too pushy or by not being patient with the process. "This can take hours and you will feel frustration. That's typical. Don't let that interfere with how we handle the mediator. We will be upfront with him, but only to a degree. We'll play some poker. I don't want the other side to be able to read us by how we act."

Emily crossed her arms and stared straight ahead.

Rick laughed. "I think you understand the point."

He stacked up his papers spread across the conference room table.

"One last concept to discuss. I don't want you to get your

expectations too high. Chances are the case won't settle at the mediation. That's okay, because we can still learn something about their thinking while we're talking with them. We may throw out some major dollar figures, but I don't want you to assume the case is worth that much just because we ask for the money. I'm optimistic they will be reasonable and you can leave the mediation never having to worry about going to trial."

Arnie leaned in and added, "You're in charge. We don't make any demand you haven't approved first and the only way the case resolves is if you agree. It's your case and you're the boss."

They glanced at each other and then at Emily. "You got any more questions?" Rick asked.

She shook her head. "Nope. I understand much better than I did." She stood and gave both attorneys hugs. "Thanks guys. I'm glad you're in charge."

They walked her to the front door and watched her trot down the front steps. Once they shuffled back to the offices down the hallway, Arnie leaned against the frame of Rick's door with his hands in his pockets. "Think this mediation will be productive?"

Rick sat on the edge of his credenza and cocked his eyes towards the ceiling. "Who knows? Wouldn't it be amazing if we can settle and have some money flowing into the firm? With your buddies Spencer and Crotec on the other side, anything might happen. Problem is, I won't trust a word coming out of their mouths. So, I guess that makes reaching an agreement a little more difficult."

Arnie turned to leave, but stopped. "In fifteen minutes we do it again with your tiger dude."

Rick grabbed his phone. "Wait till you meet this guy. He will blow your mind."

"You've been building him up for weeks. No way can he

meet my overblown expectations."

CHAPTER THIRTY

NOT FIFTEEN MINUTES after Emily left the office, Billy Blevins banged on the door ready to prepare for his mediation, scheduled the morning before Emily's. Never had Rick participated in two mediations on the same day, let alone with the same mediator.

Billy sauntered into the conference room, dressed in a green silk shirt and wide-legged white pants. He poured himself a glass of water and bowed in Rick's direction. Rick wondered if doing back-to-back sessions was too ambitious, and perhaps, overly optimistic.

Without saying a word, Billy took the seat at the head of the table.

Rick walked over and stood over him until Billy sheepishly removed himself and slunk over to the next seat.

"Thanks. That's my seat," Rick mumbled, sliding in the vacated chair.

After introducing Arnie to Billy, Rick went into a similar spiel as he had with Emily, explaining the ins and outs of mediation, what Blevins should expect to happen, and how he should handle himself. Billy stared at the wall without giving any indication of listening. Within minutes, it was apparent Billy wasn't as compliant as Emily and more willing to disregard the instructions of his attorneys and pursue his own agenda.

"Billy, focus!" Rick demanded. "You aren't listening and your attention is somewhere else."

"Sorry, man. I'm hearing what you're telling me, I'm just on a different page. You guys don't understand how this is screwing with me. When Frank Francisco first called me, I didn't know who he was. He wanted to invest in my parks. Against my better instincts, I took him in as a minority investor, yet he's trying to take over the whole business right under my nose."

Rick glanced up from his yellow pad. "It's not so simple. You both are pursuing breach of contract claims against each other. He has a separate tortious interference with contract lawsuit against you and your federal court suit claiming Francisco secured a contract through fraud for another business of his by taking proprietary information from your zoos is pending."

"His claims against me are bullshit. I have the bastard over a barrel with mine."

The last remark made Rick squirm. He leaned his head forward, placing it in his hands.

"Your claims are not as strong as you think, and his claims against you aren't crap. They are legitimate. The evidence suggests you made a series of phone calls to a company with whom Mr. Francisco was about to enter into a significant supply contract. After your calls, the other company backed out and it took him six months to fill the gap. As a result, he lost a bunch of clients and lots of money. Sounds like a decent claim."

A couple of small beads of sweat appeared on Blevins' forehead. "That slime bag is trying to screw me over and you're taking his side." Blevins stared Rick in the eyes.

Neither blinked.

"Listen," Rick said, "my job is to gather the facts and then analyze them for you. I'm not going to blow smoke up your ass and tell you your case is a winner when it's not. That doesn't help either one of us."

Rick paused to allow Blevins a chance to regain his composure. "Your claims have some merit and so do his. That's my analysis."

"He's trying to steal my business and you're letting him get away with it."

Rick focused on the ceiling. "No, we're fighting for you. Now, we come up with a plan for negotiating."

The tension in the room dissipated somewhat as they discussed the best ways to extract a settlement offer from Francisco. Rick's blood pressure went up each time Blevins' neuroses kicked in causing him to veer the conversation towards imagined sleights and other irrelevant matters. By the end, Rick couldn't decide if he had participated in a preparation meeting or a counseling session.

"Don't know what that was all about," Arnie said after Blevins departed. "I didn't say anything of value. I wanted to help, but it went off the rails right from the beginning."

"Nothing for you to do. He's Billy Blevins and sometimes he talks, but rarely does he listen. I'm betting this mediation will be going down the tubes, but it'll be interesting to witness the festivities from center ice. Sort of like watching a slow motion train wreck."

CHAPTER THIRTY-ONE

GLASS WALLS reminiscent of Hannibal Lector's jail cell enclosed the series of conference rooms. The aura, however, was much sleeker and more modern than an antiquated lockup. Ken Nisken's offices provided an impressive, yet utilitarian, venue for mediations. Each room had every electronic hook-up conceivable so attorneys and their clients would be productive during times when the spotlight shone on other participants.

Lawyers understood conferences might take as much as ten hours with the mediator moving from room to room handling the negotiations. In a complicated, multi-party piece of litigation, some defendants could hang out in their rooms, without participating in active negotiation for hours, only saved from complete boredom by utilizing internet access through a computer or cell phone.

A spunky, young receptionist held the door open for Rick, Arnie, and their flamboyant client, Billy Blevins. "Mr. Nisken will begin the mediation once all parties are here and ready. We will meet in the central conference room first and then you can break out to your own room."

She pointed across the poured concrete hallway to a larger conference room in the middle of the smaller satellite rooms. "Coffee and soda are set up in the hallway with bagels and donuts. Please help yourself to whatever you like." She made an awkward half-bow, turned, and slid out of the room.

"Nice digs," Blevins said, looking up at the halogen lights casting direct beams onto the long, dark table in the center. "This guy must pull in a lot of cash. I hope he's worth the price."

Rick stood and walked over to Blevins. "Billy, mediation only works if the parties are willing to compromise. How are you feeling about that, today?"

"Not good. I didn't sleep at all last night, worrying about how the rat tried to screw me over. Not good at all."

Rick turned away and rolled his eyes for Arnie's benefit. He mouthed, "Awesome."

Arnie nodded and directed his attention to his yellow pad as Blevins paced around the table.

Stilted conversation, mixed with an occasional uncomfortable silence, marked the next ten minutes until the mediator stuck his well-coiffed, gray haired, head into the room. He extended his hand to Blevins, "I'm Ken Nisken. I'm well acquainted with your fine lawyers."

Rick smiled, knowing he had met the mediator only once before at a conference, while Arnie didn't know the man.

"If you're ready to start, please head over to the center conference room. Mr. Francisco and his attorney are already in there."

From their vantage point looking into the other room across the hall, they had no difficulty distinguishing the lawyer from the client as they sat with their backs facing towards them at the long table. The long flowing mane of blond, teased hair draped the back of the man sporting black leather pants and tight-fitting leather blazer. No introduction was needed–this was Tiger Land owner, Frank Francisco. The gentleman with the corporate part in his jet black hair wearing the pinstriped suit was, without a doubt, Thomas Rorspot. Rorspot's well-deserved reputation of a soft spoken attorney with a meticulous, crafty mind, preceded him.

Extending his well-manicured finger, Nisken directed Rick's group to the far side of the table and then took the seat at the head to place himself between the two sides. He exchanged glances with both groups, "Thank you for providing me with your mediation statements. You gave me a lot to digest, but I believe a resolution can be found."

Rick leaned back in his chair. This was the same crap every mediator spouted. They always displayed optimism and then went into their speech about how the parties should go outside their comfort zones to reach a resolution. After five minutes of additional introductory commentary, Nisken glanced at Rick and asked if he wished to make any presentation to the other side.

Rick was about to decline, but Blevins leaned forward with his eyes not blinking, and said, while pointing at his business partner, "He better be paying me lots of money. Trying to steal my business is bad enough, but going around and spouting lies to ruin my reputation is worse. I've told my attorney to add a claim for defamation."

He glanced over at Rick, who avoided his gaze.

Francisco threw back his head and his mouth rounded. "I'm ruining your reputation?" He put his hand on his chest. "Billy, you told everyone I'm a loser and I'm incompetent running a business. I couldn't open up another zoo because you dragged my name through the mud and now everyone in town thinks I'm a moron."

"I wonder why?" Billy said under his breath, a smug expression on his face.

And away we go. . . . Rick pictured the chances of reaching a settlement melting like an ice cube on a hot sidewalk.

Nisken stood and extended his arms out to the side. "Let's take a break. Everyone should move back to their own rooms. We can talk it out separately."

"I'm so sorry, Rick," Blevins said once they returned to their conference room. "I don't know what got into me. You told me not to talk, but I'm so emotional." He fanned his face.

"That was plain stupid," Rick said. "Pissing off the other side in the first five minutes of a mediation is not the best tactic." He waved a hand at his client and walked to the far side of the room.

Arnie followed Rick, but didn't say anything allowing him a moment to calm down.

Rick turned back to Arnie and whispered, "We're screwed. Now we're just wasting our time. These two want to kill each other."

Arnie shook his head. "That's not my read. There's so much emotion–something else is at play. They both are mad, but I don't think it's about the case. You won't believe this, but I think the best thing might be to put them back in the same room to talk it out."

"They'll maul each other."

Arnie put a hand on Rick's shoulder. "I think if we keep them apart, Billy's just going to fly off the handle. They need to be in the same place and talk about what's bothering them."

"How are you so sure?"

"My family growing up–we all acted like this. Way too emotional. We yelled a lot, because we cared. The biggest problem was when one of my brothers spent time alone the anger just built up, but when we got together, we managed to work things out. There were some broken dishes and scream-ing, but letting out our emotions worked and by the end of the night we would be outside playing basketball. These guys are a little different, but I think it's a similar dynamic."

As Arnie finished his thought, the conference room door opened. Nisken stuck his head in and apologized for how the mediation had begun. He said, "Francisco's pissed at what your client said and has threatened to leave the mediation."

Rick caught Arnie's glance, who nodded his head. Rick lowered his eyes, but said, "Before they go, we think it may be productive if we put everyone back in a room and let them yell at each other."

"Are you nuts?" Nisken asked. "You saw what happened a few minutes ago, didn't you?"

Rick walked behind his client, whose eyes remained little, narrowed slits. "Do you think it might help if you two talked?"

Billy appeared confused. "Why? He's only going to insult me more. But I got more to say. I guess it can't hurt."

Nisken shook his head. "If you think it's best. I'm willing to give anything a try."

They followed Nisken back to the center conference room where they took seats across the table from Francisco and his lawyer. Nobody spoke as everyone's eyes darted from one person to the next like the moments before the shootout in a Leone spaghetti western. Rick half expected The Man with No Name suddenly to appear and gun them all down.

Instead, it only took an apology to break the ice.

"I'm sorry, man," Blevins said, reaching his hand across the table. "I thought you were trying to screw me out of my zoos. I'm not sure what the truth is and if I find out that you are doing anything to hurt our business, I'm going to string you up by your balls."

The apology wasn't much, but Francisco laughed. "Billy, I'm not trying to screw you out of anything. I want to learn from you and, someday, run my own set of zoos. You're the best in the industry."

Blevins blushed. "C'mon man, you're just talking. I wanted to work with you because you are a technology wizard and would help me update how we run our business. I never wanted to cause you any problems."

"Then why the hell did you sue me?"

"Because you sued me first."

Both men laughed and then fell silent. The three lawyers and mediator watched without saying a word amazed that so much progress had occurred in three minutes.

Billy tilted his head. "So, do you think we can work this out?"

Francisco leaned his head to mirror Blevins. "Possibly, but you're going to pay me cash for the trouble you caused and to settle my lawsuit against you."

"And you will pay me money to get rid of my suit against you."

Francisco nodded his head with deliberation. "It's going to cost you ten thousand dollars to make me drop my claims."

"Funny, I was about to say the same thing about my case."

Francisco rose and extended his hand. "Then we have a deal. You pay me ten thousand dollars to settle my claims and I will pay you ten thousand dollars to settle yours."

Billy stood to shake Francisco's hand. "I think we've come to a settlement."

Not wanting to let a deal fall through, Nisken pounced and smacked both litigants on the back. "We have a deal. We will write this up so both parties can sign. I believe we can call this mediation a success.

Billy glanced at his attorneys and with sincerity said, "Thanks guys, you were a huge help. Can you give us a few minutes to discuss how we will handle our businesses moving forward?"

"Sure, Billy, we'll give you a few minutes."

Rick and Arnie returned to their conference room and couldn't control their laughter once inside. "Careful," Rick said, "they still can see us."

Arnie moved towards the sunlight streaming in through the oversized window. "That was unexpected."

"Never saw that coming. Won't be much of a fee out this and now my best client is free of litigation."

"Don't worry," Arnie responded. "He's enough of a wildcard that he'll be involved in more litigation within six months. I promise. He's happy now. I think their relationship runs deeper than we thought. I think this all boils down to 'feelings'–and once they said something positive, they realized their relationship was more important than the lawsuits."

The sun broke through a cloud outside and the room brightened. Rick walked to the side table and grabbed a bottle of water. "This was almost too easy. We didn't do much to facilitate the settlement."

"Sometimes just getting them in the same room is enough. You earned your fee for today. Think reaching a resolution will be as easy with our next case?"

Rick glanced at his watch and shook his head. "It's an hour until Emily gets here and no, we can't expect the next mediation will end as easily as this morning's proceedings. Remember, your buddies, Spencer and Crotec, are coming. We're going to be slimed by the time the afternoon is over."

The two lawyers grabbed their suit jackets and nabbed some food from the hallway. They ate in silence, waiting for the afternoon session to begin.

CHAPTER THIRTY-TWO

In the minutes before Emily Hawkins' scheduled arrival, clouds covered the sky, causing the conference room to dim. Its illumination now consisted of a fluorescent glow, rather than natural light pouring in from outside.

Further dampening his mood, Rick received two emails which interfered with his focus. The first, from Judge Markum's chambers scheduling an argument on a summary judgment motion on a small matter Rick was confident he would lose. The second, a diatribe from Molly, detailing another long night of screaming from Samantha.

Rick recited a brief summary of the email to Arnie, who replied somewhat non-responsively, "You married way above your batting average. How did you let her go?"

Arnie's passing comment caused a flood of conflicting emotions that encapsulated his three year marriage: overwhelming love, frustration, and guilt. Seemingly simple concepts, but at this point still mish-mashed together in a conglomeration he couldn't separate without years of therapy–a ritual he was unwilling to undergo during their marriage and one he still wouldn't commit to pursuing.

"It's a long story," he mumbled. Arnie did not follow-up.

They stared at their phones, prepared for the second mediation. They understood the strengths and weaknesses of their case. Perusing the file wouldn't put them in a better position for negotiations. The chances of settlement depended on whether Spencer and Crotec viewed their case in a similar light.

Edginess crept into Rick's gut. Typical for him before any court appearance, but somewhat unusual for a mediation. Today there would only be one of two outcomes. The first, they settle, the case is over and Rick collects a fee without having to prepare for trial. The second, they don't reach a settlement, and they are one step closer to a trial. Although a settlement under most circumstances is a positive outcome, the lack of an agreement isn't always bad.

Rick took a deep breath, and while exhaling, extinguished any extraneous thoughts of his ex-wife, so he could focus on negotiating for the next four hours.

The door to the room swung open and a voice in the hallway said, "Your attorneys are right inside." Rick and Arnie stood to greet Emily dressed in a pale green, flattering, yet simple, pants suit.

She entered with her head erect and arm extended towards Rick. "I went out yesterday and bought this outfit at TJ's. I hope it's appropriate."

"It's perfect. You come across as smart and sophisticated."

Rick pulled out a chair for her. She sat and stared back and forth between her attorneys.

"Anything else I need to think about? When do we start?"

Arnie noticed movement in the conference room across the hall. "They're here." He pointed, "Spencer is the tall one and Crotec sports the bushy hair."

Emily nodded and added, "The African-American man is the manager I spoke to when I went to the store. He wasn't pleasant when we met."

The air conditioning in the conference room clicked on trying to cut through the rising heat from the unseasonably warm weather outside.

Rick put a hand on Emily's shoulder. "Remember, this is business. We all keep our emotions in check."

"Got it, boss."

Two minutes later, Nisken poked his head into their conference room and invited them to join the other side in the center conference room. With deliberate calm, Rick led his delegation out of the room, the gnawing in his gut inhibiting his ability to project confidence. Rick wiped the palms of his hands against his pants as they entered the room.

"A pleasure to see both of you," Spencer said, a huge grin plastered across his face.

"You also, Virgil," Rick extended his hand. *You're a lying, piece of crap* were the actual words formulated in his head, but which he exchanged for what came out of his mouth.

"How are you, Seb?" Arnie asked Crotec. Rick had little idea what words were bouncing around his partner's head, but he remained confident they included some choice expletives.

Emily and Wayne Oliver nodded at each other and introduced themselves to their counterpart's attorneys. The seven people in the room took seats around the conference table.

Silence consumed the room allowing Nisken to provide a similar introduction as in the first mediation. He paused after completing his monologue and asked Rick if he wanted to say anything to the other side.

Hoping to introduce some tension into the proceedings, Rick stood and moved to the white board on the wall by the immense window.

"I don't want to take up a lot of time rehashing facts everyone in this room already accepts," he began, "but let's make sure we're on the same page. The following is uncontested: An overzealous assistant manager from B & D chased down Jerry Hawkins in the parking lot. He deputized two other shoppers to imprison Mr. Hawkins by sitting on him, not allowing him to move or to breathe. They never made sure he was okay and when the police arrived, they got off him, but not before they killed him. We have no doubt they violated Pennsylvania law and are responsible for paying damages to his estate."

Rick paused and picked up a marker. "Emily, as his surviving spouse, is entitled to the following types of damages:" He scribbled on the white board while saying, "Jerry's conscious pain and suffering, his past and future lost wages, humiliation and Emily's loss of her husband's consortium. These are the primary forms of damages, but if we end up at trial, we will pursue other categories of recoverable damages."

Spencer and Crotec jotted notes on yellow pads while on occasion looking up.

Not having any paper to write on, and unsure where she should be looking, Emily took in her attorney's presentation, staring straight at him.

Rick spent a few minutes discussing the elements of damages and why for each Emily expected to receive substantial money from a jury. With his back to his audience, Rick jotted a number underneath the list, placed a dollar sign before it and circled it. He turned around with his body blocking his writing. "On behalf of her dead husband, Emily Hawkins demands that the defendants pay her . . . ."

Rick stepped aside to reveal his client's demand. " . . . the sum of five million dollars."

The room remained quiet. Spencer and Crotec barely acknowledged the presentation was complete. They glanced at each other without speaking until Crotec stood without moving to the front of the conference room. "That was unfortunate, but expected."

Turning his head ever so slightly in Emily's direction, he continued, "Losing a spouse is difficult and the people of B & D appreciate the difficulties you have suffered as a result of your husband's death. They regret he died on their property. Unfortunately, with such a demand, it's clear Mr. Waterston's client expects a windfall—which B & D is not now, and will not at any time prior to trial, be prepared to pay."

Crotec directed his attention to the mediator. "What they failed to discuss—or take into consideration—is Mr. Hawkins brought his own death on himself. He stole from the store. He did not heed warnings and when lawfully detained, he resisted. No settlement can occur unless Ms. Hawkins accepts the fact her husband bears significant responsibility for what happened in the parking lot. We come here today in good faith—in recognition of Mrs. Hawkins' loss. This said, B & D cannot, and will not, be told the actions of its employees were the sole cause of his death."

Crotec grabbed a stack of papers and thumbed through them allowing him time to take a deep breath.

"We were hopeful coming into today, that reasonable heads would prevail and a settlement might be reached. We are much less confident in light of the exorbitant demand presented today. When we talked to our client yesterday they provided us with significant authority to settle, but with this demand, we are in two different ballparks and miles apart. In light of this demand, we must call our client to determine if there is any hope of settling and until we have this discussion, on behalf of B & D, we offer ten thousand dollars."

Crotec dropped his head and shrugged his shoulders. He raised his eyes and caught the eye of the mediator. "B & D provided us with additional authority they wish to offer to Mrs. Hawkins. This, however, will only be done after a major reduction coming from the plaintiff." He shifted his gaze to Emily and then to Rick before sitting down.

The air in the room seemed heavier. Rick and Arnie grabbed their yellow pads and signaled to Emily to follow them as they returned to the other conference room.

Tears formed at the corners of Emily's eyes. "They think that's what his life is worth?" She collapsed into a chair.

"Of course not," Rick said. "This is where we begin. We have room to negotiate."

Nisken entered and sat across from Rick. They talked about the pros and cons of the case and of presenting evidence to twelve strangers sitting in judgment. Nisken focused on how Jerry's theft might influence a jury. Consistent with their prior discussions, they reduced their demand by two hundred and fifty thousand dollars to four million, seven hundred and fifty thousand dollars.

Less than ten minutes later, Nisken returned shaking his head. "They've raised their offer to twenty-five-thousand dollars."

"Dammit," Arnie said under his breath, and then made his voice audible. "They're screwing with us. This will never work."

"I understand." Nisken frowned. "Can we cut to the chase and make a more measured demand?"

Rick glared at the mediator. "They suffocated him on their property. We *are* being measured." He glanced at Emily who nodded her head. "We can go to four million, but we're walking if their next offer isn't in seven figures. Got it?"

"I will convey your offer," Nisken said on his way out of the room.

It didn't take long for the mediator to return. "They're offering 50k."

"Fifty thousand dollars. You're kidding," Arnie smacked the table.

"They said their authority is capped at a hundred thousand." Nisken didn't bother to place his whole body in the conference room.

Sensing they'd been played, Rick stood to gather his materials and place them in his bag. "We're out of here. This was a complete waste of time."

After collecting their belongings, Rick, Arnie, and Emily walked into the hallway.

Spencer and Crotec met them in the void between conference rooms.

Rick wanted to avoid saying anything, but Crotec approached with his hand outstretched and a plastered smile back on his face. "I thought we might resolve this, but sometimes you don't arrive at where you want"

Rick placed a hand on Emily's back and whispered to her, "Give us a minute." He returned after depositing her down the hallway, placing her out of earshot.

Crotec stood next to Spencer, his hands tucked in the pockets of his pants.

Rick threw his shoulders back. "You guys don't want to settle. You wasted our time."

Crotec gazed at Spencer. "We didn't think we wasted our time. We got what we wanted out of this. Rick, you should take our money. The guy's a thief–perhaps worse. Plus, aren't you in a little over your head with a case like this?"

Rick felt his face go red. "What are you talking about?"

Crotec smiled. "Nothing. We can deploy the full resources of our firm to fight this case. You have–well–your firm. It's not a fair fight."

Arnie stepped forward and put a hand in front of Rick's chest. "Don't respond. These clowns like to talk trash. The problem is they don't know how to back it up. It's style over substance with these boys–except their style is substandard. They spend a thousand dollars on their suits and somehow still make them look cheap."

Rick turned his head from the other attorneys. "Excellent point, Arnie. Let's go retrieve our client. She's classier than these ass clowns."

Rick's disdain oozed from his pores. He turned on his heels to walk down the hall. Before they got within hearing distance of Emily, he said, "Settling for a chunk of change would have been satisfying, but getting the money from a jury is going to be even sweeter."

Arnie smiled and nodded.

CHAPTER THIRTY-THREE

WITH THE DOUBLE mediation behind them. Rick and Arnie hung out in their oppressively hot conference room back at the office. They took off their sports coats, rolled up their sleeves, and kept their arms lowered to avoid displaying the sweaty pits of their dress shirts.

They stood on opposite sides of the table covered with folders, files and miscellaneous papers comprising the *Hawkins vs. B & D* file. The gloom, which permeated their mood when the mediation failed to produce a settlement had morphed into near mania with the two attorneys exchanging dueling theories of liability, synopses of evidence and outlines of additional discovery and investigation they needed to perform prior to completing their preparation of the case prior to trial.

"Good point. We got them on violation of the merchant's law and basic assault. I'm more concerned with getting the jury pissed at the company, not just the manager," Rick said, waving a pleading above his head and then lowering it.

"That's what I've been arguing from the beginning," Arnie

countered. "We need to get more discovery on their training procedures. We don't know from a corporate perspective what their philosophy was, and we don't know whether the store actually followed corporate rules."

Rick scribbled on a yellow pad and rolled his hand in a circular motion to get Arnie to continue his thinking.

"So we need more depositions of the corporate reps and some more of the store personnel. We need to depose the store director, Oliver. He attended the mediation, but didn't say a word. Not sure what kind of witness he would make. We also must take Morgan Askew's deposition. I want to find out what was going through his head and why he thought he should tackle Jerry rather than let him go."

"That's helpful. You will be in charge of the store workers. I will handle the corporate people and after we finish with those depositions we can compare and see if they're playing from the same playbook." Rick strode over to the pot of coffee and refilled his mug. He filled Arnie's cup when he waved it at Rick.

While placing the pot back on the burner, Rick continued, "What about experts? How many do we need?"

Arnie shook his head back and forth, and then shrugged his shoulders, so Rick answered his own question. "We need a security expert–someone to talk about how a store is supposed to handle shoplifters. I assume we can find someone who thinks people shouldn't die even if they were shoplifting. We also should get a medical witness to discuss how Jerry died."

Arnie shot a hand in the air. "You're right. We need to make the death sound horrific to get the jury pissed off. You know what–you read the autopsy– it sounded bad. I think we talk to the coroner who did the autopsy. He should be willing to help out–for a fee."

"Perfect. You take care of the liability expert and I will work on the medical side of things. Too bad we had this meeting– now we realize how much more work we have before we even think about getting this scheduled for trial."

CHAPTER THIRTY-FOUR

Every day is like any other at B & D as the shelves must be stocked, floors cleaned and customers allowed to make their purchases. The store walk was one of Morgan Askew's favorite job activities. Twice per shift he, like all managers, walked the perimeter of the store and attended to any issue that could pose a risk to a shopper or didn't allow for a customer to get a desired product.

The job breakdown for store walks established that the manager should pick up any debris or foreign substance from the floors. In addition, they were to block the displays by moving all product forward so no gaps appeared between items on the shelves. This increased sales dramatically as customers responded better to a stocked display than one which customers had picked over.

Walking through the store scanning the floors and shelves made Morgan appear busy without putting out a lot of effort. Occasionally, he bent over to pick up a stray wrapper or move a box on a shelf to position it better, but for the most part, his store walks allowed him to get in some steps and shoot the breeze with some team members working in the aisles.

Excellent at remembering everyone's name, Morgan would shout out, "Hey, Betsy, excellent job getting the oil filters on the end cap. Do you need any help this afternoon?" He knew people liked when management recognized them for doing their jobs and was confident his offer of assistance would be rejected.

The store walk took most managers thirty minutes to complete, but Morgan often took longer. He left one of the experienced cashiers in charge up front. As he approached the front end, ready to resume his responsibilities, he felt a strong hand on his shoulder.

"Morgan, you got a minute?" a deep voice asked from behind. He turned to find the store director, Wayne Oliver, dressed as he was every day, in dark blue dress pants and a crisp button-down shirt. Oliver towered over Askew and with a subtle pull on his blazer guided him to a corner of the aisle uninhabited by shoppers.

"I'm letting you know," Oliver said in a hushed tone, "corporate appreciates how hard you've been working and the extra shifts you took when that flu spread through here."

Morgan didn't add anything hoping for more positive critiques and word on a possible promotion.

"You heard the case with the guy who died in the parking lot didn't settle like we hoped. Almost certain it's going to trial. The suits are concerned about it. Worried bad publicity will cause us to lose business. They wanted to make sure you're willing to do your part."

Askew leaned in. "I am."

Oliver lowered his voice another notch. "What they wanted is to make sure you're ready to paint a picture at trial which helps the company. They don't want people to think our managers are running rogue in the stores."

"I'm following you."

"They told me to remind you that your performance review is coming up at the end of the year. The store's profits and your review will be dependent on what happens at this trial." Oliver paused. "If you want your promotion, you'll have to do your part. Got it?"

Askew nodded his head and muttered, "You can count on me."

Oliver smiled and walked away. The drip of sweat down Askew's back remained the only tangible reminder of his boss's warning.

CHAPTER THIRTY-FIVE

THE MARBLE TRIM SURROUNDED the imposing, black plate glass doors. The façade to the three story converted Victorian was designed to impress anyone passing by the building. Signage in front demanded attention with a cursive font reading, *"Wyatt Creft: Coroner, Renowned Historian and Scientist."*

As Rick trotted up the front steps, he presumed his scheduled meeting with Creft would be among his more memorable encounters with a prospective expert.

After pushing the buzzer and being let into the foyer, Rick found Creft's office without effort as it took up the entire first floor. A tall, bald man in his seventies greeted him with a warm smile, who, without uttering a syllable, projected an overwhelming aura of confidence.

Rick's two hour review of Creft's thirty-nine-page curriculum vitae left him impressed and, somewhat in awe. It contained Creft's undisputed credentials in at least three specialized areas of science, including Forensics. Creft had met with more world-famous people in the past year than Rick would ever hope to meet before he died.

As he entered the suite, Rick noted the considerable importance in his mission to retain Creft. He needed something to spice up Emily's case and a witness he could rely on to rise the ire of the jury. In short, he hoped Creft would breathe some life into Jerry Hawkins' death.

The items displayed with evident care throughout the office paid homage to the sports, political, and scientific superstars Creft had encountered during his career. Signed photographs of him shaking hands with luminaries lined the walls from the entrance to his well-appointed office. Four presidents, three hall-of-fame baseball players and some unrecogniz able faces of men and women in lab coats were included in the gallery.

Rick chided himself for not knowing the identities of the people of science recognizing that to gain the trust of a man like Creft, he had to up his game and be able to discuss Creft's areas of science as if he possessed similar expertise.

Creft's chair, with gleaming polished leather, dwarfed the seat in front of the desk to which Creft directed Rick. Rick sat up erect attempting to compensate for any perceived lack of stature, wanting to establish rapport with this character in the hopes he would agree to testify and allow his weighty credentials to add gravitas to Emily's claim.

"Love the photos and memorabilia." Rick said, sweeping his hand around the room. "Not the typical décor found in the offices of other experts." Rick wanted to let Creft know he'd attended other rodeos.

Creft took a moment to take in the pictures. "I get involved in many interesting cases. Met lots of interesting people."

Famous for ingratiating himself in national investigations, Creft wrangled roles in high profile cases. His picture plastered on the front page of many newspapers, as well as being a favored talking head on national news shows, made his shiny pate recognizable across the country.

"As you can see, we've handled the lion's share of well-known murders, rapes, and abductions over the past quarter century. The recent spate of cases where the police strangled people of color has garnered my attention and I have testified in many of the trials the aggrieved families have pursued. I maintain a well-deserved reputation for diligence and honesty in how I perform my autopsies. Plus, I have testified as an expert witness over one hundred times in federal and state courts. I don't worry much about cross-examination because I am prepared and will tell it like I see it."

None of this surprised Rick, as most experts believed that no lawyer, no matter how talented, could impeach their qualifications and that their testimony always fell on the right side of the truth. This despite the reality that one side paid the expert money to testify, reviewed the expert's report and prepared the witness, often causing him to shade his testimony without the expert realizing he no longer was completely objective.

"I'm sure you know your way around a courtroom and can handle any type of questioning. I'm trying to decide what I want in an expert witness for this case. There are lots of forensic experts available. I'm looking for someone with a strong opinion consistent with our theory of the case."

"Which is that the store manager asphyxiated the deceased."

"Of course." Rick leaned back to let Creft speak, for which he didn't need much prodding.

"You know I performed the autopsy on the deceased. I was inside his body and reviewed every mark on his body. Any other person you pick to testify would only be reviewing my work. Any expert the other side retains will not be able to say he attended the autopsy. I know more about this case already than anyone else will be able to learn in the future."

"True," Rick added, though Creft didn't pause. "Don't you think any jury will want to hear from the guy who stuck his fingers inside the man, who felt his skin and examined the marks on his body? We both know I'm the person who is in the best position to expound on how and why this guy died."

Rick was having troubles formulating questions, which didn't pose a problem for Creft because he didn't require prompting to continue his soliloquy. Despite having interviewed a variety of potential expert witnesses, Rick had never spoken to one who so unashamedly pitched himself as the only reasonable option, and so sat back, not blinking. He couldn't decide if Creft's confidence was a positive, or a personal flaw the other side could exploit.

Before Rick finished contemplating these issues, Creft moved ahead. "We should discuss the costs associated with retaining me. Given the extent of my experience testifying as an expert witness, my office is adept at getting files reviewed and making sure you receive everything you need from me. We are organized and will provide you with billing statements at the appropriate junctions."

"I hadn't asked yet about compensation, but please go ahead."

Creft cleared his throat. "My fees are substantial and non-negotiable. Those who retain my services are, without fail, satisfied, so I am confident whatever you pay will be a worthwhile investment in your case. Many attorneys utilize my reports as leverage to achieve remarkable settlements, and if the case doesn't settle, my testimony will be a decisive factor in a positive jury result. Accordingly, these are my fees: five thousand dollars up front to review the file materials. An additional five thousand to draft my report. It's ten thousand dollars to prepare for testimony, if necessary, and another ten thousand dollars for my one day in court."

"That's thirty thousand dollars," Rick spit out.

Creft nodded and offered nothing further.

Rick understood it was time to make a decision. He balanced the benefits and risks of retaining Creft. The primary benefit, as he pointed out, was his expertise and intimate knowledge of the details of Jerry's autopsy. Another forensic expert could review the same information, but would suffer from not being the one who conducted the autopsy. On the other hand, the cost was, to say the least, high.

In a case with this much potential upside, getting cheap with experts wasn't an option. Creft was a wild card, but also brought attributes no other expert could bring.

High risk/high reward.

Rick tried to focus on the positive side of the equation and realized he had little choice.

"Send me an invoice, and we can get you our file. I'll expect a report within sixty days."

"Won't be a problem and I'm sure you'll be satisfied with my conclusions." He grabbed Rick's hand and shook it with vigor.

For that kind of cash, I better be. He left the office pleased to have scratched off one item from his trial preparation list. He knew when he returned to the office his focus would shift to the other ninety-nine.

CHAPTER THIRTY-SIX

RICK AND ARNIE stood behind counsel table. To their right, Spencer and Crotec preened for the court, offering an almost primitive need to please. A sense of disdain, long dormant, rose inside Rick as he turned his head slightly to see his adversaries out of the corner of his eyes. The genesis of his feelings, stemmed not only for how they humiliated him when he worked at the firm and how they treated Arnie with a comparable level of degradation, but also for their work representing well-heeled corporate entities willing to shell out six hundred dollars an hour for attorneys they could command to do their bidding. This was repugnant to Rick when he was under their thumb, but even more so now that he was on the opposite side of the courtroom.

The tinge of superiority evaporated as Judge Markum took the bench. The judge waved his hand to signal everyone to take their seats. The judge's tipstaff handed him a folder which the judge threw to the side. "We are here for the second pretrial conference in *Askew v. B & D, Inc., et al,*" the judge announced.

The court reporter dutifully tapped at the keys on her machine, so she could produce a complete transcript of the proceedings in the unlikely event any party desired to review what would be said this day in court.

"What's the status of settlement negotiations?" the judge demanded, avoiding any pleasantries.

Rick glanced over at Spencer and Crotec, but when they stared straight ahead, he stood. "Your Honor, the parties engaged the services of a mediator. We didn't resolve the case, primarily because defendants refused to engage in good faith negotiations."

Markum raised his eyebrows and rotated his head, glancing at Spencer for a response. "Your Honor," Spencer said, "obviously the defendant engaged in negotiations with the highest level of good faith. Evaluating a case differently than Mr. Waterston does not suggest bad faith—only a difference of opinion. I agree with opposing counsel, however, we couldn't resolve the case. It appears as though both sides believe a trial will be necessary to reconcile our differences."

Markum jotted notes on a yellow pad without making eye contact. He sat at his bench above the other participants in the courtroom. "We will set this for trial at the end of the conference. How are you on discovery?"

Spencer stood and cleared his throat. "Your Honor, it's nearly complete. All written discovery is done. There are still a couple of witnesses whose depositions we will take in the next two weeks."

The judge nodded at Rick. "Mr. Waterston, anything to add on discovery?"

"I agree with Mr. Spencer. We have completed most discovery and there's no reason the rest can't be finished soon."

Markum said, "Where are we on dispositive motions?"

Spencer glanced at Crotec who shook his head. Spencer

stood and said, "Despite our belief that the law supports the actions of the store, the defendant does not intend to file for summary judgment."

The judge smiled. "If you are so confident in the law, why don't you file a brief? You might get rid of the case without a trial."

"Judge, we would value your input; however, our client does not believe the cost of presenting such a motion is worth it given the limited grants of summary judgment the court has entered recently."

Markum scoffed. "Usually, these issues are better resolved by a jury rather than by me wading through all the evidence." He motioned to Rick. "Does plaintiff intend to file any pretrial motions?"

Rick stood as Spencer sat. "No, plaintiff is prepared to go to trial."

"With discovery nearly complete, settlement explored and no pending dispositive motions, I can set this for trial." Markum glanced at his computer to find the court's schedule. "No need to let this case sit. I can set this trial for the first week in September. Is three months enough time to finish discovery and get ready for trial?"

Both attorneys stood and assented to the schedule. Markum thanked the attorneys for their time and left the bench followed by the court reporter and his tipstaff leaving the four attorneys alone in the courtroom. The sun streamed in though the wooden windows facing the jury box casting a heavenly light on the seats the jurors would occupy once the trial began.

The sound of Spencer and Crotec slamming papers into their brief cases and chuckling grabbed Rick's attention. The faint scent of cigarettes wafted over to him from Crotec's suit. Despite the voices in his head telling him to be quiet, he turned to the two attorneys with a three alarm smile. "Guys, I am so looking forward to spending a week in the same courtroom watching you sweat. Your clients killed this guy, and they're going to pay. You won't be so smug watching the jury return its verdict."

Spencer finished putting the papers in his bag. He then turned to Crotec and spoke to him as if he was the only other people in the room, "Seb, are you concerned about going to trial?"

Crotec grabbed Spencer's arm. "Not really. The law and order citizens who'll inhabit our jury will dislike anyone who goes into a business and steals. I presume they will find he received his just rewards."

Spencer nodded. "I agree. I think we should go back to our swanky offices. We can get some lunch delivered to us."

They left the courtroom without looking at Rick and Arnie.

CHAPTER THIRTY-SEVEN

"You know I can probably get you put in jail," Molly said without any evidence of a smile.

Rick blanched, not having an appropriate response, and not wanting to test the will of his ex-wife. He stumbled for something to say, but all that came out was a series of sounds which didn't actually form words, causing him to blush.

"This is serious. You're six months behind on alimony and four months on child support. I'm not making much money and I'm getting behind on my bills. If my car gets repo'ed, I'm taking yours."

The chatter in the diner wafted over their heads as Rick searched for words to ease his guilt. The smell of greasy fries and hot turkey sandwiches almost overwhelmed his ability to think.

"If it's any consolation, I'm also getting far behind on my rent." He forced a smile, but she remained impassive. "Listen, Moll, I thought my tiger zoo guy would be in litigation for the next ten years and his legal fees would help me get even with you. Unfortunately, he made happy with his partner and settled all his cases so that well has effectively dried up."

Molly rubbed her thumb over her forefinger to depict their former joke of the world's smallest violin. "Your daughter, Samantha, you remember her?"

The rhetorical nature of the question stung. He sat back and let her continue.

"She's having trouble. You know that, but we've started therapy. That's another bill I'm paying. There's enough tension in our house already. Adding money issues will only make her situation worse."

Rick hung his head, but Molly paused, waiting for him to respond. "I'm trying. The practice is picking up. Arnie is a huge help and I think he'll help attract some new clients. The money's not flying in, yet, but it will. I promise."

Molly held up a finger. "Stop. I don't want to hear any more hollow promises. I need to feel confident I can trust you. Please tell me you're not drinking again."

Rick felt the pain in his lower lip as he bit down hard. How far had he fallen in her estimation that she would have to ask? "C'mon, Molly. I haven't had a drink in months. I'm still attending meetings. That's not the issue."

"Then what is?"

"It's not easy starting a new practice. At the old firm, there was always work to do and I didn't worry about bringing it in. Now I have to get the clients, do the work, and pay the bills. It's not easy."

The coffee steam rose from her mug and twirled upwards before dissipating as she took a generous swallow.

Rick's gaze drifted off to the side the familiar patterns in their conversation again hammering him. Somehow they always managed to turn a small problem into a polarizing argument, or a nothing conversation into an analysis of each other's issues. He knew he hadn't been there when she needed him and despite the bitter falling out, he still wanted to earn her respect.

"We just got scheduled for trial in the parking lot case," he said. "It's in a month. With some luck we get a verdict and my firm's financial troubles are taken care of for a short period. I should be able to catch up then."

"Why don't you get the case settled? There's a lot less risk."

"You think? We've tried, but the other side hasn't put as much effort into it. We're headed to trial."

"What makes you so sure you'll get money quickly? Aren't there appeals and motions, and other lawyerly things to do?"

Molly was never one for the details of how the legal system worked, but she wasn't far off with these questions.

Rick looked past Mollie. "You're probably right. Even if we win, it might be awhile until the company pays."

"Awesome. Apparently, Sam and I are on our own until you get your act together."

Rick slunk back in his chair shaking his head. "Please don't talk like that. I will get you what I owe you. I promise–I mean–I'm sure I will."

Molly looked down at her phone. "I also want to let you know that Sam is going to have to be in the hospital for a couple of days. They want to run some tests and perhaps change her medication. The doctor said it would be easiest to admit her for a night to monitor her. Looks like that's happening right when your trial is starting. Don't worry about it, I can take care of it."

Rick grimaced. "Thanks for handling everything, but I'll be there. I want to show my support."

The frown on Molly's face disappeared. She reached for her purse, but Rick threw a twenty onto the table. Molly mouthed, "Thanks." They walked out the front door together and separated to head to their respective automobiles.

CHAPTER THIRTY-EIGHT

EMILY'S quiet confidence jumped out to Rick as she sat at the conference room table hands clasped, not saying a word.

Lawyers and clients usually did not have deep and personal relationships. A lawyer wants to get to know some details of a client's life, but most of the time, only to help with the case–to provide necessary information to answer interrogatories or to provide depth so a jury could relate to the person on the witness stand. Many lawyers don't want to socialize with their clients. There are exceptions, but the risk of crossing ethical lines ordinarily served as enough of a bar that lawyers and clients didn't mix much outside of the office or the courtroom.

Rick had liked Emily since the first day she came to his office. With the exception of the mediation, he never met with her at any other location. For those meetings, she arrived promptly, was always courteous and ready to tackle any task.

With some clients, reviewing discovery responses often devolved into bitch sessions. The client avoided the difficult job of providing precise information and utilized the time to complain about how the case was not proceeding fast enough, how the other side's lawyers weren't so smart or to raise other personal issues floating in the client's head that happened to surface during the meeting. These diatribes serve little beneficial purpose and merely extended the duration of meetings and interfered with creating rapport between attorney and client.

During each session with Emily, however, the pair focused on the impending tasks and completed them without much dithering on unrelated issues. After finishing the work, Emily would rise to say her goodbyes, allowing Rick to move on to the next item on his work agenda. Rick appreciated this consideration of his time and hoped it portended a similar appreciation from the jury when their approaching trial date arrived.

The purpose of this day's meeting was to begin Emily's preparation for trial. It likely would not be the last, but Rick wanted to lay the foundation for how Emily would testify at trial and how she should react during the parade of witnesses, many of whom might offer disparaging information about her husband or her case. He did not know how she would respond to cross-examination, but he needed her to understand the grueling and unrelenting nature of the process and how she couldn't let her guard down at any point.

At times, Rick wondered if Emily was too meek and would not hold up during trial. Today he would probe the contours of her life's story, trying to fill in gaps of what he already knew about her, wanting to paint a picture for the jury of a woman devastated by the loss of her husband. He needed to figure out how compelling her story was and whether she would be able to withstand the rigors of trial.

Stacks of folders spread across the length of the conference room table. Arnie waited at the far end, his role to watch Emily and evaluate, while Rick questioned her.

At this point, it didn't really matter how well Emily

performed. They were stuck with her. So, no matter how pitiful her presentation might be, they couldn't exchange her for someone different. They couldn't go to central casting and find a better actress to play the role.

Emily was the star, and their production depended on her to shine and hit all the high notes. In fact, if she truly excelled, her luster would cover up the warts on their case and dazzle the jurors into awarding her an astronomical amount to compensate her for her loss—at least they could dream.

Rick started the session by describing how the trial would unfold. First, the judge's opening instructions to the jury, continuing to the parties' opening statements and then through the evidence. After all the witnesses testified and the parties introduced any exhibits, each side would give a closing argument. The judge then would instruct the jury on the law that governed her case and the jury would deliberate, culminating in the jury's verdict.

"It's sounds kind of simple, when you put it like that," Emily said after Rick's quick description.

"It is," Rick said. "The hard work is in the details. Arnie and I are responsible for making sure we have the exhibits and to deal with the witnesses. Your responsibility is primarily in your testimony."

"I figured I'd better get that part right." She blushed and smiled.

"You will. If you tell the truth, you'll be fine."

"I think I can do it." She looked down and touched the cuff of her sleeve.

"Your testimony is rather simple. You'll tell the jury about yourself, your husband, and your life together. You'll paint a picture of what your life was before this incident and how his death has changed it."

Emily rolled her eyes. "You're right. Completely simple."

Rick twisted his hand in front of him. "I get it. It's not that simple, but it's stuff you know, and only you know. There's not much they can do to question you on the changes to your life, because you're the only one who has lived your life. You paint the picture for the jury so they see you in the best light possible." Rick paused. "One thing you won't talk about is the incident. You weren't there and you don't know what happened. There's other witnesses for that."

"Good. I've barely been to the store. Jerry did most of the shopping."

Rick and Arnie spent the next two hours talking with Emily about the trial, trying to make her relax about spending a week in a courtroom. They explained to her how she, like the other witnesses, would be cross-examined by the other side's lawyers and to be careful about agreeing to too much, especially when they included arguments in their questions.

With many clients, this first prep meeting caused their heads to spin and their anxiety levels to rise. More than once, a client of Rick's left the initial session screaming that Rick was dumping too much information on him. Yet, Emily displayed nothing to indicate she would cave-in at trial. Maybe it was two lawyers talking to her in different tones that helped her, but by the end of the day, Rick was confident Emily would be an asset at trial, rather than an anchor tied around their necks.

"There's more to discuss at our next meeting," Rick said after reaching three hours of preparation without a break, "but you're handling this like a trooper. I'm looking forward to seeing you testify."

Emily stood and grasped Rick's hand. "I'm not sure I share your enthusiasm, but I couldn't get through this without you. Thanks." She grabbed her coat and slipped out the front door.

Arnie turned his head slightly and stared at the door as it closed. "Who is that woman?"

Rick laughed and slapped Arnie on his back, "She's the woman who'll be getting this firm out of debt."

CHAPTER THIRTY-NINE

RICK AND ARNIE faced each other at the far end of the conference room table with refreshed mugs of coffee steaming in front
of their respective yellow pads. Both poured over their notes
from the just completed prep session with Emily—the snapping
of the thin sheets of paper as they flipped them was the only
sound in the room. They finished reviewing their scribbles at
nearly the same time.

Arnie clasped his hands in front of his body signaling his
intention to allow Rick to speak first.

"I'm rather happy." A slight smirk appeared on Rick's face.
"She's reserved, reasonably articulate, and paints a realistic
picture of their life before Jerry's death and the difference now
with him dead and on her own."

"Keep talking." Arnie didn't raise his head, continuing to jot
notes on his pad.

"I don't know. I feel like if I could build a plaintiff from
scratch, Emily would be close to the ideal. She's personable, but
I didn't think she was overselling. I found her believable. She
gave details, but not too many. I felt like I understood what

she's been going through, without her shoving it down my throat." Rick glanced at his notes and shook his head. "I guess it's nothing specific, I'm almost convinced a jury would view her favorably."

"I hear what you're saying," Arnie said. "She presents rather nicely and acts the part. She's cute, but not drop dead gorgeous. The guys on the jury will like her, but the women won't hate her thinking she wants to steal their husbands. I agree with you—she's smart. There's a certain caginess to her where she finds the perfect word to describe what she's talking about. I also agree that she's able to paint a cozy picture of her family, but somehow it seems a little too easy."

"What are you saying?"

"Not sure. It's like she knew exactly what we wanted to hear and said it. She made her life with her husband before this accident sound almost like a romance novel. They met, they fell in love, they dreamt of the future, and then he got killed."

"Don't you think any jury will relate to her situation?"

"I'm not sure. You know it's hard predicting how people will respond to someone. You're right. She checks all the boxes with us, but will the jury be looking for the same things? I don't want her to sound rehearsed or make their life sound better than it was."

Rick shook his head. "I thought she tried to tell us what her life was like. I didn't get the sense she embellished it to sound better. You try describing intimate details of your life to strangers and get it perfectly right. You won't. You'll highlight the best parts. It's only natural."

"Don't get pissed with me. I love her, too. I'm telling you there's something making it hard for me to connect with what she says. We don't know her very well." He paused to gather his thoughts. "It really doesn't matter because she's our plaintiff, and we can't hire some actress to play the part. I'm hoping a jury reacts to her the same way you are."

"I'm not pissed. I'm surprised you're having doubts. After watching her today I want to call Spencer and gloat a little. Tell him how she's going to make him wish they hadn't taken this case to trial. Ask him if he wants to reconsider their ridiculous offers."

"It's clear we're not getting any more money from them before trial. Our friends, Spencer and Crotec, are bent on making us look stupid for not taking what they've offered. I'm hoping your evaluation of our client is accurate, because if it's not, they are going to be two happy lawyers when the jury comes back."

Rick took a seat and read through his notes again. He tried to discern if he had any bias in his view of his client and felt a slight sliver of panic when he couldn't determine if his need to win influenced his view of Emily.

CHAPTER FORTY

I⟋ wasn't often that Rick got mad at other attorneys. Sure, some liked to play games, but mostly they stayed within predictable lanes and despite advocating for their clients, didn't stray from the understood boundaries that governed attorneys' conduct. Judge Markum, for the most part, forced lawyers to follow these unwritten rules and punished behavior which didn't conform to professional expectations.

Rick stood in Markum's courtroom having difficulty keeping his anger under control. He perused the six-page motion, styled *Emergency Motion to Dismiss Plaintiff's Claims or in the Alternative to Continue Trial,* emailed to him at 4:49 p.m., the day before.

Upon receipt, Rick realized Crotec would present the motion without giving the customary ten day notice causing Rick to let out a torrent of expletives he had not deployed since the worst days near the end of his marriage. The explosive outburst shocked Arnie who came running in from his office to find Rick standing near his window, muttering while pointing at his computer. It took him five minutes to collect his thoughts and explain to Arnie how outrageous it was for Crotec to present the motion the following morning.

They printed out copies of the motion and reviewed it together, each yelling about the factual inaccuracies as if the words on the pages might change in response to their tirade. Despite their entreaties, the words remained the same, so Rick and Arnie spent the next two hours formulating an appropriate response to present to the court.

Rick took his copy of the motion and moved to counsel table when Markum sauntered to the bench without a trace of bemusement on his face. Courts took emergency motions seriously and Markum did not appear in the mood to be summoned unexpectedly to the bench.

"Mr. Crotec, tell me what your emergency is that necessitates the Court deal with your motion without the required ten days' notice."

Crotec stood while buttoning his suit jacket. "Your Honor, we came across a peculiarity with plaintiff's discovery responses and it appears they are withholding evidence from us. Due to the plaintiff's vexatious conduct, we are seeking sanctions including the dismissal of plaintiff's claims against our client. If the court is unwilling to order this remedy, we request a continuance of the trial to complete discovery."

The judge peered out over the top of his glasses. "Those are fighting words, counselor. Please educate the court so it can understand what plaintiff did wrong here."

"Thank-you." He glanced at his notes before lifting his head, first taking a quick glance at Rick and then locking eyes with the judge. "In our discovery requests, we asked numerous times and in every way conceivable manner, for all evidence to support her claim against our client, B & D. We sought all records regarding her husband's shopping at the store and all evidence of anyone having similar claims against the company.

160

To date, despite our requests, we received no such information from the plaintiff.

"The failure to provide this information has prejudiced the defendants who request the court dismiss plaintiff's claims for failing to conduct discovery in good faith. In the alternative, order plaintiff to provide the requested information and move the trial to the next available trial list. We would also request the court sanction the plaintiff by ordering that she cannot present evidence of other potentially similar incidents."

The judge kept his eyes directed at his pad and waved his pen at Rick who stood to respond.

Rick stared straight ahead and took in a big breath of air. "The court is aware the trial in this matter is scheduled in ten days. The parties completed discovery with each side having every opportunity to serve interrogatories, request documents and take depositions of every conceivable witness. In fact, to date, the parties took sixteen depositions. The defendants had the opportunity to take any deposition they requested–and so did the plaintiff."

Rick paused, hoping the judge understood the parties conducted a significant amount of discovery without much interference from either side.

He continued, "The parties had every chance to take discovery and the parties cooperated during the process."

Markum interrupted, "Counselor, your opponent suggests the plaintiff hasn't been so forthcoming and you are withholding information necessary for them to present their defense. How do you respond?"

Rick nodded his head. "B & D claims it asked us about other people who had similar experiences to Mr. Hawkins. We responded that we don't have such information. It's not that we are hiding any information, we just do not possess any to provide to them. We've wondered about similar incidents and don't feel like B & D has been upfront with us about similar incidents which have occurred despite being in a much better position to provide such information than we would be. However, they are correct, we are unaware of such evidence and this is why we haven't provided any."

Markum stared at Crotec shaking his head. "What are they supposed to do if they don't have any evidence of other incidents? Should I sanction them for that?"

The judge leaned forward over his bench and pointed his pen at Crotec. "They won't be able to present any information of similar incidents—not because they are being nefarious, but because they aren't in a position to know what happens at your store."

He stopped and glanced away before returning his glare to Crotec. "Apparently, you provided the plaintiff with no information related to prior incidents, correct? Should I sanction you? Given the aggression with which the store is trying to prevent this information from coming into evidence I am led to believe there are other incidents and you are playing rubber and glue with the plaintiff."

Rick kept his head down while the judge spoke, enjoying the tongue lashing directed at Crotec.

Although Markum had asked Crotec a series of questions, he wasn't really looking for answers. He was blowing off steam outraged at the defense's shameless maneuvering. Any lawyer knew that success with arguing motions before a judge was at times dependent on the mood and whims of the judge. Sometimes the judge might mutter three words during an argument without offering an indication as to his thinking. Then there were times, like this day, where a judge, leaving little doubt as to his mindset, might stick a little prod in the backside of an unsuspecting lawyer.

Rick didn't raise his eyes, hoping the judge would keep his attention directed at Crotec.

Crotec remained motionless and unresponsive, trying to formulate an answer to the multitude of outstanding inquiries.

Judge Markum waved his hand. "Counselor, please sit. There's no need to respond. Your motion is baseless and I am denying it. Let this serve as a warning–unsubstantiated allegations don't do well in this courtroom. Don't bring them here." The judge stood, grabbed his folders and disappeared out the door to his chambers.

Rick followed the judge's lead and grabbed his materials. With the judge's contempt for his opponent's tactics still playing in his head, he couldn't resist the temptation of twisting the knife. "Nice job, Crotec, you guys really nailed that one. Keep making arguments like that and I won't need to put on evidence when we get to trial."

Crotec caught Rick's stare and tried to generate an appropriate comeback, but nothing came out of his mouth.

CHAPTER FORTY-ONE

RISK and its always present partner, anxiety, are constant companions for lawyers during any trial. The possible unexpected answer to even an innocuous question worries every attorney until the jury returns its verdict. This insidious, looming cloud of uncertainty hung over every meeting Rick and Arnie had getting ready to put on Emily's case.

Rick wanted to wall off the rest of his life from the trial and not deal with typical day-to-day responsibilities, but, paying bills still was necessary and if the car broke down, it had to be repaired–the demands of preparing for trial be damned.

The text came at 6:30 p.m. Receiving it was no surprise, and Rick probably would have sent a similar one had he been in a comparable situation. Yet, after spending the prior eight hours reviewing deposition transcripts, interrogatories, medical records, and everything else he needed to know inside and out, he didn't welcome it.

Even Arnie, who generally displayed little outward evidence of internal turmoil, was beginning to show the first signs of cracking. They'd been working in the conference room for nearly two weeks, focusing their vast energy on preparing for Emily's trial, learning the weaknesses of their arguments, while honing their examinations to focus on the strengths of the case.

So when the notification appeared on his phone, Rick tried to avoid it by turning his phone face down on the table. Three minutes later he read it. Despite his overwhelming desire to delete it and pretend he'd never seen it, he knew his only option was to deal with the fallout. The piles of documents on the conference room table and Arnie's incessant, yet relevant, questions, could wait. Ignoring the text would only open the festering wound further. He needed to respond.

"I'm taking a break," Rick said to Arnie, who was scribbling furiously on a yellow pad.

Arnie barely acknowledged Rick's announcement, nodding without taking his eyes off his writing.

Cell phone in his right hand, Rick scampered out of the conference room and ducked into his empty office. He collapsed into his chair and let himself ease backwards, allowing a change in his blood flow and a slight reduction in the stress coursing through his body. He stared at the phone and felt the pangs of guilt gnaw at his insides once again.

Dammit. The trial is bad enough, but now I have to deal with this.

His body balanced almost horizontally in the chair, inches from tipping over onto his head. He let the phone rest on his chest contemplating the response he would issue. Acerbic possibilities whizzed through his head, each, in his mind, more brilliant than the previous one. He knew he would never send any of the wittier ones, and he urged himself to write down some of them to save for another time, but he understood he needed to respond to the text before returning to his trial preparation.

By pulling his head forward, the chair tilted back to its upright position.

The game was over and once again he was the loser. If only this were golf, and he could pick up his opponent's ball to concede the putt, or chess, where he could knock over his king to surrender with grace—but this was life and his failures had consequences. He read the text again:

Rick, my financial situation is getting out of control. I got a notice from the bank that they are going to repossess my car next month. I'm three months behind on the mortgage. Sam needs help. Her new doctor is a pro, but it's getting expensive. The school wants her to get tested, but won't pay for it. You still owe me money. I talked to my lawyer (more cash). He's to send you a threatening letter. Grow a set already, so I don't have to call a reporter. Let me know when you're sending the money.

The brilliant responses which fluttered through his head minutes before vanished. He typed:

Mol, the trial is in two weeks. We're working hard getting ready. Arnie's been an amazing find. I know (and I know I said this before) I owe you the money. You're going to get it right after this trial. Please tell your lawyer to hold off a little so we can get through this trial without any more distractions. Tell Sammie I miss her.

He pressed the send arrow and hoped he wouldn't hear the ping signaling a new text arriving until at least he got home. He raised his head and offered a little prayer Emily Hawkins would hold up as a witness, and pave a path to making things right with his ex-wife and daughter.

CHAPTER FORTY-TWO

Morgan Askew stood before his mom who straightened his tie and then pushed his hair out of his eyes. "Now, you're ready. I hope you make me proud."

Morgan didn't respond and continued to stare up at the ceiling, causing his mom to grasp his chin and pull his head down so he made eye contact. "You're going to be a star," she said while nodding her head.

He slapped at her hand and broke away. "I don't know ma, this isn't so easy."

She squinted her eyes at him. "Don't talk like that. You know what to say."

"I do. They've told me what I need to say and told me if I do it wrong, I may not have my job any longer."

"Don't worry, honey, they need you as much as you need them." She engulfed him in a huge hug, his head buried in her bosom. A quiet moan escaped from his mouth. Monica patted him on the head until he broke free.

"You don't understand. If I don't get this right, those prosecutors could reinstate the charges against me. Prison was horrible. I can't go back."

"Look at me, Morgan." She grabbed both of his hands with hers. "You aren't going back to that jail. You said the lawyers helped you get ready to testify, didn't they?"

"They did, but who knows. Those guys are trying to help me, but the other lawyers, the ones representing the woman whose husband died, they won't be so kind. Their job is to put words in my mouth. They want to confuse me. I'm worried they're going to mess with my head. I won't be able to think too fast with so many people watching me."

Monica's hands flew up to her chest and her head rocked backwards. "You have to do whatever it takes to make sure you don't go back to jail–I couldn't handle it again. Don't you dare do that to me, you understand?"

Morgan's head bobbed up and down. "I do, mamma. Trust me, the last place I want to go back to is there. Our lawyers promised me that if I did what they said, I would be okay and the company would make sure I would stay out."

The green couch behind Monica caught her as she collapsed backward, causing the small polyester cushions to bounce a few inches in the air. She fanned herself with her right hand. Morgan leaned over and put his head in front of hers while grabbing her cheeks with both of his hands. "Don't worry. I will make sure you are proud of me."

"Like I always am." Monica smiled weakly and turned her head away.

CHAPTER FORTY-THREE

THE ROBE WAS BUTTONED HALFWAY REVEALING a white t-shirt and a paunch. Judge Markum paid no heed to his manner of dress as he traipsed around his chambers in black socks, oblivious to the small hole that allowed his left pinkie toe to peek out. The few extra-long hairs curling at the edges of his eyebrows completed the image of a judge devoid of care for his personal grooming.

Rick and Arnie sat on the felt green couch shoved against the wall to the side of his desk, while Spencer and Crotec wedged into two tiny wooden chairs placed on the other side of the desk. They didn't have enough space to put their yellow pads and other documents, and sat in silence as Markum held the floor.

"Once we're done in here," Markum said, his back to the attorneys, "you will head to the jury selection room and pick your jury. You can come back on Monday, and we will start the trial. Any questions?"

"No, Your Honor," Rick said, assuming nothing they said would make much difference at this point.

Crotec, however, wanted to be heard. "Defendants would like to discuss a few matters before we select the jury."

Markum spun on his heels and placed both hands on his desk. "Go ahead, counselor. What would you like?"

Crotec leaned forward holding his yellow pad before him. "Your Honor, defendants filed three motions *in limine* to preclude certain evidence we believe plaintiff will attempt to elicit during trial. We provided your chambers with the motions and the supporting law in corresponding briefs last week. Plaintiff did not file a response." Crotec pulled a stack of documents from his bag and grabbed the one on top. "Our first motion is to preclude any evidence of prior stops made by any B & D employee because such evidence would be irrelevant and highly prejudicial to the defendant because. . . ."

Still leaning on his desk, Markum quietly stated, "Denied, next."

"But you didn't hear our argument," Crotec's voice squeaked a little.

"I read your brief, and your motion is denied."

Crotec shook his head. "Our next motion is to preclude evidence of work the deceased did in the past as he was not working at the time of the incident."

Markum leaned forward a little more so his face was closer to Crotec. "Denied."

"But," Crotec attempted to continue to argue his motion.

"Denied, Mr. Crotec. You may not know, but I'm not a fan of motions *in limine*. I find I do much better hearing the evidence at trial and making rulings on the fly. Do you think I should change my practice, counselor?"

"Well," he stammered, "this is the purpose of motions in limine–to review evidentiary issues before we begin the trial. These are issues that are germane to the evidence the jury will be hearing, and we want to make sure that the court is aware of these issues to avoid any possibility the jury considers improper evidence."

Markum responded in a slow, steady voice that bordered on patronizing. "I understand the purpose of motions *in limine*. I also went to law school. It wasn't one of those fancy law schools you big firm attorneys seem to always attend, but we studied evidence. I like to make my rulings in the context of the testimony a jury hears and I find I do a much better job at avoiding the introduction of improper evidence by doing it this way." He smiled at Crotec, who did not reciprocate. "Mr. Waterston, any need to respond to defendants' motions?"

Rick shook his head. "Plaintiff understands how this court handles evidence. We did not file a responsive brief yet, understanding these issues may come up during trial. We will be prepared to support any evidence we intend to proffer with an appropriate legal basis."

"I look forward to it," Markum said, returning his gaze to his notes. "Any need to discuss settlement one final time? I know mediation didn't resolve the matter, but sometimes the threat of trial is enough to move parties to reevaluate their positions. I'm at your disposal if you think it can help."

Arnie patted Rick on the arm and said, "As you are aware, plaintiff came to the mediation in good faith, ready and willing to discuss settlement. Defendants were looking to get rid of a substantial case at a major discount. They never actively participated in the settlement process. We remain willing to discuss reasonable terms to a settlement. Ms. Hawkins will respond once defendants make a significant offer."

The judge's chair squeaked as he angled himself to face defense counsel. "Sounds like the ball is in your court. You prepared to swat it back?"

Spencer shook his head and exhaled. "The defendants believe they made a reasonable offer at the mediation and their offer was refused. Defendants are not prepared to raise their offer unless plaintiff substantially lowers her demand."

Huffs of air escaped as both Rick and Arnie scoffed simultaneously.

Markum turned his head back and forth between counsel waiting for the logjam to break, but neither side gave any indication of the potential for further movement. "This is why we call in jurors. They will make the final decision as to the value and merit of this case. We will begin at one o'clock this afternoon with jury selection with the goal to have opening statements first thing on Monday."

The judge stood and extended his hand. "I don't need to tell any of you this, and please remind your clients of what I am about to say. There is significant risk on both sides. An individual died on defendant's property. That certainly can be troubling to jurors."

He paused, looking Rick in the eyes. "Please remind your plaintiff there are no guarantees at trial. Yes, her husband died, but the jury will also evaluate his conduct. They may not like it and there is the possibility she gets nothing. Please continue talking and I will see you later today for jury selection."

The words of the judge's warning reverberated in Rick's head as he left chambers.

CHAPTER FORTY-FOUR

COUNSEL SETTLED at their respective tables with Rick and Arnie sitting closer to the jury box as is the custom in every courtroom. The sound of folders and binders dropping onto wood came from their right as Spencer and Crotec emptied their document bags and then made tidy piles of their papers and exhibits.

Thick, choking tension enveloped the room, causing the lawyers to communicate in hushed whispers as if in church.

Jury selection was scheduled to begin in ten minutes. Both sides made sure to be ready long before the anointed hour, not wanting to risk raising the ire of the judge and creating a bad impression with the jury before any witness took the stand.

Rick and Arnie sat next to each other flipping through their notes and documents, killing time, having no desire to engage their counterparts in meaningless conversation. Picking the jury was only the appetizer until the main course and having witnesses testify.

Ten minutes after the hour Markum meandered out of his

chambers to climb the three steps up to his perch. Without acknowledging the presence of the attorneys, their clients, or the handful of other people scattered in the back rows of the courtroom, Markum waved his hand to instruct those in the courtroom to sit.

Avoiding emotion, and for that matter, much volume, he stated, "We are present for the trial of *Hawkins v. B & D, Incorporated and Morgan V. Askew.* We will begin with picking the jury." He turned to his tipstaff, a young woman with heavy eye liner and a skirt much shorter than any female attorney would dare to wear. "Is the panel ready to be brought in?"

With a nod, she headed to the back of the courtroom and motioned through the open door. A minute later, a line of residents from the county streamed into the courtroom, led by the tipstaff. The bailiff led the first twelve to the seats in the jury box and placed the next group in the chairs behind the counsel tables, until all forty sat, awaiting instruction from the judge.

Markum addressed the panel. "Ladies and Gentlemen, you've each received a summons to appear today to be part of the panel for potential jurors in the case of *Hawkins versus B & D Incorporated and Morgan V. Askew.* My tipstaff will administer your oath. If selected as a juror, you will take a second oath."

The tipstaff stood and instructed the jury panel to stand and raise their right hands. She then made them, as a group, swear to tell the truth to the questions the court and counsel would ask them. They all agreed and retook their seats, staring at the judge, waiting to get involved in the proceedings.

Judge Markum perked up at his opportunity to address a group of potential voters in his next retention election and spoke to them without looking at his notes. The prior malaise wiped from his face, so no juror could detect a hint of boredom, he explained their role as part of a panel of potential jurors.

Trial would begin after the weekend, assuming they finished picking the jury by the end of the day. He thanked them for their service and attempted to head off any potential attempt to avoid jury service by explained he would only let people out of jury duty if they provided documentation of a provable medical condition which prevented them from listening to testimony, a trip scheduled in the next week when they could show proof of purchase for the trip, or a family member who needed their assistance in a life-and-death situation with no other person available to provide care. Insufficient excuses for dismissal included financial hardship, short of being thrown out of their homes.

Markum had heard every excuse and expected all potential jurors to take care of their affairs before entering his courtroom so they could listen without passion or distraction to the testimony, whether the trial took one day or an entire month.

"Your juror questionnaires are complete," Markum said, while holding up a sample of the two-sided document each worked on earlier in the morning. "The lawyers for both sides have copies of your answers and I will give them thirty minutes to review them before we begin *voir dire*."

None of the jurors knew what the term meant, but they sat back as the courtroom settled into near silence as the four attorneys reviewed the jurors' responses and scribbled notes on their yellow pads. Occasionally, one of the attorneys would glance up, examine a juror, and then return to jotting notes on his pad.

After a half hour, the judge announced, "I will question you about certain topics as a group, and then we will call each juror up one-by-one and question them out of the hearing of everyone else in the courtroom. Please keep your voices down so the court reporter can take down what everyone is saying."

Markum asked the four attorneys to approach. They complied, standing in front of his bench tilting their heads up as he leaned forward. The court reporter placed her machine in the middle of the four attorneys and nodded once she was ready to transcribe the conversation.

"So we are on the same page," Markum said. "Each side will get four strikes. Motions to dismiss a juror for cause must be made before the end of interview with that juror. You will retain your remaining peremptory strikes if I strike a juror for cause. You must utilize your strikes for jurors currently sitting in the box. If you don't want to strike one of those jurors, you can pass, but you lose one of your strikes. The twelve jurors remaining in the box at the end of striking will be the jury. Any questions?"

Neither side indicated they wanted to discuss anything further.

Markum dismissed the attorneys with a wave and began lobbing questions towards the potential jurors.

"Do any of you know any of the lawyers?"

"Are you familiar with this case?"

"Do you know any of the parties?"

Nobody admitted to having met any of the lawyers before. A few indicated having some knowledge about the case, likely due to the publicity Jerry Hawkins' death received for a few days after the incident. A bunch of hands went in the air acknowledging a familiarity with B & D.

Raising a hand did not guarantee getting out of jury duty, but portended additional inquiry from the judge and lawyers.

Upon completion of the group questions, Judge Markum glanced at the woman in the first seat in the jury box. "Juror number one, please approach."

The African-American woman tried to appear nonplussed, but everyone watched her closely knowing they would be in the same position at some point soon and none wanted to violate some unknown rule of decorum. A small portion of the rising level of stress in the room dissipated when she stood before the judge and was not admonished.

After a few questions from the judge, outside the hearing of the other potential jurors, and a couple from the lawyers on each side, she returned to her seat. Mindful of the rule against speaking about the case to anyone, she kept her gaze straight ahead and did not speak.

The procession of potential jurors continued unabated with no evident sign of harassment or admonishment. The non-lawyers couldn't hear any of the conversation, but nothing appeared heated or out of the ordinary, until one person walked straight out the courtroom after the lawyers questioned him. Markum briefly explained that he might dismiss some people for cause, but those remaining should not read anything in their departure or attempt to discern the reason he had dismissed them.

Those awaiting questioning pondered what type of answer they could give to get dismissed.

It took almost two hours to interview a sufficient number of people to create a large enough pool of potential jurors. Markum indicated jury selection would pause to allow the attorneys to review their notes.

Rick and Arnie huddled to discuss the order in which they would strike jurors, having to make the first selection in each of the four rounds. They were in lockstep as to which jurors they would excuse. Ordinarily, it took less than ten minutes for the lawyers to make their peremptory strikes.

Rick first struck a juror, the owner of an importing business, who Arnie suspected would identify more with a corporate entity than a person like Emily.

Spencer and Crotec dismissed a young unemployed male

who Rick wanted on the panel, but knew would never make it through four defense strikes.

After Rick struck a well-dressed woman whose husband worked as an executive at an insurance company, Crotec returned the sheet with a line through the name of a black woman who worked for a major computer company as an analyst.

Arnie grabbed Rick's arm. "I told you they would strike the African-Americans. We should make our motion."

Rick shook his head and leaned into his partner. "Patience. You know their next strike will be the black woman in the back row. That's when we move."

Arnie relented and watched Rick make their third strike and then their fourth after getting the sheet back from Spencer and Crotec, who snatched it out of Arnie's hand to make their final strike. When the sheet came back, Arnie scoffed while handing it to Rick, who rose and asked to approach the bench.

Markum waved the attorneys forward and motioned for the court reporter to rejoin them.

"What is it counsel?" Markum asked.

Rick nudged forward. "Your Honor, defendants struck two African-Americans on the panel in violation of the U.S. Supreme Court case of *Batson v. Kentucky*."

Markum nodded and turned to Spencer. "Counselor, plaintiff makes out a *prima facie* case of a violation of *Batson*. Can you articulate a legitimate, non-discriminatory reason for dismissing these jurors?"

Spencer cleared his throat and examined his yellow pad. "We can. With respect to the first woman, she indicated she brought two personal injury lawsuits where she sought compensation against large companies like the defendant in this case. We struck three potential jurors because they were plaintiffs in other cases."

"The second African-American," Markum interjected, "what is the reason you struck her?

Again Spencer studied his notes. "According to what I wrote, this woman is a teacher and we believe educators generally empathize with plaintiffs."

Rick jumped in. "That's a complete pretense. There are three other teachers on the panel and they didn't strike any of them."

Markum turned towards Spencer. "Is that accurate?"

Spencer shuffled his feet. "I guess it is, judge. In reviewing my notes, it appears this woman also is twice divorced and our research indicates this to be a negative factor for defendants."

"Ridiculous," Rick said, cutting off Spencer from adding more. "I think they made that up, but there are other multi-married individuals on the panel."

The judge put up a hand. "Not hearing any additional basis for striking this juror, counsel has not presented a legitimate, non-discriminatory basis for making this strike. Although defendants proffered a valid basis for striking the first black juror, they failed to provide the court with one for the second. Given this, it would be within my power to put both jurors back on the panel, but I'm not going to do that. I will overrule the defendants' strike of the second black juror and return her to the panel. Defendant can strike another juror."

Markum handed the sheet of paper with the strikes on it and handed it to Spencer, who sheepishly took it. Within seconds, he drew a line through a juror's name, finishing the selection of the jury.

"Gentlemen, this is our jury. We will seat them, and then we can return tomorrow for opening statements."

The four lawyers stepped back to return to their seats.

Arnie sidled up next to Crotec. "Well played. Now a court

179

has found on the record that you guys are racists. Congratulations."

Arnie smirked and returned to sit next to Rick. They
exchanged glances to signal a readiness for the real work to
begin when they returned to court after the weekend.

CHAPTER FORTY-FIVE

THE ALARMS of both cell phones went off at 9:00 p.m. The activity in the conference room came to an immediate halt. Rick and Arnie glanced at each other and began putting their papers in the proper folders while setting their binders into the appropriate boxes. Fifteen minutes later the seven banker boxes crammed with the plethora of outlines, exhibits and notes they needed for trial rested by the front door of the office.

"We promised we would stop at nine," Rick said. "If you allow me, I would keep reviewing my notes."

Arnie shook his head. "We talked about this. We've been preparing for weeks and we're ready. Home is where we need to be to get some rest."

The desire to slog through some depositions still gnawed at Rick. "You're right, but I don't want to be caught short when we start tomorrow."

"Don't worry. We know every exhibit and deposition from front to back. I think I could do your examinations after hearing you practice them so many times. Your opening is excellent and the jury will know what evidence to expect and hopefully be on our side by the time you're though with it."

Rick leaned against the wall taking a sip of water from a plastic bottle. "I don't want to let Emily down. She deserves the best we can offer."

"She's getting it." Arnie held open the door and gestured for Rick to leave. He didn't move.

"Let's make sure we've planned everything properly," Rick said as Arnie slowly closed the door.

"We're good. The AV guy will be there in the morning to set up the video and get our exhibits ready to display on the big screen. Audrey and her son are coming in the morning to get these boxes. They'll be in the courtroom long before we get there. What we need for opening is in the first box. She organized and collated everything. Staying here will only make us more nervous and less rested."

"I know, but I'm pretty freaking nervous already. We've spent a lot of time on this case and unless we win, none of us—Emily, you, me—will get a penny for the work we've put in —not to mention the money I already paid for the experts. There hasn't been a lot of checks coming into the firm for the past few weeks."

A comforting smile appeared on Arnie's face. "Try not to put too much pressure on yourself. Don't worry about me. I love the law and if I don't ever get paid, that's okay because I enjoy what I'm doing so much."

Rick shook his head and opened the door gesturing for Arnie to lead the way out. "You're full of crap, but you're a good partner."

CHAPTER FORTY-SIX

RICK NEARLY PANICKED WALKING the five steps to the lectern which held his notes, The first lines of his opening statement, which he thought were indelibly etched into his memory, were lost and random thoughts, having nothing to do with Emily Hawkins, filtered into his brain. He forced himself to stand motionless before the jurors, seeking to make eye contact with each one before he uttered a word. This delay created tension, but also provided him the opportunity to clear the distracting thoughts impeding his initial presentation to the jury.

The morning had begun with the judge's preliminary instructions, during which Markum deployed a deliberate tone to emphasize to the jurors that they were the finders of fact, while the judge would decide what law they would hear at the end of the trial. Markum told the jurors that the lawyers would object to some testimony, but they shouldn't concern themselves with his reasons for allowing them to hear certain evidence or wonder about testimony excluded from the trial.

The butterflies which kept Rick up most of the night disappeared when the judge called the trial into session. He felt waves of confidence during the fifteen minutes the judge instructed the jury on the order of the trial. He was calm when Markum explained how plaintiff presented her case first and the defendants offered their evidence afterward. He had no internal reaction either when Markum instructed how the lawyer calling a witness would question him first, while the other side would be able to follow-up by cross-examining the witness.

After the judge completed the preliminary instructions, the jury appeared eager to hear the case. This jury seemed different from others he had heard about which were disinterested and bored from the first minute of trial, and which returned verdicts with little deliberation just to complete their service.

Rick controlled his emotions, until Markum pointed his gavel at him and asked, "Is plaintiff ready to open?"

With the attention of everyone in the courtroom focused on him, the realization of carrying Emily's hopes on his back kicked in. Rick forced himself to rise and muttered, "Yes," but in the time it took to answer the judge's customary inquiry, the butterflies returned with a vengeance.

As Rick scanned the jurors, he wanted to project calm, but the disparate, irrelevant thoughts swirled. He knew if he couldn't articulate the first part of his opening without error, the rest had the potential to fall flat.

He glanced down at his feet and ignored the fleeting thought to run out of the courtroom or, at least to grab a glass of water in a stalling maneuver to recapture the mental outline of his remarks. He took one final, deep cleansing breath and locked eyes with a young juror he thought resembled Emily.

"On a cool, June evening last year, Jerry Hawkins entered the B & D store on Beadle Avenue as an invited shopper and when he left the parking lot, he was on a gurney in the back of an ambulance. The paramedics raced to restart his heart and get him breathing again. They failed as did the doctors in the ER. He didn't suffer a natural death. To the contrary, a manager of the store had organized a mob which strangled him to death. All because the manager thought he was a shoplifter."

This opening paragraph, rehearsed for weeks, conveyed the text and subtext of what Rick wanted the jury to hear. Getting it out without stumbling gave him a shot of confidence, allowing the nauseous rumbling in his gut to subside, replaced by a readiness to battle.

Rick introduced Emily to the jury by asking her to stand. She rose and nodded at the jurors wearing a demure navy pants suit and dark flats. Rick warned Emily not to wear any flashy jewelry which Rick presumed wouldn't be an issue because he hadn't seen her wear anything close to tawdry since they met. While Emily exchanged glances with the jurors, Rick offered a couple of informational tidbits about her with the implicit assurance they would hear more about her life when she testified. Rick also introduced Arnie, informing the jury they would split the labor at the trial.

The jurors returned his gaze as turned back to them. He knew they wanted to hear more.

"Jerry Hawkins was killed at B & D because their employees never received training on how to detain potential shoplifters, and they allowed their managers to play police officers, unchecked and uneducated. Emily Hawkins sits alone because of this, widowed and unable to get answers to why that company allowed its employees to play god."

Rick added a little emphasis to the last word while pointing a finger at Spencer and Crotec.

"How did this happen?" Rick asked rhetorically, and then provided the jurors with his answer. "B & D is a regional chain of stores. You all have probably shopped at one at some point.

Sometimes people steal. Everybody knows it's going to happen and stores want to stop it. The law even gives them the right, within reason, to stop it. Under what is known as the Merchant's Act, stores can stop suspected shoplifters under two conditions. First they have a reasonable suspicion that someone committed theft, and second, they detain suspected shoplifters for a reasonable period and in a reasonable manner. I will talk to you later in the case about whether the store maintained a reasonable belief Jerry shoplifted, but for now I want to talk about how the evidence will prove they did not detain Jerry in a reasonable manner."

Rick grabbed a plastic cup with water on the table to his right and took a quick sip.

"The manager of the B & D store, a man named Morgan Askew, will tell you he thought Jerry stole a few items even though he paid for many other products. Before he could assure himself Jerry stole anything, Mr. Askew accused him of being a thief and then chased him out of the store, determined to catch Jerry at any cost.

"In the parking lot, Mr. Askew realized Jerry was too far in front of him, so he called for help from a young cart person who tackled Jerry. It's apparent Jerry was stunned, suddenly accosted in the parking lot, so he tried to get away. Ultimately, the cart person, the store manager and two other people sat on Jerry to prevent him from moving. Jerry was helpless and couldn't breathe. He desperately tried to free himself so he could get a breath into his lungs, but Mr. Askew insisted that his band of vigilantes not relent. They were going to sit on top of Jerry until the police arrived—no matter how long that took."

He stared at one of the jurors in the back row for a moment.

He continued: "It took nearly seventeen minutes for the police to answer the call a customer placed to nine-one-one. They pulled their squad car alongside the four people imprisoning Jerry and instructed them to get off. When they did, Jerry was lifeless. Despite the attempts by the paramedics, they were unable to resuscitate Jerry. The store had killed him."

Rick paused again hoping to see a glint of furor in the eyes of the jurors hearing Jerry was killed even though he shopped at the store. After surveying the members of the jury, he couldn't determine what they thought.

"You may be thinking to yourselves, 'Did Jerry have to die?' No, of course not. Jerry Hawkins was killed because B & D never trained its employees how to detain shoplifters. During this trial you're going to hear all about how shoplifting is a problem for all retailers. How people come into their stores and take items without paying. What you aren't going to hear about is a coherent training program at B & D to give their employees the skills to confront and detain shoplifters without harming that person or other shoppers in the store. What you won't hear from their employees is that they understood how to deal with shoplifting or how the store provided them with appropriate techniques to deal with shoplifters who become aggressive.

"Because B & D never trained its work staff, managers like Morgan Askew would physically challenge accused shoplifters. The company told them to lower the rate of shoplifting at the stores, but never warned them how accusing someone of shoplifting could lead to violence—and in this case the death of Jerry Hawkins.

"You will hear from experts in retail shoplifting and medical experts and what they will tell you is simple—Jerry Hawkins died as a result of the negligence of B & D in failing to follow industry standards in establishing a training program so its employees could detain Jerry Hawkins, if appropriate, without killing him."

Without allowing his gaze to stray from the jurors, Rick

flipped a page in his binder to signal his movement to a new topic.

"Emily Hawkins will tell you how she has suffered because B & D killed her husband. She lost her husband, her rock, the man she relied on to cope with the problems life would throw at them. She lost his future income. No Jerry didn't have a job at the time of his death, but he was working hard to educate himself to become a computer programmer. They lost every dollar he would earn in the future, which he will never earn because B & D ended his life prematurely.

"Emily is also seeking to recover for Jerry's pain and suffering for the seventeen minutes they sat on him and squeezed the life out of his body. She is seeking to recover for losing her husband and what he brought to the household and to their marriage.

"She is also seeking compensation for the loss of Jerry's income, his conscious pain and suffering and her loss of the services and society of her husband. Emily can't get her husband back and you can't return to her their future. The only thing you can give her is money and although it won't change what her future is now, it will compensate her for her losses. Her losses are significant and under Pennsylvania law we can't ask for a specific amount of money from you, but you will understand the extent of her suffering and will have the tools at your disposal to compensate her appropriately. It feels crass to ask for a large sum of money from you, but it would be so much worse not to."

None of the jurors blanched in the slightest at Rick's suggestion they would award her a huge amount of money—an amount most of the jurors would not make in fifty years of working. He neared the end of his opening statement. "Ladies and gentlemen, the negligence of the defendants stole Emily Hawkins' husband away from her. We are asking you to compensate her for this enormous loss. We thank you for taking time from your busy lives to hear our case and know you will listen to the evidence with care."

Rick stepped back, away from the jurors. The courtroom remained silent.

CHAPTER FORTY-SEVEN

SEBASTIAN CROTEC EASED out of his chair and reached forward to grab his yellow pad. His slow walk towards the jury caused Rick to imagine a peacock preening for a potential mate. The same punch in the gut sensation that hit Rick when Crotec made no attempt to hide his enjoyment of terminating Rick's employment years before, struck him again as Crotec waited to speak to the jurors.

Rick's desire to help Emily motivated him as they prepared for the trial. He now realized his antipathy towards Spencer and Crotec was nearly as strong of a motivational force. He wanted to win, but humiliating opposing counsel at the same time would make victory so much sweeter. He exchanged glances with Arnie as they steeled themselves for the body blows they both knew their case was about to endure.

"Good morning, members of the jury," Crotec said in an easy manner, as if addressing the school PTO. "It's a shame Jerry Hawkins died. It's a shame people like Morgan Askew have to get involved in stopping a shoplifter, and it's a shame people like Morgan, and companies like B & D, get sued when trying to protect the public against thieves. Jerry Hawkins didn't need to die, but he continued to fight–trying to avoid being caught and handed over to the police. Jerry Hawkins was out of control and never stopped trying to get away. Because of his actions, he died.

"Myself, Mr. Spencer and the people from B & D will say the same–it's a shame Jerry Hawkins died–but one thing none of us will say is Jerry Hawkins died because of anything wrong anyone from B & D did. Nothing could be further from the truth. The evidence in this case will prove to you that the people from B & D acted appropriately, within the bounds of the law and did not act negligently on the afternoon Jerry Hawkins died."

Crotec placed a fist near his shoulder. "The following facts are not in dispute: One, Jerry Blevins tried to steal from B & D." Crotec lifted his index finger away from his hand. "Two, all retailers, including B & D, have the right under the law to stop shoplifters and detain them until the police arrive." The middle finger on Crotec's hand joined the first. "Three, Morgan Askew verbally told Mr. Hawkins to stop and warned him a B & D employee would use force to detain him." Crotec raised his next finger. "Four, Mr. Hawkins ignored the demand to stop and continued to flee the scene. And five, even after Mr. Askew stopped Mr. Hawkins, he continued to struggle, forcing people passing by to assist Mr. Askew and ultimately leading to his death."

Crotec extended his fifth finger and let the image of a stop sign linger before the jury. "Mr. Hawkins would be alive today if at any point in the process he heeded these warnings and stopped."

Crotec lowered his hand and took a step backwards. "This

case is simple. Yes, it's a shame Mr. Hawkins died, but when a person decides to steal, he elects to take on risks and one of those is getting caught. A person assumes the risk he will get hurt if he shoplifts, gets caught and then attempts to fight his way out of it. Mr. Hawkins assumed those risks that night and as the evidence will prove to you, this is the reason he died.

"You're going to hear evidence from the people at the store and expert witnesses about the prevalence of stealing. Most of you might be surprised, but it is a constant threat that stores are under. The people from B & D will tell you about how its employees are trained to be diligent about being aware of what people are doing while in the store, and if they suspect a person is about to steal, they are given tools to stop the person from shoplifting or on how to detain the person until the authorities arrive."

Crotec turned to Rick. "Mr. Waterston suggested the employees from B & D want to be law enforcement officials. Wrong! The police are the experts and B & D relies upon their expertise to get the shoplifters out of the stores and to prosecute them when they are caught. The police need the help of merchants to properly observe shoplifting when it occurs and then to reasonably detain shoplifters until the police arrive. This is laid out in the law as the judge will instruct you at the end of the case.

"Ultimately, what we have here is a store and its employees doing exactly what they should be doing to prevent and deter shoplifting. Under the law, B & D is supposed to detain shoplifters until the police arrive. What B & D did was entirely reasonable under the circumstances. Jerry Hawkins would be alive today if he hadn't stolen from the store or resisted the efforts of the B & D employees to detain him. That is why his death, although a complete shame, was not the fault of the defendants and that is why at the end of the trial we will ask you to return a verdict in their favor."

Crotec drifted back to his seat.

Emily Hawkins' muffled crying was the only sound in the courtroom.

CHAPTER FORTY-EIGHT

JUDGE MARKUM ASSESSED the state of the jurors after having heard the opening statements. He turned to Rick. "Counsel, there is almost two hours before the end of the day. Let's see how much testimony we can get in."

Rick stood and announced, "Plaintiff calls Deandra Bortz to the stand."

The order a party calls witnesses at trial is monumentally important. The first witness must be strong and compelling-a dud as a first witness risks losing the jury before they hear the meat of the testimony. On the other hand, the first witness must lay the groundwork for the entire case and put it in context. Sometimes, a witness's testimony, without an appropriate foundation laid by other witnesses, can be incomprehensible to the jury and its impact muted.

The obvious witness for Rick to bat lead-off would be Emily. The jury needed to hear from her and bond with her if it was ever going to award her the amounts of money Rick wanted it to. She, however, didn't observe Jerry's death, so couldn't offer any insight into the events in the parking lot.

Her job in testifying was to lay out her damages, paint a picture of their life before this happened and to engender sympathy. Rick needed to paint a picture of what happened to Jerry before letting the jury hear from Emily. He planned to call some B & D employees as part of his case, but felt it too risky to lead with one of them.

Those fireworks could wait just a little. No, the independent and spirited Deandra Bortz would take on this role, even if she didn't comprehend how important she was to the future of Emily Hawkins.

The jurors' eyes followed Bortz as she walked from the back of the courtroom until she stood in front of the tipstaff with her right hand in the air. Her hair, pulled back into a ponytail, gave her an approachable air which contrasted with the tight green sweater which emphasized her ample bust. She swore to tell the truth and walked up the two steps to sit in the witness chair. After fiddling with the long, skinny microphone, she raised her head and smiled.

Rick offered a small Hail Mary she would limit her answers without providing too much extraneous information. He knew in court prayers often go unanswered.

He led her through some preliminary introductory questions so that the jury knew her name, her address and that she lived with her dog and Princess the cat. Bortz's smile radiated when she described how much she enjoyed shopping at B & D, which Rick hoped would emphasize her independence as a witness, not wanting to stick it to the big company, but only trying to recollect the details of a tragic evening.

Rick moved into the meat of her testimony. "Why did you go to B & D the night Jerry Hawkins died?" He asked, not wanting to provide too much unnecessary personal detail and seeking to steer their conversation to the events that lead to her helping to detain Jerry Hawkins.

"No particular reason," Bortz said, "I go there sometimes after work. I'm a massage therapist and when I'm done, I like to find something for dinner or maybe buy some clothes."

Inwardly, Rick groaned, realizing that reining in Deandra Bortz and having her provide limited responses would prove to be difficult.

"Did you ever make it into the store?"

"No, I didn't. I wanted to, but then I got caught up in the situation in the parking lot and before I knew it, the police arrived and then I got upset. So, I just left and never shopped." Bortz blushed, realizing she was rambling.

Rick smiled at her paternally and held up a hand. "Tell you what–let's all slow down. I will try to ask you simple questions and you just try to answer those, okay?"

Her head bobbed.

"What happened when you got out of your car?"

"I noticed a disturbance close by."

"Please describe the disturbance."

"Two men were fighting, rolling around on the ground."

"Did you notice other people?"

She shook her head. "At that moment, no. I believe I was the only person in the vicinity."

"How did you get involved?"

"I really didn't want anything to do with it. I planned on just walking to the store, but one of the men involved yelled at me to help him."

Rick moved to the far corner of the edge of the jury box, wanting to make sure she spoke loud enough that every juror could hear her. "What did he say?"

"While he wrestled with the other guy, he identified himself as a manager and said the other man stole from the store and was trying to escape. He claimed the man was dangerous and might hurt other people."

"So what did you do?"

"At first I didn't think he was speaking to me, so I pointed at myself–like, 'are you talking to me?' He repeated he needed help. They continued to roll around on the ground, so I figured I might be able to help out."

"Did you?" Rick scrunched his nose a bit.

"Yes." She responded. I walked over, and he started giving me detailed instructions. He told me to grab his arm. So I did– which didn't seem to help too much. He then yelled at another gentleman to help and that man came over and grabbed his other arm. Another kid from the store also came to help. With the three of us helping, we subdued the man."

"Ever seen the man who directed you before?"

"Yes, I knew he was the manager of the store."

"Is he in the courtroom today?"

"Yes." She extended her index finger in the direction of the defendant's counsel table.

Rick turned his head to where she pointed "Let the record reflect she has identified B & D manager, Morgan Askew."

He turned back to the witness. "After you subdued Mr. Hawkins, what happened."

"The manager told us not to get off. He kept giving us orders–mainly to stay on top of the guy."

"Did anything ever change?"

"Well. . . ," Bortz turned pensive. "After a while, it seemed to get quiet. Some people gathered around. We didn't talk much, but I asked the manager at some point if we should get off of him."

"How did he respond?"

"He told us not to move."

Rick moved to the front of his counsel table, but noted that most of the jurors were jotting notes on their pads. "Tell me the positions of everyone assisting the manager."

197

Bortz lifted her head towards the ceiling. "Lets see–I held his right arm and the other gentlemen secured his left. The young cart person laid on his legs and the manager straddled his back."

"How was Mr. Hawkins positioned?"

"He faced the ground. The manager told us not to move until the police showed up. That took forever." She threw her hands in the air.

"What happened when the police arrived?"

"I was so tired when they got there. It's not easy lying on the ground, trying to make sure someone doesn't move." She took a breath. "Two officers came. One of them told us to get off of the man, so they could take charge. We got moved away, but the man didn't move. Not at all. One of the policemen turned him over and his face was lifeless–his eyes closed. They immediately started to do CPR and then the paramedics took over when they showed up. I gave my name to the other police officer and left. He called me a couple of days later and I gave him a statement."

Rick took a step back and turned to opposing counsel. "No further questions. You may cross-examine."

Spencer stood and moved to the lectern in front of counsel table, placing his notes and clearing his throat. "Ms. Bortz, Virgil Spencer representing B & D, we met at your deposition." Bortz nodded and waited for his question.

"Ma'am, you would agree that when you got out of your car there was a huge fight ten feet from where you stood."

"I'm not sure I'd call it a huge fight. A disturbance, perhaps."

Spencer moved forward towards the witness. "Do you remember four months ago the lawyers in this case all asked you questions while you were under oath at your deposition?"

"Yes."

Spencer waved the bound copy of her deposition. "I direct

your attention to page forty-nine, line twelve; didn't you say, and I quote, 'I got out of my car and there was a huge fight ten feet from my car.'

He handed her a copy of her former testimony, and she read it.

She looked up. "Yes, that's what I said."

"Didn't it appear as if Mr. Hawkins was the aggressor?"

Bortz paused while Spencer pointed a finger at her deposition transcript.

"I guess that's accurate," she responded.

"Mr. Hawkins acted like a maniac?"

"Yes, that's what I said," she said, her words barely audible.

Spencer moved closer. "You worried about the safety of the manager as Mr. Hawkins continued to fight him?"

"Yes."

"You felt you needed to help get the situation under control."

"That's probably true, but Mr. Askew requested my help."

"Which you willingly gave."

"That's true."

Spencer paced in front of Bortz, whose eyes moved to the side to follow him. "After you began to help out, Mr. Hawkins continued to resist," he said.

"I guess. The situation was out of control."

"In fact, two other people joined in to stop Mr. Hawkins."

"Sir, I don't know why they came in. I think the manager requested more help."

"Ma'am, even with four people on top of him, the man continued to struggle."

Bortz paused and Spencer again lifted her deposition, so she could see it. "I think that's right," she said. "The manager told us not to let go."

"The whole time you sat on top of him, you worried about

your safety and the other good Samaritans holding down the shoplifter."

"Yes, that's true."

Spencer smiled. "No further questions."

The judge dismissed the witness when Rick indicated he had no follow-up.

As Bortz walked past him, he forced a smile while scribbling a note to Arnie. "*She helped—but they scored some serious points on cross.*"

Arnie nodded as the judge turned to address the jurors.

CHAPTER FORTY-NINE

JUDGE MARKUM FACED THE JURORS. "It's getting late in the day. We've accomplished a good amount today, and we'll hear from one more witness before adjourning." He turned back towards the lawyers. "Who's the next witness?"

Arnie stood to address the jurors. "Plaintiff calls Officer Peter Mitinger."

A uniformed officer arose from the back of the courtroom and swaggered without hesitation to the front of the courtroom. The cop locked eyes with the bailiff and raised his right hand. After she swore him in, he moved into the witness box upon completing his oath and adjusted the microphone.

A copy of Mitinger's police report detailing Jerry Hawkins' death rested in front of Rick. Yellow marker highlighted the word "shoplifter" the eighteen times it appeared in the report. Rick squirmed in his seat hoping Arnie would be able to elicit the few facts they needed without the cop emphasizing his conclusion Jerry stole while in the store.

"Please state you name," Arnie said in a conversational tone.

"Peter Mitinger."

"You are a police officer for Mahoney County, is that correct?"

"It is."

"For how long?"

"Seventeen years."

Arnie reached to adjust his tie. "Did you respond to a call from the B & D parking lot on June, twentieth?"

"I did."

"What did you find when you got there?"

"My partner, officer Menendez and I responded. I got out of the car first. I identified a group of people holding down a suspect in the northeast portion of the lot."

"Were they on the ground?"

"Yes."

"How many people were involved?"

"May I review my report?" The officer requested.

Arnie nodded.

Mitinger reviewed what he had written. "Five people total. The shoplifter and four people trying to detain him."

A scowl snuck across Arnie's face. "Officer, when you arrived, you didn't know if the person held down was a shoplifter or not, did you?"

Mitinger pondered the question. "I didn't."

"In fact, you never did any investigation into whether this person had stolen anything, did you?"

"Didn't see much point to it, by the time we got there."

"Perhaps," Arnie responded. "But you never tried to figure out why the B & D manager decided to hold down Mr. Hawkins, did you?"

"The manager told me he was a shoplifter."

"So, you didn't do any investigation. You obviously never talked to Mr. Hawkins. You relied on what the manager told you after he just killed the man."

Crotec shot out of his seat. "Objection, Your Honor. That is incredibly argumentative."

Markum shook his head. "Sustained. Mr. McBride, please rephrase."

Arnie smiled and turned back to the witness. "You use the word, 'shoplifter' only because this is what the manager told you, but not because you did any independent investigation?"

Mitinger relented. "I guess that's true."

"Can we refer to him as the victim, since we can agree he died and because you don't have any independent knowledge of what Mr. Hawkins did while in the store?"

"I guess that's fair." A small concession, but the use of the word "shoplifter" would be avoided until, at least, cross-examination.

"Thank-you." Arnie moved closer to the jury box. "So, when you and officer Menendez arrived, four people laid on top of the victim."

"There were four people around the victim. I wouldn't necessarily say they were all on top of him."

"Fine. Will you agree each of the four people was touching the victim."

"Yes."

"Did each of the four people hold down the victim?"

"It appeared that way." Mitinger's lips curled at the edges.

"Did the victim move at all?"

"No."

"Did it appear these four people prevented the man from moving?"

"I don't know that. I can only say he didn't move."

Arnie shook his head and moved closer to the witness. "So what did you do?"

"I ordered them to get off the man."

"Did they?"

"Yes."

"Then what did you do?" Arnie asked as slowly as he could.

"I noticed the man didn't respond. He was face-down. I directed a question to him, but he didn't answer. I became concerned." Mitinger's eyes narrowed. "I touched the man, but there was nothing, so I turned him over. His face was bluish. I didn't think he was breathing, and I couldn't find a pulse."

"This was serious?"

"Absolutely. My partner immediately got down on the ground and began to perform CPR. I called for an ambulance and for backup. I then started to do crowd control. A few minutes later the ambulance arrived. They took over treating the man. While trying to revive him, they got him into the ambulance. I don't believe he ever regained consciousness. I checked on him at the hospital and learned he passed away."

Mitinger looked down briefly.

Arnie let the testimony sink in with the jury before proceeding. "Officer, did you get statements from the people involved?"

"I spoke with the four individuals on the ground with the man when we arrived."

"Did any of those people identify him or herself as being in charge?"

"Well, the manager of the store indicated he instructed the lot kid to stop the man because he thought he took something. He also said he asked for help in detaining the man. So, yeah, I guess he was."

"Thank you, Officer Mitinger. I have no more questions."

Crotec stood with his yellow pad in his right hand, his other rubbing his bushy hair. "I only have a couple of questions for you."

Arnie nudged Rick. They figured the cop would be helpful for them because he established how Jerry died, but couldn't offer much on the shoplifting issue. No matter what Crotec did with the cop, they would still be left with a dead person on the store's pavement once he left the stand.

"Officer, Seb Crotec. I represent the defendants in this case. You weren't in the store when Mr. Hawkins was in there, correct?"

"No, I got there when he was detained in the parking lot."

"So, you can't say what he did in the store or if he left the store without paying for certain items."

"That's true."

"When you interviewed Morgan Askew immediately after you arrived, did Mr. Askew offer you his view on what Mr. Hawkins did when he was in the store?"

"He did. He said Mr. Hawkins stole merchandise from the store."

"He said this right away. Right then and there?" Crotec asked, waving his arms.

"Correct."

"You, however, didn't investigate whether Mr. Hawkins committed theft while in the store?"

"No, I didn't."

"Why not?"

Mitinger twisted a bit in his seat. "It didn't seem to make much sense at that point. He was dead."

"You mean if Mr. Hawkins was alive, if a store manager said someone stole from the store, you would've investigated to determine if it was true."

"Sure. We do it all the time."

"I know, and it's because theft is common?"

"That's correct."

"Final question, sir. A store maintains the absolute right to stop shoplifters, doesn't it? To put it another way, the law allows it to detain shoplifters if it has a reasonable suspicion the person stole from it."

"Absolutely. In fact, that's what it should do. They should detain a person, call the police, and let us do the investigation."

Crotec shook his head. "That's all the questions I have. Thank you."

Arnie stood behind counsel table. "Let me follow-up. The law also says a store detaining a suspected shoplifter must do it in a reasonable manner."

"It does."

"Is strangling someone to death a reasonable way to detain someone?"

Before Arnie completed his question, Crotec shot to his feet. "Objection. Move to strike counsel's question."

Arnie smiled and said to the court. "I'll withdraw the question. I know it would be a hard one for him to answer." Arnie returned to his seat and signaled he was done with his questions, hoping the jury caught the significance of the withdrawn question.

Noting the questioning was complete, the judge dismissed the witness and said to the jury, "That's a fair amount for one day. I'm dismissing you until tomorrow morning."

As the jurors filed out, Rick patted Arnie on the shoulder. "Nice job. We ended right where we wanted with the image of Jerry dead in the parking lot. I'm going to visit my daughter in the hospital. I'll try to catch you in the office later–if I can make it."

Arnie packed up the remaining papers and Rick allowed himself the luxury to focus on Sammie for the first time since he entered the courtroom in the morning. He grabbed his bag and dashed out the door.

CHAPTER FIFTY

THE SWEET, antiseptic hospital smell smacked Rick as he forced his way through the revolving door. The guard at the security station nodded as he made a direct path to the elevator. The ride up to the eighth floor seemed to pause on every floor, and with no one else in the elevator, Rick kept pushing the button for Sammie's floor.

It was a fifteen-minute drive from the parking lot next to the courthouse to the hospital, during which for the first time since the judge gaveled court into session, Rick allowed his thoughts to focus solely on his daughter. This wasn't life threatening, he kept reminding himself, but he still couldn't wrap his mind around how his daughter was lying in a hospital room or how potentially life affecting this might be for her

Sammie's floor at the hospital treated kids who faced the enormity of a variety of cognitive and emotional issues. A few days earlier, he heard out-of-control screaming coming from a room down the hall. That experience, with the doctors and staff rushing to the situs of the noise, unnerved Rick as he imagined what they did behind closed doors to help the child calm down.

From everything he'd seen in his limited time at the hospital, the staff maintained high levels of professionalism despite constant calls for their attention for children who lacked certain innate control mechanisms.

Relief flooded Rick turning into Sammie's room, finding her resting peacefully in bed, a small, over-loved doll lying in her arms. He waited at the door resting his head against the frame, watching her rhythmic breathing. On the far side of the bed, Molly dozed in a chair, her legs stretched out on the bed. As he eased into the room, Molly's eyes opened, following him as he slipped into the seat next to her.

Molly removed her legs from the bed and stretched her arms above her head, smiling at Rick. "You're wiped out. You shouldn't have come."

Rick scoffed and shook his head.

"How's your trial going?"

"It's fine. How's she doing?" He touched Sammie's leg, releasing a torrent of emotion—part love, part guilt and part fear for what his daughter might face.

"Today was a little rough. They're figuring out how to adjust her meds. It might take a little time."

"How's Sammie taking all this?"

"I'm not sure. She's happy most of the time, but then she isn't."

"How long is she going to be in here?"

"They say probably one more night, but they're also telling me that it's going to be a long road once we get home."

Rick stared straight ahead and mumbled, "I'm sure."

Silence engulfed them as they watched their daughter sleep. Rick leaned his head back against the cinder block wall. After a few minutes, he turned to Molly. "I haven't been a responsible father—or ex-husband for that matter. I need to do better. I will be better and do whatever I can to help out."

Molly turned her head to Rick. "Don't make promises you can't keep. I want more from you. I just can't depend on you at this point."

Rick nodded and then lowered his head. Molly placed a hand on his leg. "She's probably not waking up before morning. You're in the middle of this trial with lots of work to do. I'll tell her you came here, but you should go."

Rick shook his head. "No, I'm staying for a while. This is more important."

Molly gazed at the wall above Sammie's bed and smiled. At eleven, a young nurse came in to inform Rick he had to leave. He put on his suit jacket, kissed Sammie's forehead and waved to Molly as he walked out of the door.

CHAPTER FIFTY-ONE

Byron Hucklesbee, big as a tree and dressed in baggy jeans, sat in the back of the courtroom with a blank stare on his face. The jurors studied him, assuming he would be the next witness, but he never looked in their direction.

The dilemma facing Rick was excruciating, but similar to ones lawyers deal with in every trial. How hard should he crush a witness? The quick answer laypeople might give is to destroy every witness when given a chance.

Rick knew better.

Sometimes, even adverse witnesses offer helpful testimony, obviating the need to resort to extreme cross-examination. Most lawyers knew to put aside questions designed to make a witness look like a fool when he actually helps their case. Avoiding making the witness look silly when not necessary can score additional points with jurors who understand that other options exist to circumvent the witness having to bow at the lawyer's feet.

As much as jurors enjoy watching a witness squirm on cross, sometimes withering questioning ticks off a jury. Even green, inexperienced lawyers know elderly witnesses are exempt from in-your-face, overly aggressive questioning–same with the infirmed.

Rick needed to avoid offending the jury with intense questioning of any witness whose ability to respond was at issue or who engendered sympathy with them.

Byron Hucklesbee presented such a conundrum for Rick. Tall, overweight and displaying minimal apparent intelligence, he'd worked at B & D for ten years as a lot attendant. He managed to pass his high school equivalency examination, but the B & D managers testified at their depositions that he may have reached the zenith of his employment opportunities when he was given supervisory responsibilities for the parking lot. The people in charge at the store knew he was hardworking and followed directions, but when pressed, admitted that any instructions with more than two steps was more than he could handle.

At his deposition months before, Byron could barely articulate a complete sentence, offering incoherent responses to the simplest questions. With even a limited use of leading questions, Rick could get him to admit to almost anything.

Because Byron worked for the other side, Rick could call him as an adverse witness and deploy cross-examination by leading him through his testimony. Though confident he could get Byron to admit on the stand he had killed his own mother, Rick knew there was limited utility to any of Byron's admissions as the jury might disregard his testimony and hold it against Rick for beating up a naïve person.

Rick mentally took off his boxing gloves and replaced them with an empathetic smile when he called Byron as the next witness. He would allow Byron to tell his own story without putting too many words in his mouth.

After taking his oath and placing himself in the witness

box, Byron's eyes darted around the courtroom, unable to focus on anything in particular. His attention moved from the judge to the jurors and then to Rick, before circling again.

Rick waved his fingers to grab Byron's gaze and inwardly preached patience to resist the urge to get confrontational.

"What's your name?" Rick asked, confident Byron would not get flustered handling it.

"Byron."

Two jurors smiled.

Close. "What's your full name?"

"Byron Hucklesbee." He nodded and his wide smile was returned by three more jurors.

It took almost ten minutes to establish Byron's work history with B & D and his routine of returning lines of shopping carts to the store from the parking lot each shift. One thing Byron had a handle on was his job duties, as he did the same tasks every day he worked.

Without trying to get any extraneous details from Byron, Rick turned to Jerry's death. He asked, "Byron, were you involved in trying to stop a shoplifter in the parking lot?"

Byron nodded. "You mean when the guy died?"

"Yes. How did you become involved?"

"My manager, Mr. Askew, told me to stop the man. He had stolen something from inside the store."

"Where were you before Mr. Askew asked you to stop the man?"

"I was getting carts from the return place in the parking lot."

"Did you know that Mr. Askew was chasing someone in the parking lot?"

"I don't think so," Byron answered. "I was just grabbing the carts."

"Was Mr. Askew near to you when he asked you to stop the man?"

"No, he was far away. He had to yell to me."

"So, what did you do when Mr. Askew yelled to you?" Rick asked.

"The man he told me to stop was close to me and not that close to Mr. Askew. I tried to tackle him, so he couldn't escape. I missed. He shoved me out of the way. He may have hit me." Byron eyes now focused on Rick who took two steps back, away from Byron.

"Did you need help from anyone else?"

"Yes Two other people helped me and Mr. Askew."

"What did the four of you do?"

"Mr. Askew told us not to let him go until the police got there, so I made sure he couldn't leave."

"How did you do that?"

Byron smiled. "I sat on his legs. He wasn't going nowhere. I'm pretty big."

The jurors chuckled causing Byron to blush.

Rick shifted forward grabbing a binder of exhibits off of his table. "Thanks, Byron. I only have a few more questions. I'm showing you an employee manual. Did you receive this document?"

"I did when I started working there."

"Did the manual teach you anything about how to deal with shoplifters?"

"I don't know." Byron's face turned red. "I don't think I ever read it."

"What did the store teach you about dealing with shoplifters?"

"I can't remember anything. I just do what my bosses tell me to do."

"Are you supposed to help stop shoplifters?"

"I don't know. I had never been asked before."

Rick opened the employee manual and flipped to a tabbed

page. "Byron, the manual says, 'no employee shall approach a suspected shoplifter. If you suspect someone of shoplifting, report it to a manager.' Is that what you were taught?"

"I guess. I just do what Mr. Askew tells me to do. He told me to stop the man, so I did."

"And he told you to make sure the man didn't leave until the police got there?"

"So that's exactly what I did."

"Thanks, Byron. Your attorneys may want to ask you some questions."

Byron grinned, making Rick believe he hadn't been too rough on him.

The jurors turned their heads to Spencer, who stood. "Byron, a couple of follow-up questions. Is stealing wrong?"

Byron looked quizzically at Spencer. "Of course."

Spencer nodded. "Should people be allowed to steal from your store?"

"No, they shouldn't."

"How does it feel when you know people steal from the store?"

"Lots of people do it. It's wrong."

Spencer sat at counsel table. "That's all we have for this witness."

Rick turned to Arnie and whispered, "Now's when we start having some fun."

Arnie responded, "Hopefully," and grabbed the binder marked "Askew."

CHAPTER FIFTY-TWO

"PLAINTIFF CALLS DEFENDANT, Morgan Askew, to the stand."

All twelve jurors turned their heads to find the B & D assistant manager sitting alone in the spectator seats. He rose and headed to the front of the courtroom to be sworn. His newly purchased gray suit and fresh haircut didn't impress Arnie, who awaited his opportunity to expose the company's claims it acted reasonably while detaining Jerry Hawkins.

Unlike Byron the lot attendant, Askew was about to receive the Full Monte of cross-examination, with the goal to give the jurors permission to work up a healthy dose of antipathy, not only for the witness, but also for his employer. Arnie didn't mind that Askew's mom sat in the front row of spectators, smiling as her son swore to tell the truth. He placed his body between Askew and his mother, preventing Askew from making eye contact with her.

Askew sat, crossed his hands, and nodded at the jurors.

Arnie waited for him to return his gaze. When Askew locked eyes with him he launched his first grenade. "You are the store manager of B & D who took charge of the group of people who killed Jerry Hawkins, aren't you?"

Crotec shot out of his chair screaming, "Objection. Compound question, misleading and argumentative," beginning the short list of Crotec's objections.

Before he could finish, however, the judge interrupted. "Slow down, Mr. McBride. Let's ease a bit into your questioning of this witness. Objection sustained."

Arnie had the jury's attention and paused to re-start his examination. "Mr. Askew, you are the manager of the B & D store, correct?"

Askew responded, "I am the assistant manager of the store."

"It was your responsibility to be in charge the afternoon Mr. Hawkins died, correct?"

"Yes, I was the key carrying manager at the time."

"You were twenty-seven years old, in charge of the store, and responsible for the safety and well-being of your customers?"

"Yes."

"You failed, didn't you?"

"I don't think so." Askew wouldn't concede without a fight. "I stopped the shoplifter from stealing."

Arnie shot a glance at Askew. "We'll get to that part in a minute. You failed to protect the well-being of Mr. Hawkins, didn't you?"

"I don't think so. We were waiting for the police."

"He died—with you in charge."

"That wasn't the plan." Askew crossed his arms and then uncrossed them.

"I would hope not." Arnie was ready to move on—the jury understood Jerry died while Askew was in charge.

"Your company knows shoplifting happens at the store every day."

"Yes, people steal from every department–in every way imaginable."

"You are trained to stop shoplifters."

"We are trained to protect the assets of the store and if we can safely detain a person, we maintain the right to try to get back items that are stolen."

"Are those the talking points your company told you to use when you testified?"

Crotec jumped back to his feet with the exasperated look returned to his face. "Objection. Argumentative and seeking information potentially in violation of the attorney-client privilege."

"Sustained." Markum peered over his glasses at Arnie. "Let's try to establish some facts, counselor."

Arnie turned back to the witness. "Did your company ever teach you people can get hurt when you try to arrest them?"

Askew stared back smugly. "We don't arrest people. We detain them until the police arrive."

"They don't resist quite as much when they're dead, do they?" Arnie waited for Crotec's objection and nodded when the judge sustained it. Arnie knew he was close to the line and told himself to back off a little, yet intended to bore in. He held the remote control for the video player stationed on a small table in the middle of the room.

Arnie said, "I want to go through the video of the day in question."

Askew nodded, as if Arnie required his consent.

"Let's examine Jerry Hawkins' entire trip through the store. We've spliced video together from the time he arrived at the store until he left in the ambulance. You've reviewed this video and you would agree it's an accurate compilation of Jerry's trip through the store."

"I do."

Askew's agreement circumvented the necessity of calling witnesses to authenticate the video and testify that it was an accurate compilation of the events of the day. Arnie relaxed slightly knowing they had avoided hours of potential tedious testimony just to get the edited video admitted into evidence.

He spent the next ten minutes playing the initial portions of the video showing Jerry entering the parking lot, selecting a cart, and then traveling up and down various aisles. Nothing he did appeared out of the ordinary—from placing various items in his cart to continuing his journey from one end of the store to the other. Askew offered no resistance to the suggestion that Jerry Hawkins appeared to be a typical shopper who did nothing to garner suspicion prior to entering the checkout line.

"You didn't noticed Mr. Hawkins before he began to check himself out, did you?" Arnie asked.

Askew nodded. "At that point, as you can see, I'm helping out on the front end. I never noticed him before that, even though on the video it appears we passed each other earlier while he shopped."

"In fact, he almost completed his transaction before you decided to monitor his actions."

"That's true. You can see I am about fifteen feet away from him, but I maintained a clear view of his activities. I noticed as he was almost finished scanning his items, he left some product in his cart without paying for it."

On the video Jerry Hawkins placed the green plastic bags the stores provided into his cart with the items he scanned. Askew pointed at the screen. "There, at the bottom of his cart, some product remains. He put the bags with the scanned items on top of the product he didn't purchase."

"You had no idea what he intended to do, did you?"

"He hid the unscanned items. I was confident he did this on purpose."

"You waited until he left the registers before you approached him."

"Exactly how they teach us to do it. You can't accuse anyone of stealing before they leave the registers."

"You could've approached him and reminded him to pay for the items at the bottom of his cart."

"That's not how we're trained. I suspect if we did that, customers would get mad because you're telling them how to do things. They get angry when we do stuff like that."

"So you were setting him up?"

"Not at all. We don't want our customers to steal, but if they do, the law lets us stop them to get our product back."

Askew sat up straight. Arnie wondered how confident he would be when he honed in on his method of detaining Jerry that evening.

"Looking at the video," Arnie said, "Jerry completed his transaction and you didn't stop him near the registers."

"I wanted to stop him there, but I got momentarily delayed moving around another customer. That's when he started to head for the door. I tried to stop him before he got there, but as you can see he ducked around me."

On the video, Jerry juked to avoid Askew, and then made a beeline for the exit.

Arnie renewed his questioning. "At this point, he left the store."

"Correct. I didn't stop him at first."

"So let's talk about the company's policy when you can't detain a shoplifter before he leaves the store. What is the company's policy?"

Askew shot a questioning gaze at Arnie. "I was never aware of one. We have the right to stop shoplifters, so we do."

Arnie moved closer to Askew. "Who is Blaze Rondowsky?"

"He's the head of Loss Prevention for the chain. Smart guy."

"He will be testifying later in this trial. He developed your company's shoplifting policy. Did anyone from the company teach you, 'When they are out the door, chase no more?'"

Askew shook his head. "Never heard of it."

"If you had been taught this, you wouldn't have chased Mr. Hawkins into the parking lot."

"I don't think I chased him, but I did follow him into the parking lot."

"You ran to try to keep up with him." Arnie pointed at the video screen where Askew is pictured in a steady jog with Jerry moving at a quicker pace towards his car."

"He was so far in front of you, you couldn't catch him?"

"Probably not, but we had other people in the parking lot."

Arnie smirked at the witness. "So, just to be clear, you continued to chase the supposed shoplifter even when he was out the door?"

Askew returned Arnie's smirk. "First, he was not a supposed shoplifter—I saw him leave the store with product he didn't paid for. But, yes, I continued to pursue him into the parking lot."

Again, Arnie drew everyone's attention to the video. "Your cart kid, Byron, he was shagging carts. You called to him to stop Mr. Hawkins, didn't you?"

"I yelled that the gentleman stole some items from the store."

"Had Byron Hucklesbee ever been trained on how to detain a shoplifter?"

"I don't know."

Arnie shook his head. "Yet, you yelled for the kid to stop the shoplifter. Byron jumped in front of Mr. Hawkins and without warning grabbed Mr. Hawkins, didn't he?"

"I heard Byron tell the shoplifter to stop. The guy didn't slow down. So Byron did what any person would do. He made sure he got him to stop."

"He grabbed him and tried to wrestle him to the ground."

Morgan took in the images on the video. "It's not clear who grabbed who."

"Because the kid you yelled at to stop Mr. Hawkins suddenly started to wrestle him, Mr. Hawkins, not surprisingly, punched your employee."

"Yes, the shoplifter escalated the event by not submitting to the store's authority."

"You're suggesting Mr. Hawkins *had* to submit to Byron's authority," Arnie stressed his incredulity.

"I guess. But he didn't and then he punched me in the face." Askew pointed at the screen.

On the video, Byron and Askew attempt to hold down Jerry, who keeps trying to escape. Askew yells to passing customers.

"You and Byron are attempting to subdue Mr. Hawkins and then you get two other customers to help you out, don't you?"

"Yes. The shoplifter kept fighting."

"Once the two other shoppers decide to help you, you take charge and instruct them to hold down Mr. Hawkins."

"True."

"You tell them each to grab a limb and hold on tight."

"Yes."

"And not to let him up."

"Yes, he continued to struggle, even though I told him to calm down."

"Didn't he tell you that he couldn't breathe?"

"He kept struggling. I couldn't understand anything he said."

"Perhaps, because he lay face down on the pavement with four people on top of him?"

Askew sneered at Arnie. "Maybe because he kept struggling and wouldn't settle down."

"At some point he calmed down didn't he?"

"I think he continued to struggle almost to the time the police came."

Arnie let out a small scoff. "It took the police seventeen minutes to get there. You and your posse held him so he couldn't move, and you didn't relent. When the police came, he was dead."

"I was surprised when we stood up that he didn't respond."

Arnie turned and leaned over counsel table to grab a paper and muttered, "I bet you were." He stated louder, "Sir, you will agree your company never gave you any training on how to detain someone who didn't agree to be detained."

"Correct."

"In your experience in stopping shoplifters, some won't automatically *submit to your authority*, will they?"

"No, some get testy."

"People can get hurt when they get testy."

"No one will get hurt as long as people provide us appropriate respect."

Arnie shook his head. "C'mon, a shoplifter is not going to show you respect. They're stealing from you. If you get physical with them, someone's going to get hurt."

"I never had an issue before."

"You saw he tried to get to his car once you went into the parking lot"

"Yes."

"You had video of him from when he shopped in the store so you could identify him."

"Also true."

"If you let him go without provoking him, you could've gotten the license plate of the car, called the police, and they could have arrested him without you having to play police officer."

"I didn't play anything. I did what I thought was appropriate, consistent with my training."

Arnie stared at Askew before slowly repeating, "If you called the police before taking charge nobody would have gotten hurt."

"I always try to handle these situations in a manner so that it reduces the risk of people getting hurt."

"C'mon Mr. Askew, your decision to chase Mr. Hawkins out into the parking lot and instruct a lot attendant to wrestle him to the ground, that was risky, wasn't it?"

Askew paused to think. "I don't agree. It was in an open area. No innocent customers had a chance of getting hurt. We were within our rights to get our product back. No, I made the proper decision."

"Even though Mr. Hawkins died because of your decision?"

"An unfortunate consequence."

Arnie knew he couldn't get Askew to admit he did anything wrong and hoped Askew appeared cavalier and remorseless in minimizing his role in causing Jerry's death. Still wanting to beat a confession out of the hostile witness, Arnie waved his hand at Askew and released him for questioning from the store's lawyers.

Spencer handled the questioning of Askew for the store. He spent a considerable amount of time reviewing all the training he received, even though the vast majority had nothing to do with handling shoplifters. The evident goal was to make Askew appear like a well-trained, conscientious manager. The second part of Spencer's examination focused on the prevalence of shoplifting in his store, as well as, all the other company stores. By the time Askew completed his testimony, they had painted a picture of bands of roving thieves constantly hauling goods from the store and the store futilely attempting to keep up, foiling its primary concern of trying to keep its wares affordable for its customers.

"Every product in our store costs probably twenty percent more just to account for the stealing that takes place," Askew explained with raised eyebrows and his palms facing the ceiling.

While Spencer paced in front of the jurors, Arnie wondered if the jury lumped Jerry in with the bands of marauding cons who apparently roamed free at their stores.

Finally, Spencer questioned Askew about how he verified Jerry stole product. He feigned disbelief when asking, "Mr. Hawkins pulled his cart up to the check out and purchased thirty-two dollars of product from your store. Thieves don't go through the checkout line. It doesn't sound like he was stealing, does it?"

Askew's lips curled into a smug smile. "It's an old trick. Pay for a few cheap items so you look legit. Cover up the expensive items on the bottom. That's exactly what he did. His receipt showed him paying for thirty-two dollars' worth of product. He didn't pay for one hundred and forty dollars of goods which were in his cart. I verified this information after the ambulance left, and double-checked how much the other product cost if he had paid for it."

A picture of a shopping cart filled with product appeared on the screen. "What are we looking at?" Spencer asked.

"We took that picture immediately after. We brought the cart into the store. We printed out a new copy of his receipt. You can see some product was in bags, but most was underneath those bags. He paid for a few items, but the vast majority he clearly was stealing." Askew scanned the jurors, planting a serious look on his face.

Spencer's face mirrored Askew's while the picture contrasting what Jerry purchased with the additional items in his cart hung over the courtroom. Without making a sound, Spencer flicked the projector off. The image, though no longer visible, still resonated.

"No further questions," Spencer announced as he returned to his seat.

Arnie stood intending to score at least one point to counter the lingering impression of Jerry stealing from the store. "Mr. Askew, you believe it's your right to detain Mr. Hawkins don't you?"

"Absolutely."

"You also had the right not detain him, correct?"

"I guess. Life is filled with choices."

Arnie inched towards the witness. "If you made virtually any other choice, Jerry Hawkins would still be alive?"

"I don't know that. He might have. . ."

Before finishing his thought, Arnie cut him off. "You've answered my question. I'm done with you."

Without any further questions, the judge dismissed Askew from the stand. "The hour is late. This is a fine place to stop for the day. We will see you all in the morning."

Rick exhaled a huff of air and turned to Arnie. "We did fine today. No knockouts, but we're setting up our important witnesses for tomorrow."

Arnie nodded while throwing papers into his document bag. "I think our case will rise and fall with our last two witnesses to end our case tomorrow."

Rick offered a quick prayer in case anyone was paying attention.

CHAPTER FIFTY-THREE

THE MORNING SUN shone through the windows of the courtroom casting a sheen onto the tile floor in front of the jurors. Rick scribbled on his yellow pad, double checking his outlines for the three witnesses they intended to call in the morning.

Arnie sat staring straight ahead, the table surface in front of him devoid of any papers. They did not stir when the court personnel appeared, and ignored opposing counsel when they returned lugging their bags.

Not until the jurors shuffled in from the side door and Judge Markum entered to take his seat did they acknowledge anyone, including Emily, who sat silently in a seat immediately behind their counsel table.

Markum waved his gavel to indicate they should proceed.

"Plaintiff calls Virginia Montooth."

A young woman wearing a long sleeved, dark navy, polo shirt, black pants, a dark fleece pullover sweater paired with steel-toed boots, walked to the front of the courtroom. The insignia on her shirt read "Powers Ambulance." The subpoena Arnie served on her three days before hung from her hand.

This witness would not elicit strong questioning from the other side. Her testimony was not in dispute, although each side wanted to shade it their way.

Arnie took her first through her responsibilities as a paramedic, starting with her training and experience, and then through a typical day riding in the ambulance. After establishing that she had the proper qualifications and experience, Arnie asked her about the call to the B & D parking lot.

Arnie didn't much care what she said, as long as she painted the picture of Jerry lying motionless on the parking lot, unresponsive, his face an unnatural shade of gray.

The paramedic, her blonde hair pulled back behind her ears, provided straight forward testimony, trying to present an accurate accounting of the events. It took Arnie ten minutes to elicit her testimony, and he was satisfied she established that Jerry stood no chance of regaining consciousness by the time the ambulance arrived.

She finished by stating, "Despite our efforts to resuscitate the victim, we never could get him breathing or find a pulse. I performed CPR until we arrived at Memorial General, without any apparent success."

After Arnie took his seat, Crotec stood to announce, "Defendant has no questions of this witness."

Exactly as we expected, Rick thought.

Wanting to establish some momentum, Arnie called Sarah Bishop, one of the emergency room doctors to testify next.

Dressed in scrubs, Bishop presented as a medical dynamo consistent with the expectation of a doctor who dealt with numerous significant traumas each shift. She sat erect, but still relaxed and confident, as she spoke to the jurors. Again, Rick and Arnie needed only one fact from this witness, but wanted to highlight what it's like when a person is brought non-responsive into the ER.

"Mr. Hawkins was not breathing, and we could not find a pulse. A team of two docs and two nurses immediately attempted to restore breathing, but despite our efforts, he never regained consciousness. We pronounced him twenty minutes after he arrived."

"He was dead?" Arnie clarified.

"Yes," Bishop nodded as if this was fairly obvious from her testimony.

Arnie released the witness and before he returned to his seat, Crotec announced they again would ask no questions of this witness.

I guess they won't argue he wasn't dead, Rick thought, as he gathered his materials for the next witness.

Without delay, because he wanted to avoid the judge calling for the morning recess, Rick called Buster Toomey, their expert witness. Tall, paunchy, and wearing a tie a little too wide by present day standards, Toomey lugged his file to the stand, swore to tell the truth and gracefully, at least for a man of his size, took his seat.

Rick felt a bit conflicted. He understood the importance of the witness's testimony, but the credentials he presented took too much time to get through. He hoped to keep the pace moving, as he took the witness through his experience as an expert in store security, knowing that Toomey's testimony probably wouldn't do much to sway the jurors, who understood B & D retained its own expert whose opinion would be the exact opposite of this witness.

Rick took him through the depositions he had read and the documents, including the store's shoplifting policies, which he reviewed. They showed portions of the video to explain what Toomey thought Morgan Askew did incorrectly, highlighting the decision to chase Jerry outside of the store and having the cart boy try to tackle him.

It was no surprise when Toomey concluded, "Clearly, B & D did not have the appropriate policies in place and its training of its employees was nearly non-existent. Whatever policies B & D formulated. Mr. Askew failed to follow. No one should be held down against their will and when the training of employees is so poor, it is especially foreseeable someone will get hurt. Jerry Hawkins' death, though tragic, was completely expected given B & D's failure to train its workers, and Morgan Askew's failure to withdraw in the parking lot."

Rick hoped Toomey sounded knowledgeable expressing his opinion and conveyed the point that the company came across as unprepared to deal with the onslaught of shoplifting it knew it would face daily. His testimony, designed to highlight the inadequacies of B & D's policies, tied a bow for the jurors around his conclusion the failure to train properly precipitated Jerry's untimely demise.

Rick sat at counsel table and crossed his arms, ending his questioning.

As Crotec began, Rick could've written his script, almost word for word: "Shoplifting is a scourge that every retailer faces, isn't this true, Mr. Toomey?"

Toomey conceded, and as Rick expected, had to respond to a series of questions about how often thieves came into stores and how much gets stolen off the shelves every day.

Crotec threw statistics and graphs at Toomey, who admitted theft is ever prevalent, but kept deflecting by pointing out, "Every store knows it's happening, so they must train, train, and train their employees for the possibility of detaining a shoplifter under a variety of circumstances. B & D failed to do this?"

When pushed to admit that the law allows stores to stop suspected shoplifters in their parking lots, Toomey shook his head. "I disagree," he said. "Many stores I work with tell their staffs–the non-managers, they will never try to stop a shoplifter. It's not part of their job. To me, that's the safest route. If you miss some shoplifters who get away, I think it's better than having an hourly worker, not trained, try to stop someone."

Each time Toomey turned the subject to training, Crotec would emphasize how it was within the rights of the store to detain shoplifters.

Toomey almost jumped out of seat to explain, "Yes, they maintain the right to detain people who steal, but only to reasonably detain. I guess that's why we're here." He shrugged at the jurors.

Toomey conceded little beyond how much shoplifting occurs at stores. He remained resolute on the important point that B & D did not train its employees appropriately, and therefore improperly caused Jerry's death.

Not wanting to give Crotec another shot to ding Toomey's credibility, Rick released him, allowing him to leave the courtroom.

Judge Markum glanced up at the clock and informed the jurors it was time for lunch.

Once the jurors vacated the courtroom, Rick huddled with Arnie. "That was fairly predictable. We established this morning Jerry was non-responsive in the parking lot, dead on arrival at the hospital and the store's failure to train caused Jerry's death. All of which is necessary to prove, but our two witnesses this afternoon better put some more emotion into our case. The jurors want to feel some."

Arnie nodded his head. "We're sunk if we don't let the jurors feel something strong by the end of our case."

CHAPTER FIFTY-FOUR

"PLAINTIFFS CALL as their next witness, Blaze Rondowsky," Arnie said while facing the jurors. Rondowsky had lead the Safety and Loss Prevention Department for the company for the past thirty years, from the time it operated three stores, to now when its footprint included over four hundred locations.

Arnie was confident the jurors, after hearing Rondowsky's testimony, would believe the company grew quicker than its implementation of appropriate safety policies. As the skinny exec in the semi-wrinkled, off-the-rack, suit swore an oath to tell the truth, Arnie waited by the edge of the jury box.

"You are Blaze Rondowsky, head of B & D's Loss Prevention Department, correct?"

Before the witness agreed to the basic information, Crotec stood to object. "The question is leading, Your Honor."

Markum nearly rolled his eyes, but caught himself and without looking up from his notes said, "Response, Mr. McBride?"

Arnie smirked at Crotec. "The witness is an executive with the defendant company. Under the rules of civil procedure we can call any of their employees as on cross-examination, and then we can lead the witness during questioning."

Markum, still not raising his eyes, said, "It's pretty simple, counselor. Do you have a response?"

Crotec didn't bother to try. "Defendants withdraw the objection."

Turning to Arnie, Markum said, "You may continue to cross-examine the witness."

Arnie moved to the center of the courtroom. "Sir, you have been director of Loss Prevention for thirty years for the company haven't you?"

"I have."

"You have no education in that field, do you?"

"I did not study that area when I was in school, but I have been a constant study for the past thirty years. I have been to many, many seminars and have reviewed so much written materials in the area I wouldn't be able to list it."

Arnie pursed his lips. "It's your responsibility to make sure every employee of your company is trained to prevent shoplifting."

"You're correct, but every category of employee will receive different training. Our managers receive the most extensive training on how to deal with shoplifting. I'm rather proud of how we make our stores safe for our customers."

"Then you agree that shoplifting is a serious problem your stores have to deal with every day."

"Absolutely."

"And you have a responsibility for dealing with it safely, to protect your customers."

"I would agree."

"You train your employees to know they are allowed to detain suspected shoplifters until the police arrived."

Rondowsky smiled. "You know that counselor. I've been

sitting in the courtroom the whole trial. We all know the law allows, even expects us, to detain shoplifters. It's the best way to reduce shoplifting and the police appreciate it when we turn over a thief to them."

"Even after you killed them?"

Crotec screamed, "Objection."

The corners of Markum's lips curled up, "Sustained. C'mon, counselor, drive within the lines."

Arnie nodded. "Let's put it this way, you know people shoplift. You prime your managers to stop them, but you never trained them on how to detain them—without killing them?"

Before Crotec could renew his objection, the witness responded, "Counselor, we train our managers to be courteous, yet firm, when dealing with shoplifters."

"You do? Show me one training document which says that. Show me one that tells me how managers are instructed to detain suspected shoplifters."

Rondowsky frowned. "Our company has a culture of in-person training. We don't throw a bunch of manuals at people knowing they will never read them. We have seminars and we stress everything we're talking about in our face-to-face training sessions."

Arnie stepped closer to the witness stand. "Sir, you have no documentation any manager ever went to any training session. You have no sign-offs, nothing to indicate anyone actually received any instruction."

Rondowsky face scrunched together. "What I can tell you is we spend lots of time and money in training. If we don't have a list of signatures it's only because we are more concerned with instructing than having what you call 'documentation.'"

"Also known as proof. Okay, we can agree you have no backup to prove your company did any training, so let's move onto one final area. You testified in your deposition that you have taught your managers not to chase suspected shoplifters outside. You have a pet phrase, 'When they are out the door, chase no more,' don't you?"

"I have utilized this expression to teach our managers they should be careful if they get outside with a shoplifter. It's to remind them they could get hurt or an innocent customer could get in the way. Here, no employee got hurt and neither did any innocent customer get injured. Unfortunately, Mr. Hawkins died, but I don't think he would have been hurt had he listened to the directive of the manager and not tried to escape."

"Easy to say now, isn't it? Nobody at the store ever heard of your pet expression. None was aware that company policy prohibited them from chasing a shoplifter in the parking lot?"

"From my review, Mr. Askew appeared to be well-trained. He approached Mr. Hawkins only after having witnessed him stealing and dealt with him in a professional manner. Let me repeat, it's unfortunate Mr. Hawkins stole and even more unfortunate he failed to heed Mr. Hawkins' instructions stop."

Arnie shook the yellow pad he held. "Sir, can we agree that if Mr. Hawkins had been properly trained and didn't chase Mr. Hawkins into the parking lot, Mr. Hawkins would not have died."

Rondowsky displayed no outward signs of agitation and only smiled at Arnie. "I can't agree with much of your question. Mr. Askew was well-trained and handled the situation appropriately. He followed the shoplifter into the parking lot without creating commotion. No one would have been hurt if Mr. Askew listened."

"Can you agree that getting the lot attendant involved when Mr. Askew couldn't catch Mr. Hawkins violated company policy?"

"I cannot. Our policy is that non-management employees should not make decisions as to when to detain a suspected shoplifter. Mr. Hucklesbee made no such decision. I have no issues with a manager utilizing an hourly employee where appropriate. Here, I believe was just such a situation. Mr. Askew directed Mr. Hucklesbee the entire time."

"Did the company ever train its managers how to detain a shoplifter who doesn't want to be detained?"

"You can't anticipate every situation which might arise. We teach our managers to think and to be pro-active, while anticipating potential negative outcomes, so as to avoid them. I believe this was how Mr. Askew responded to this situation."

Arnie shook his head while expelling a breath. "Wouldn't you agree that if Mr. Askew had followed your advice and not chased Mr. Hawkins into the parking lot, all information necessary would have been available to report Mr. Hawkins to the police so they could arrest him, if necessary, somewhere else?"

Rondowsky didn't twitch. "Sir, I am not in the business of speculating. I cannot say with certainty what might happen if different paths are taken. What I can say with absolute confidence is that Mr. Hawkins acted appropriately and consistently with our training. It is within our rights to detain shoplifters. Mr. Hawkins stole and we have the right to get our product. No innocent customer nor any employee was hurt. That is what I know."

Pain etched across Arnie's face. He looked down at his feet. "I have no further questions."

Crotec stood glancing through his notes appearing as if he was deciding to ask any questions, but took a step forward. "Sir, a few follow-ups."

"Is it your company's policy that Mr. Askew should not go into the parking lot if a thief runs there?"

"Of course not. It would be a poor decision to let the man run away without making sure the customers in the parking lot weren't in any danger. I would have been upset at Mr. Askew if he stayed in the store."

Crotec eyes lit up. "What about asking Mr. Hucklesbee to get involved?"

"Similar response. Mr. Askew has to make quick decisions all geared towards protecting the assets of the store and the customers. Getting Mr. Hucklesbee's assistance was smart as it helped to get the product returned and protected the customers from Mr. Hawkins running scared through the lot."

"Finally, do you believe Mr. Askew should be reprimanded?"

"Of course not. I wish we had more managers with his attitude. It is a shame that Mr. Hawkins died, but he had so many opportunities to stop this from escalating. I only wish he had taken one so none of us would be here."

"Thank you Mr. Rondowsky, I have no more questions."

Arnie stood to indicate they would ask nothing further of the witness. He walked over to Rick and whispered, "He would never agree anyone ever did anything wrong. I hope the jurors understand his lack of objectivity."

Rick shrugged.

CHAPTER FIFTY-FIVE

He could tell all eyes in the courtroom locked on him–like every other time he testified. Wyatt Creft understood his reputation proceeded him into the courtroom, but it was why lawyers always forked over the money to pay his fee. The starstruck expressions he saw on the jurors' faces told him that every dollar he received was a value to whomever retained him. Like so many times before, his testimony would be the jet engine propelling the jury to award a huge hunk of cash.

He had never met Emily Hawkins and barely offered her a nod when he sauntered up to the witness stand. She might reap the benefits of his testimony, but it was he who would make the jurors want to reach into B & D's pockets, and grab its money.

The microphone blocked part of his vision to the jury box, so he pushed it aside. His training as a stage actor decades ago would allow his voice to carry to the back of the courtroom. No one would have difficulty hearing him speak, and he knew how to enunciate each syllable to project subtle innuendo, as well as, any needed subtext.

Rick began with the preliminaries, but didn't rush, allowing Creft the opportunity to expand the cold entries on his resume. He gave Creft space to work in stories of meeting celebrities or of particularly gruesome autopsies, so the jurors would feel like insiders in a world they never got to experience.

Creft told of his medical training and how a mentor during his internship pushed him into the field of pathology. Ultimately, he became the head of the coroner's office in Cleveland, but his work stretched to all parts of the world, as he consulted on many of the world's most infamous deaths.

The jurors sat forward as Creft told them about examining the remains of the passengers killed when terrorists blew up their plane over Lockerbie, Scotland, and about his involvement in the murder of a Washington Post reporter in Saudi Arabia.

He touched on his role in recent high profile killings where police officers utilized choke holds to detain black citizens, which caused their deaths. At this point, Creft knew not to give too much detail about these cases as the plan was to circle back when discussing Jerry Hawkins' death.

Confident the jury anticipated the meat of his testimony, Creft leaned his long frame forward, awaiting Rick's transition away from his qualifications.

"Did I request that you review the entire file of Jerry Hawkins' death before offering any opinion?" Rick asked as he pointed to seven file folders lined neatly next to his counsel table?"

"You did ask and I did review the entire file."

"How did your experience as a pathologist and coroner assist you in formulating your opinion?"

"My experience has taught me how to review medical records and witness testimony to get a picture of how a person died. The fact that I conducted the autopsy on Mr. Hawkins gives me the unique perspective of being able to evaluate his injuries. With this information, it was rather simple to determine not only the cause of his death, but the circumstances giving rise to them. Piecing together what the witnesses said about what happened with the physical, objective trauma he suffered, I maintain a clear picture of what lead to his demise."

"Did you also review the video of his detention?"

"I did, but truth be told, it did not inform my opinion much. The quality of the video was rather poor and it was not a significant factor I utilized to determine what happened to Jerry Hawkins when he was killed."

Rick paused for a moment. "Sir, you said, 'when he was killed.' Are those the words you want to use?"

Creft smirked. "Absolutely. Jerry Hawkins did not just die that afternoon. It was an act of a group of people intentionally holding him down against his will which caused him to die. I am quite comfortable with the phrase, 'he was killed.'"

Creft noticed the jurors not taking notes and leaning forward. They wanted to hear more.

Rick moved ahead, "What did you do to determine how Jerry was killed?"

First, I performed his autopsy. I will speak about that in a moment. I also reviewed all the deposition testimony to determine how Mr. Hawkins was subdued. It's clear the store employees tackled him. He then struggled to get free. The store manager, Mr. Askew, and the cart person tried to hold him down, but Mr. Hawkins continued to struggle. Two customers joined in and the four of them held him down. Mr. Hawkins was face down on the concrete with each of the four individuals restraining one limb. Mr. Hawkins could not move and Mr. Askew placed a knee on his right arm and his other knee immediately below his neck. This is borne out in the photographs I took at the autopsy."

Arnie tapped the video remote to control the images on the screen and placed a blowup of bruising on Jerry's back.

Pointing to the screen, Creft said, "This is a picture of the marks on Mr. Hawkins' back. They measured six inches in length, four inches wide. The bruises spread deep into the subcutaneous tissues."

More pictures appeared for the jurors to view. He narrated, "There was also significant bruising on his arms, leg and the lower part of his torso."

"What other findings did you make during your autopsy?"

A close-up of a deep incision in the front of Jerry's neck with his skin pinned back appeared on the screen. Creft stated, "This image shows Mr. Hawkins' trachea, or his windpipe. It's severely damaged. It's effectively crushed."

Emily, who was sitting quietly behind Arnie, gasped loud enough for the jurors to hear. She threw her hands over her mouth and lowered her head when she realized the jurors had turned their attention to her.

To regain his momentum, Creft modulated his voice, and like a cat transfixed by a beam from a laser, the jurors turned back to him. "To impart such damage, Mr. Askew must have placed nearly his entire body weight centered on one spot just below Mr. Hawkins' neck–right on the location of the bruise we just reviewed."

Rick moved a few steps closer to the witness, and asked, "Mr. Askew testified that Mr. Hawkins continued to struggle up to nearly the time the police officers arrived at the scene. What did your investigation reveal about this contention?"

Creft tilted at his waist in the direction of the jurors and spoke with less volume than before. The jurors matched his lean to catch each word.

"I will proffer two points in response to this contention and each is significant. First, Mr. Askew did not understand Mr. Hawkins' response to being denied oxygen. The manager suggested Mr. Askew continued to struggle so his group increased their restraint on him. This was not what was happening. Rather, when a person suffers from a lack of oxygen—is being suffocated—the body's natural response is to convulse. This is not, as Mr. Askew suggested, a fight, but a natural bodily response. The way to have gotten Mr. Hawkins to stop was to release the restraint. Instead, they tightened their hold on him, which caused his body to respond. It was a vicious cycle about which Mr. Askew apparently knew nothing. Had he been taught better, perhaps he and his group would have eased up."

He had the jury where he wanted, begging to hear more. He would make them wait a little longer, so he pulled out a handkerchief and wiped off his round glasses. After inspecting them, he put them back on.

"The second, and perhaps, more important point," he continued, "is Mr. Hawkins stopped breathing and died minutes before the police arrived. Despite this, Mr. Askew and the people assisting him maintained their holds, denying Mr. Hawkins any opportunity to breathe."

Rick waited to let the answer sink in with the jurors. "How do you know this?"

"It is clear from the autopsy. My examination of the blood saturation and the oxygen levels in Mr. Hawkins' tissues indicate he died at least three minutes before the police came. The witnesses testified they released their holds only upon the instructions of the police. It stands to reason they held their deadly restraints on a dead person for minutes before getting off him."

Rick inched towards the jurors. "Dr. Creft, was how Mr. Askew detained Mr. Hawkins dangerous?"

Creft's lips stretched into a scowl. "Absolutely. Anyone with any training knows that sticking a knee in the back of a person will deprive him of his ability to breathe. This is exactly what has happened with many of the police incidents where people they have held down ended up dying. I have testified in some of those cases and I don't want to address them directly, but it's a similar situation. The problem is police officers receive much more training on how to deal with unruly people and still they end up making huge mistakes. Here, you have a grocery store manager trying to forcibly detain someone against their will. He's untrained on how to do it. It's no surprise someone got killed."

Rick took three steps and faced the jury box. Without looking at Creft he asked, "Final question sir: In your opinion, was there a reasonable way for Mr. Askew to detain Mr. Hawkins if he suspected him of stealing, without killing him?"

Creft nodded his head. "Of course. Let's start with the opposite question. Was Mr. Askew's detention reasonable? I say 'no,' because he died and almost by definition if the man dies, in my opinion, it's unreasonable. Conversely, there are many ways to detain a person. One simple way might be just to ask him to wait. What's the worst that could happen? He leaves? I submit that is a much more reasonable response than to kill a person while waiting for the police to arrive."

"Thanks, doctor. That's all my questions."

Crotec rose as Creft stared at him without worry or concern. Creft did this often enough he was confident of his ability to deflect any difficult inquiry and remind the jury that Jerry Hawkins didn't have to die.

"Dr. Creft, can we agree Jerry Hawkins was stealing?"

"I can't agree. I never investigated that issue—not my area."

Crotec grimaced. "I understand, but you said you read every deposition. Morgan Askew clearly explained how he thought Jerry was stealing?"

"He did."

"You can't dispute his testimony."

"I can't. I didn't witness what he did."

Crotec stepped closer to the jury. "Next point–stores have the right to detain suspected shoplifters."

"Again, I'm not a lawyer, but yes, that is my understanding."

"They have the right to stop shoplifters until the police arrive, whether the person actually stole, so long as their suspicion is reasonable."

"Also my understanding," Creft conceded.

"So now we get into the manner of how the store detained Mr. Hawkins."

"I guess we do."

"You said the store could ask Mr. Hawkins to stop. Isn't this exactly what Mr. Askew did when he approached Mr. Hawkins inside the store?"

"I guess."

"Yet, Mr. Hawkins bolted from the store."

"He certainly did not remain."

"In the parking lot, when approached by the lot attendant, he sucker-punched him, didn't he?"

"I guess, he was the aggressor, yes."

Crotec edged closer to the witness. "When Mr. Askew again tried to detain him in the parking lot, Mr. Hawkins tried to fight his way out to escape."

"I suppose you could say that."

"So now there is a bloody cart attendant and a man trying to fight his way out of the parking lot, correct? Wasn't it reasonable, at this point, for the store people to take down Mr. Askew to prevent a further escalation?"

Creft sucked in a gulp of air and pulled out his handkerchief, but this time to dab his brow. He knew he had strayed from the autopsy results in his direct examination and offered his thoughts on the manner of detention. Now, opposing counsel was pointing out the ways Jerry had exacerbated the situation. He wanted to get his testimony back to where it belonged.

"I never condone the use of violence, especially if it leads to someone dying?"

A smug smile stretched across Crotec's face, "Wouldn't it be fair to say that by throwing the first punch, it was Mr. Hawkins who started the cycle of violence that led to his death?"

Knowing full well he couldn't just acquiesce, Creft said, "No, I can't agree with it. I would suggest the situation got out of control when four people sat on Mr. Hawkins waiting for the police."

"Sir, didn't things start to get out of control when Mr. Hawkins stole from the store?"

"No, stealing is expected, killing someone in the parking lot, that's out of control." The bass quality of Creft's voice was beginning to desert him as its timbre moved higher.

"Will you agree, had Mr. Hawkins not stolen, he would still be alive."

"Probably," Creft's voice was now higher and meeker.

"If Mr. Hawkins didn't punch the lot attendant there wouldn't be any need to physically detain him to prevent injury to others."

"Perhaps."

Crotec turned to the judge. "That's it for this witness."

Rick followed with a few questions so Creft could again discuss the manner of Jerry's death, but Creft had already inflicted significant damage. Crotec, without getting into how Jerry died, had punctured the doctor's aura of invincibility.

Despite a few head shakes from a couple of jurors, Creft left the stand still confident his testimony had impressed them.

Rick collapsed back into his chair and whispered to Arnie. "What a wimp. Couldn't handle cross."

Arnie nodded. "It's up to Emily to rescue her case."

CHAPTER FIFTY-SIX

No TRIAL PROCEEDS EXACTLY as planned. Despite solid preparation, complete knowledge of the case, and an understanding of the applicable law, no lawyer can predict how the evidence will unfold. Too many variables collide to disrupt the best made plans. Lawyers could prepare witnesses for days, but withering cross-examination under the scrutiny of twelve jurors can waylay even the most confident witness. Other unforeseen influences, like an offhand remark by a judge, can fundamentally alter the perception of a jury.

Rick understood the risks of trial; the wreckage of Creft's weak, parsimonious testimony on cross was smacking him in the face like an MMA punch. The world renowned pathologist had not delivered on what he promised. The jury might have been impressed with his qualifications, but the tailspin brought on by Crotec's questioning left them with no more margin for error. With one remaining witness, Rick sensed if Emily didn't hit it out of the park, the jury wouldn't slam B & D in the way he had hoped in his fantasies leading up to trial.

Emily had impressed Rick from the day he first met her.

Her smart, understated, and self-assured demeanor provided Rick sufficient confidence to save her for last. He avoided talking with her about how the jury might be responding to the case, because he wanted her to focus on what she had to say and not feel like she was the cleanup batter. The fear in her eyes as she approached the witness stand told him everything–she understood Creft had crapped the bed, and she was the only one left who could clean up the mess.

Emily sported a long-sleeved, silk blouse and raised her eyes while adjusting her seat to catch the supporting gaze of the jurors.

Rick waited a moment to allow her an opportunity to bond with the people who sat in judgment of her.

Her voice was quiet, not meek, as she gave the basics– name, address and the fact she had been married to Jerry. Rick didn't want to ask long questions and liked when Emily talked freely to the jurors.

"I was twenty-one when we got married. Maybe a little young, but we were in love and wanted to spend our lives together." She blushed and lowered her eyes. "The plan was to have three kids–maybe four, but despite trying, and trying, we hadn't had any yet. We remained hopeful." She raised her shoulders.

"Tell the jurors what Jerry was like," Rick requested.

The edges of her mouth curled up. "He was really sweet and smart. Funny most of the time. It was just easy to spend time together. We didn't spend a lot of time with other couples. We enjoyed hanging out with each other."

"What did Jerry do in his spare time?"

"He read books. All kinds of books. He was trying to write a book, but I guess it's never going to get finished. There were lots of things that interested him–something always grabbed his attention. He fixed everything around the house, and he kept our garden."

"Was he working at the time he died?"

Emily's head shook back and forth. She started to talk, but hesitated. A tear snuck out of the corner of her eye. "He wasn't working at that time. He worked as a waiter for a bit after we married. He was wonderful. I thought he could make a living doing that, but he wanted more. Constantly he talked about becoming a computer programmer. He started to take some courses and began to hunt for a job in that field. I know that's what he wanted to do long term." She glanced at the jury.

"What do you do for work?"

"I've taken a variety of jobs over the years–receptionist, delivery person, mail carrier–there were a bunch. That's the thing. The plan was for me to work for a little. Help us save money. But we both wanted me to stay at home and raise the kids. Jerry would be the one working full-time–making the money. It may be a little old-fashioned, but it's what we wanted. We did our best to get there."

"Is that what Jerry wanted?"

She dropped her gaze briefly and then raised it towards the ceiling. Her lips scrunched together. "Absolutely. He wanted what was best for us, for our family. Every day both of us worked towards our goals."

Rick paused, ready to switch gears. He glanced at the jury allowing Emily a moment to recompose. "Emily, what happened the day Jerry went to B & D?"

"It was a normal day for us. We ate lunch together. I remember he made some tuna salad while I watched t.v. We sat and ate it together. After we finished, we realized we needed some groceries and some other things for the house. I didn't really want to go, so he said he would. I wish. . . ." She didn't finish the sentence.

"When did you find out what happened at B & D?"

"I guess it was a couple of hours later. He was gone for a while, but I didn't think much of it. A policeman knocked on the door. He told me Jerry had been murdered. I needed to go to the hospital to identify him."

"What were you thinking?"

"I have no idea. I didn't know what happened." Emily's eyes darted back-and-forth. "I called a friend for a ride to the hospital. In the emergency department a sweet nurse and another policeman took me to Jerry. He was in the basement on some slab. I remember seeing bruises all over his face. I think I collapsed." Emily reached in her pocket for a tissue and dabbed at the tears running down her face.

This was the difficult part for Rick—how hard to try to get the jury to empathize with Emily. He wanted them to feel her pain, but didn't want to appear like they were begging for it. If any of the jurors suspected she forced the tears, they would be hard to convince to be on their side during deliberations. But, with a dead husband, he felt like she had a lot of leash.

"So what did you do?"

Emily stared at Rick, her expression blank. "What could I do? I cried. She took me to a room and I cried some more. After a while another woman came in and took me back to Jerry, so I could say goodbye. I took his hand. I talked to him for a while. I told him I didn't know what I would do without him. He told me I would be alright. Finally, I said my goodbyes."

"What happened after that?"

"I'm not really sure. I went home. Our bed felt funny, so I slept on the couch. I think it was the first time since we got married we didn't sleep in the same bed."

"How have you been since that day?"

"I'm doing fine, I guess." She bit her lower lip. "I'm managing. I just got a new job with a manufacturing company. It's time to start a new career." She forced a smile.

"You talked about how you thought Jerry said you would be okay. Are you?"

"I miss him. I miss what we did together. I miss the security of him being around and protecting me. He always protected me and worried about me. Now I'm on my own."

She shrugged.

"Emily, did you ever go back to the B & D since Jerry was killed?"

"I drove by and tried to figure out how things went so wrong, but I couldn't bear the thought of being there. All I see is the image of Jerry dead on the concrete, and him never coming back—all because they said he stole something. I don't believe it—he would never do anything like that." She stared straight at Morgan Askew sitting behind B & D's attorneys and pointed a finger at him. "You had no right."

The tension between Emily and Askew was palpable as she did not break eye contact with him. Rick had more questions he could ask, but thought they had reached a crescendo. Two jurors dabbing their eyes with tissues convinced him to sit and let the cross-examination begin.

Spencer walked to Emily in the witness box and handed her a fresh tissue. "We are all sorry for your loss. If you need a break, please let me know."

Emily nodded, not uttering a word. She stared straight at Spencer, her eyes narrowing into slits.

Spencer flicked a switch and the projector emitted a beam onto the screen. "Let's start where you left off, Mrs. Hawkins. You said, 'Your husband would never steal,' didn't you?"

Emily's body withdrew involuntarily. "Of course."

"Ms. Hawkins, you will later hear the testimony of Wayne

Oliver, the store manager of B & D. He will testify that he reviewed video related to your husband."

"You mean, where you killed him?" Emily snarled.

"I was talking about what he was doing in the store."

"Alright."

"You know we have evidence of him stealing that evening?"

"That's what you say."

Spencer smirked. "True, but did you know it was not the first time he stole from the store?"

Rick shot out of his chair. "Objection. That's outrageous."

Markum waved the attorneys forward. "Approach." The court reporter joined them with her stenographer's machine. "State your objection," he commanded.

Rick cleared his throat, not quite understanding what the evidence was, but knowing he had to keep the jury from hearing it. "Counsel suggests he possesses evidence of Mr. Hawkins stealing on other occasions. This has no relevance to this case, especially given how prejudicial it would be."

When he finished jotting notes on his yellow pad, Markum nodded at Spencer to respond.

Spencer gave a quick glance at Rick and then said, "The evidence is completely relevant. Plaintiff opened the door to this evidence by testifying on direct examination that her husband never stole anything. It would be highly prejudicial to the defendants to allow her to make this statement and not provide us the opportunity to refute it. We are offering this testimony to rebut her statement. Accordingly, we had no obligation to provide it during discovery."

Rick's stomach twisted into a knot. On its face, Spencer's argument was correct. Her statement about her husband never stealing before was off-script and now they were about to pay dearly for her winging it.

He responded to Spencer's argument, "Generally Mr.

Spencer is correct about the law here, if Ms. Hawkins, in fact, opened the door. However, her statement was merely her belief and not a factual statement of her husband's activities. Allowing defendants to cross-examine her about what her husband did in his free time is well beyond her knowledge and the court should preclude the evidence."

Markum held up his hand to signal the end to the argument. "Ms. Hawkins clearly raised the issue of her husband's freedom from other acts of theft. If she did not have knowledge of such activities, she shouldn't have said anything. She opened the door to this evidence and I will allow defendant to question her about it."

Markum's ruling nearly sucked the breath from Rick's chest. He staggered back to his counsel table prepared to listen to evidence he knew nothing about, that he presumed was about to sink his case.

An epic smirk spread across Spencer's face as he waited for everyone to return to their positions. He nodded at Arnie as he turned to resume his cross-examination.

"Ma'am, you recall saying your husband never stole anything?"

"I do."

"What if I say that he systematically stole from our stores?"

"I would say you're a liar."

The smirk returned to Spencer's face. "Let me show you a video from the same store, three days before your husband died."

Security images flashed again on the screen. The date stamp from the video confirmed they were taken a few days before Jerry's death. A picture of Jerry pushing a shopping cart appeared.

"That's your husband, Jerry, isn't it?" Spencer asked.

Emily nodded. "It is."

"Let's follow him and see what he does."

The video displayed images of Jerry picking out items and placing them in the cart. He then pushed the cart to the health and beauty section at the far end of the store. After picking up a toothbrush and toothpaste, he headed to the cash registers where he paid for the two small items and placed them in a green B & D bag. Instead of heading for the exit, Jerry took his green bag and returned to the health and beauty section.

Spencer interjected, "Ms. Hawkins, you agree your husband never paid for the items he left in the cart?"

"I guess so."

As the video continued, Spencer asked, "Yet, as you see, your husband places the green bag with the two items he just purchased on top of the cart and pushes the cart out the café door next to health and beauty."

Emily muffled a groan. "Yes."

The video cut to a picture from the lot where Jerry is shown putting everything from the cart into his car.

"Let's review some video from five days before that."

The video showed Jerry walking in the back of the store wearing a long trench coat. Approaching the meat section, he turned his head side-to-side before picking up four packages of meat which he slid inside his coat. He headed down an aisle before walking out the front door.

"He didn't pay for those either, did he?"

Emily shook her head as her lips clenched together.

"I'm sorry," Spencer said, "but we need your answer out loud for the record."

"No, he didn't," Emily spit out.

"Thank-you, Ms. Hawkins, let's go through another."

The video jumped to a day two weeks before Jerry's death with him again walking through the store, this time pushing a cart. Boxes spread along the inside walls of the cart obscured a view inside through the sides. Pushing the cart throughout the store, Jerry placed items inside which the boxes hid. Instead of heading to the registers, Jerry pushed the cart straight out the doors and to his car.

"Ms. Hawkins, that's three times in two weeks your husband stole from our store, isn't it."

"If you say so." Emily almost spat at Spencer, with her body recoiling at the same time.

"I understand, Ms. Hawkins, this may be painful for you. In the three months before your husband died, we found on video seven occasions where your husband came into our store and stole. Mr. Oliver . . . ," he pointed to the store manager seated in the front row, ". . . will testify how he found the video and how many times Mr. Hawkins stole from our store. I don't want to cause you too much pain, so I don't think it will be necessary to go through each one with you."

Emily forced a smile. "Thank you."

Spencer held up his index finger. "To put a bow on it–based on what you've seen at this trial and how your husband systematically came into the B & D store and took product without ever paying for it, can't we agree that your husband is a thief?"

Her eyes glistened as she peered up to the ceiling. Finding no comfort there, she returned her glare to Spencer. Her voice softened. "I don't know what to say. The video is shocking and that's not the Jerry I know. I can't agree with your question because I could never see Jerry that way. Never."

Rick patted Arnie on the sleeve satisfied that perhaps Emily blunted the thrust of the question. He had no idea how this evidence affected the jury or whether it altered their view of her.

"I just have one more area of questioning for you," Spencer continued. "I wanted to talk about your husband's plan for the future."

Emily nodded, and readied herself for the next assault.

"Your husband was a high school graduate."

"Yes."

"He had no further education."

"Correct."

"He held three jobs since you met him."

"Yes."

"The longest tenure he had in any job was for seven months."

"I think that's true."

"When he was a waiter."

"Yes, and a very good one."

"Yet, he got fired from that job."

"I don't know that. I thought he quit."

"Not a huge point, but review the records we received from the restaurant." He handed her a sheet of paper. "Under reason for separation, it says, 'terminated,' doesn't it?"

She scanned the paper. "It says that, but I don't know what happened."

"Sure." Spencer slid closer to the jurors. "Tell me if you agree with this summary—your husband can't hold a job for a year—never has. He received no particularized training in any field and took two on-line courses for computer programming, but didn't receive any degree or certification before he died?"

Emily squirmed in her chair. "I believe that's accurate."

A pained grimace appeared on Spencer's face. "Yet, despite your husband's lack of credentials and lack of any fortitude in holding a job, you claim he was about to embark on a new career—one where he would work hard and make lots of money."

The witness chair creaked as Emily leaned forward onto her arms. "That's absolutely correct. He was a wonderful man and his primary goal was to provide for his family. There were going to be kids, and he was going to get an important job, so we could raise them right. It was about hard work and Jerry always was willing to do that. So, yes, it's completely true. He was going to start a new career and take care of us. You just never gave him a chance." Emily searched the jurors' faces for support.

"Ms. Hawkins, I don't have any further questions."

Before Spencer finished his sentence, Rick stood. "One question: Did you know anything about what Mr. Spencer just showed you in the videos?"

"Absolutely not." Emily recoiled back into her seat. "I'm shocked by what I saw. That's not Jerry. He would never do anything like that." She shook her head. "I don't understand why they felt like they needed to show this." Her voice trailed off.

"Thank you, Emily, that's all I have."

Emily stared at Spencer, who gave no indication of wanting to ask any more questions. She stood and walked off the witness stand trying to make eye contact with any juror willing to engage. They stared straight ahead.

Rick turned to the judge and announced, "That's all the evidence the plaintiff will present. Plaintiff rests."

Markum turned to the jurors. "It's late in the day. The defendant will begin to present its case in the morning. Let's be ready, bright and early."

As the jurors filed out of their seats, Rick turned to Arnie. "Let's talk about how badly our case has been hurt."

CHAPTER FIFTY-SEVEN

THE SMALL ROOM sat at the end of the hall, and despite the decrepit table and chairs, the county primarily used it for storage. Rick and Arnie ignored the décor and flipped through their notes from the day utilizing the light from the bare bulb hanging from the ceiling.

ARNIE SPOKE FIRST. "Today didn't play out in the way we planned. The sheets in Creft's bed are going to smell for a long time and those images of Jerry walking out of the store with stolen product are still bouncing around my head."

RICK NODDED. "That's exactly what I'm worried about. Are the jurors seeing the same thing? They planned this well. Those videos must have resonated with the jurors." Rick pouted. "This was supposed to be our best day, when our star witnesses presented the strongest part of our case. I'm not nearly as confident as I thought I would be."

• • •

"I HEAR YOU, but here's my take," Arnie said. "Emily's right. Those videos of Jerry on the other nights had nothing to do with why they stopped him when they killed him and nothing to do with Emily. I assume the jury didn't think she knew anything about this."

"I HAVE no idea what that jury is thinking. It's just like it was at the beginning. They could go either way."

ARNIE STOOD to pace the room. "I agree. Looks like it's another night of not much sleep."

RICK CHUCKLED. "The closing isn't going to write itself. Let's hunker down for a while to make sure we're ready to give them our best."

BOTH LAWYERS FLIPPED their yellow pads to a clean sheet, knowing in the next few hours they would fill up many pages with new scribbles. Rick wondered if he would be able to get the recent images of Jerry stealing from the store out of his head.

CHAPTER FIFTY-EIGHT

Never having been in a courtroom before this trial, Wayne Oliver found the testimony in the case fascinating. Observing from his perch in the second row behind the company's attorneys, he mentally compared the proceedings to a Greek drama, seeing the witnesses as contrasting heroes and villains, ultimately having to wait for the chorus to announce the victor.

Oliver swam in corporate waters and his sympathies lay with his pecuniary interests and his sense of right and wrong— so given that B & D paid his check and Jerry Hawkins was a thief, he was rooting for his company to prevail, despite a deep river of well-hidden empathy he maintained for Emily Hawkins.

Oliver enjoyed watching the other witnesses squirm under well-tailored questioning, respecting the lawyers' abilities to pick out a fact to throw back at a witness to thwart their testimony. The ramifications of the team members' actions leading to Jerry Hawkins' death might end up affecting others at the store, but they would not fall on him. He was not in the parking lot and did not lead a group of shoppers on a vendetta. In fact, he was at home that afternoon. He felt above the fray, unaffected by whom the jury believed had acted appropriately.

Chosen as the first witness for the defense, he felt comfortable in his role as representative of the company. Crotec stood before the jury as Oliver, in his deep baritone, described his rise up the corporate ladder starting as a stock person until culminating in the role of a Store Director after nineteen years of long hours of repetitive, mostly mundane, tasks.

Today his job was simple–paint the company in a positive light, highlighting its emphasis on customer safety and system of constant training. Oliver spent his entire adult life learning, and then, teaching these standards, and he remained confident in his ability to project the company's positive attributes.

"As Director, I am the person in charge. I hold the ultimate responsibility to make sure the store runs properly, which includes setting up to sell our products and providing a safe environment for our customers to allow them to enjoy a pleasing and efficient shopping experience."

Crotec nodded his head as if this was the first time he had heard these lines. "Would you tell us a little about B & D."

"Of course. B & D started in Ohio about fifty years ago. Two families ran a store that sold almost anything. Most people think the name for the company comes from the two founders, Bernie Malkin and Dan Sudsby, but its official name is actually Bargains and Discounts, not Bernie and Dan."

Oliver leaned in towards the jurors. "The store was rather successful, emphasizing product availability and pricing. After a few years they expanded. And there was more expansion until the company had hundreds of stores in the Midwest and Eastern part of the country. As our tagline suggests, we have amazing prices, but I think we also have excellent customer service. Our guests are rather loyal."

"Is shoplifting a problem at the store?"

Oliver's head bobbed in unison with Crotec's. "Absolutely. Every day it's a battle. So many people come into our store with the sole purpose of taking product without paying for it. Some days I feel like we spend all our time chasing down thieves."

"What does the store do to combat theft?"

"Like I said, it's a constant problem, but one we address through our training and our vigilance. We station a uniform police officer at the front of the store who primarily acts as a deterrent so when people see him they think twice about stealing. There isn't an officer there all the time, and he wasn't scheduled when Mr. Hawkins came into the store. We also allow undercover security guards to walk the store looking like they are shoppers, but if they see suspicious activity they will move to stop it."

Crotec nodded. "How often do they catch people stealing?"

"All the time." Oliver threw up his hands. "I've seen some of these detectives catch four people on one shift. There's so much paperwork involved when they catch someone it usually takes ninety minutes to complete the processing."

"Do any of the people working in the store other than the police officer and the security guards have responsibility for combating shoplifting?"

"In some ways we all do. We tell our team members to be vigilant in keeping an eye on their surroundings and if they see anything suspicious, they should notify a manager. The staff is instructed not to stop anyone if they suspect someone is stealing–but they can act if directed by a manager."

"What do managers do with respect to suspected shoplifters?"

Oliver's lips turned up at the edges. "We're trained to watch suspected shoplifters and only stop them if we maintain eye contact from the time they take something, until they pass the point of sale. If they stuff something in their pocket on the sales floor, we have the right to stop them right there, but we don't. We wait until they go past a checkout counter to give them a chance to buy the item. Also, if we are distracted, like if a customer asks us a question, and we lose visual contact, we are instructed not to stop a shoplifter."

"Interesting," Crotec said. "Do you want to stop shoplifters?"

Oliver paused. "What I would want is for people to pay for what they put in their carts. Then none of us would need to worry about any of this. But lots of people steal and I want to protect the store and our customers."

"Mr. Oliver, do you receive sufficient training on how to detain a shoplifter?"

"We do. We attend lots of seminars. Our Loss Prevention Department teaches us and assists us. I'm comfortable that all the managers at the store are more than competent to handle shoplifters." He glanced over at Morgan Askew and nodded.

Crotec shifted back towards his counsel table. "Let me ask you about another issue. Did you review video to find other instances of Jerry Hawkins shoplifting from the store?"

"I did. I presumed he tried to steal on other occasions. In other shoplifting situations I went back and found other instances of theft which was much easier because they used their shopper's cards, so we had a record of when they shopped in the store. Here, Mr. Hawkins didn't use a card. We utilize software that can identify people through facial recognition, and I searched it to find other times Mr. Hawkins was in the store. The hard drive automatically overwrites the video after ninety days. So once I started, I only had that much time to review."

"So what did you find?"

"Mr. Hawkins was very busy. He employed different methods for shoplifting, but we found them. In the three months before his event in the parking lot, he shopped in the store six times that we could uncover. In those occasions he purchased thirty-six dollars of product," Oliver paused for effect. "but, he took over six hundred dollars of our items without ever paying for them."

"You can't be serious," Crotec said with a slight shake of his head.

"Oh, I am. Unfortunately, this is fairly common at any retail establishment."

Crotec nodded with solemnity. "That's all my questions for this witness."

Arnie stood and approached with a scowl etched on his face. He didn't waste any time searching for a question to ask. "Mr. Oliver, your managers weren't trained in how to detain possible shoplifters, were they?"

"I would disagree with that," Oliver said, wrinkles appearing on his brow. He turned away from Arnie and toward the jurors. "Our managers undergo extensive training to help them deal with any possible situation."

Arnie held up his hand. "My question was limited to detention." He held up a binder. "There is nothing in any of your training manuals about how to properly detain someone, is there?"

"That's probably true," Oliver conceded.

Arnie stepped towards the jurors after receiving the concession. "You admit shoplifting occurs all the time."

"Correct."

"You are trained to stop suspected shoplifters."

"True."

"Yet, nothing in your training materials teaches you how to safely detain someone."

"I just told you that."

Arnie smiled. "So when Mr. Askew went to detain Jerry, Mr. Askew had no training in how to do it safely."

"I disagree. We had lots of instruction and I believe Mr. Askew had enough to do it safely."

"There was no training on the potential risks of sitting on top of someone, was there?"

"No, probably not."

Arnie approached the witness while raising the papers he held. "The lot attendant, Byron Hucklesbee, he didn't have any training on how to detain a suspected shoplifter, did he?"

"I imagine not."

"No training on how to approach a suspected shoplifter."

"No."

"So he was not aware of the danger in taking someone down and sitting on him, was he?"

"Probably not."

"Yet, your assistant asked him to do just that?"

"I'm not sure. It seemed like Mr. Askew sought some assistance, but was always in charge."

Arnie shook his head and turned his back on the witness to relocate to the front of defendants' counsel counsel table. "One more area Mr. Oliver. How many hours did you spend reviewing video following Jerry through your store on his visits before the night he was killed?"

Oliver thought for a moment. "Probably about twenty hours."

"That's a lot of time spent for something that isn't even relevant to what Mr. Askew did that night."

"We thought it was relevant that he kept coming to the store and stealing from us."

Arnie held up his hand. "Sir, at the time Mr. Askew stopped Jerry on the night he died, Mr. Askew had no knowledge of what Jerry may or may not have done on other visits to the store, did he?"

"I guess not."

"Therefore, what Mr. Askew did on those other occasions played no role in the decisions he made."

"I suppose you are correct."

"So, Jerry was killed only because of what Mr. Askew saw that afternoon and not on other days."

"I wouldn't put it that way, but I would agree that Mr. Askew made his decision to detain Mr. Hawkins based solely on what he saw Mr. Hawkins do that afternoon."

"The other times aren't relevant to the decisions Mr. Askew made?"

"I guess you're correct."

Having received one last concession, Arnie announced he had no more questions and threw Rick a weary expression of relief.

CHAPTER FIFTY-NINE

DAMMIT, *let's just get this over,* Rick thought as Marlon Copelman wedged into the witness box. He sat at counsel table with the folder marked "defendant's liability expert" opened in front of him. He had a sense of what Copelman was about to say–everything bad that ever happened occurred because Jerry Hawkins took a few things from B & D.

This is not going to be fun.

Rick turned his attention to the chubby man in the plaid sports coat who was spreading his report in front of him.

Despite his stature, the witness displayed no shortcomings in confidence. His gaze never wavered from the jurors, taking pains to make sure he spoke directly to them. He had testified in courtrooms across the country and his comfort in these surroundings was evident.

Fifteen minutes elapsed while he served up his qualifications as Spencer stood by counsel table almost as a bystander, not having to ask many questions. Copelman emphasized his familiarity with shoplifting and state statutes authorizing stores to prevent shoplifting. Despite the limitation of supposedly only talking about his qualifications, Copelman primed the jury to recognize the prevalence of shoplifting and the company's rights under the Merchant's Act to detain suspected shoplifters.

When given the opportunity to question Copelman regarding his qualifications, Rick avoided attacking his credentials head-on, but wanted to lay the groundwork for his later questioning.

"Sir," Rick said, "you have testified on behalf of individuals suing companies twice, correct?"

The witness reviewed his resume. "That appears to be correct."

"Yet, you have testified for stores and other defendants in shoplifting matters forty-seven times."

"That is also correct."

"Thank you, Mr. Copelman. I will want to discuss your opinions in those cases later." Rick sat, releasing the witness for his substantive testimony, while implicitly conceding he was qualified to offer his opinion to this jury, yet reminding them to wait before reaching any conclusions.

The witness breezed through his direct examination, offering a substantive basis for the store's detention of Jerry Hawkins and their right to utilize force, especially in response to Jerry throwing a punch at the cart boy. He pieced together his argument to make killing Jerry Hawkins almost seem like something which should happen with more frequency.

He summarized at the end: "Under the law, any retailer has the right to detain a suspected shoplifter. The shoplifter has no right to resist and no right to engage in a physical altercation. If he does and that altercation escalates, it is the shoplifter who bears responsibility, not the shop owner, which is acting completely within its rights and authority. Mr. Hawkins was an aggressor and chose to fight his way out when the store personnel confronted him. The company was within its rights. Mr. Hawkins clearly was not."

Spencer wanted to tie the bow on this testimony. "In your opinion, did the store act reasonably under the circumstances?"

Copelman held his gaze with one juror before responding. "Absolutely. The law is there to protect the store and their honest customers from the dangers of shoplifting. Not only can the store lose money through theft, but innocent bystanders can be hurt. Here, B & D employees protected not only the assets of the store, but also its customers. By detaining Mr. Hawkins and preventing him from running dangerously through the parking lot, they protected unsuspecting customers from danger. I applaud their courageous actions."

The testimony took little more than thirty minutes and allowed Copelman to emphasize that Jerry's theft put everyone else's actions in motion and had he been a law-abiding shopper, nothing bad would have happened to him.

Rick didn't have any interest in further discussing shoplifting. He stood in front of the witness, intending to emphasize the killing.

"Mr. Copelman, Jerry Hawkins died because four people sat on him with one having a knee in his back. They suffocated him."

Copelman looked uneasy and turned to the jury. "Without rehashing the chain of events, it started with Mr. Hawkins stealing. Yes, he ultimately died and yes, four people laid on top of him, but you're forgetting to include the fact he continued to struggle and fight to get loose."

"Will you agree that it's improper for four people to detain a person by sitting on him and holding him so he can't move?"

"What I will say is there are probably better ways to accomplish this objective, but when a suspect struggles, you have to do whatever works under the circumstances."

A grimace formed on Rick's face. "The reason why it's improper to sit on a person who is struggling, is because of exactly what happened here. Someone could die."

"I suppose that's true."

"None of the employees from B & D received any training on the proper method of how to detain a suspected shoplifter, did they?"

"I did not see any evidence of that specific training."

"Like you said, sometimes people when accused of stealing will not comply–they may act out."

"That's true."

"So, you agree shoplifting is foreseeable, correct?"

"Yes, all retailers must deal with it."

"It's also foreseeable that people accused of shoplifting may act out?"

"Yes."

"Based on what you said, more physical means of detention will prove necessary."

"Yes, that's true."

"If a store does not properly train its employees on how to detain someone when they act out, they will end up in a situation like what happened to Mr. Hawkins."

"Perhaps."

Rick moved forward towards the witness. "Come on, Mr. Copelman. Shoplifting is foreseeable. People don't like to be accused of stealing, so acting out is foreseeable. If a store decides to detain someone who is acting out, it will have to act physically by perhaps sitting on them."

"Yes, I agree to that."

More of the whites of Rick's eyes appeared. "So if this is all foreseeable, doesn't a store have an obligation to train its employees on how to deal with a suspected shoplifter who may act out?"

Copelman shook his head. "I'm not sure I agree. . ."

Rick interrupted. "Because if they don't train him properly that person could die."

"I don't agree. I don't believe Mr. Hawkins dying was foreseeable by anybody. The store had a reasonable policy of training, consistent with every other similar company."

"That's the best you got, Mr. Copelman?" Rick scoffed. "They didn't know they would kill Mr. Hawkins. You can do better, can't you?"

Spencer shot up. "Objection. Move to strike."

The judge held up a hand preventing any argument. "The objection is sustained. Mr. Waterston's last question is stricken. Any further questions?"

"I do." He turned back to the witness. "Mr. Copelman, the forty-seven times you testified on behalf of a corporation in a wrongful detention case, you opined that their policies are reasonable, correct?"

"I believe you are correct. That's because the policies are fairly similar and consistent with the law."

Rick continued. "The two times you were hired by a person suing a company, you offered the contrary opinion–that the company acted improperly."

"I can't say I remember my testimony from every case. It was a long time ago."

Arnie handed Rick a stack of deposition transcripts. Rick grabbed them. "I got them all here. For example, in *Myers v. Trader Vick's*, you testified on page forty-two, 'The Company's training was clearly lacking and this led to the manager improperly detaining the plaintiff.' You said that, didn't you?"

"If it's there, I said it."

"C'mon sir, I'll go through each one, but didn't you offer testimony in every case on the side of the plaintiff that the company's policies were insufficient?"

Copelman bit his lip. "I suppose that's true."

Rick smiled. "So, each time you testify, your opinion is favorable to the side that is paying you?"

"I call them as I see it, counselor. Those were well-reasoned opinions."

Rick stared at Copelman. "Well-compensated opinions, you meant to say." Before Spencer could object, he said, "I have no further questions for this witness."

Spencer conferred briefly with Crotec and then stood. "Mr. Copelman, explain why B & D's policy is reasonable in your professional opinion."

Copelman nodded and turned to the jurors. "B & D, like every other major retailer, understands that some people will come onto their property not with the intent to shop, but with the intent to steal. Like every other retailer, B & D maintains the right to detain suspected shoplifters. What this means is, it's reasonable and expected the company will deploy eimployees to make sure that when people on their property select merchandise, they actually pay for it. If they don't, B & D can detain them for prosecution by calling the police.

"It's exactly what happened here. Mr. Askew reasonably attempted to detain Mr. Hawkins, but the situation escalated, through no fault of Mr. Askew. Mr. Hawkins, as the bad actor, bears the responsibility for the consequences he set in motion by stealing and fighting."

Spencer glanced at Crotec who nodded his head. "Thank you, Mr. Copelman."

Rick stood to make sure the judge allowed him one more opportunity with this witness.

"Mr. Copelman, the assistant manager instructed the cart person, Mr. Hucklesbee, to stop Mr. Hawkins in the parking lot."

"Yes."

"He tried to grab Mr. Hawkins, didn't he?"

"All in the course of trying to detain Mr. Hawkins."

"Which is the point, isn't it? Nobody trained Mr. Hucklesbee on how to detain, so he escalated the situation and initiated the first physical contact with Mr. Hawkins. If he didn't do that, Mr. Hawkins would still be alive."

"I don't agree with your analysis. Again, Mr. Hawkins started this whole chain of events by stealing and could have stopped the chain by submitting to the store's proper authority to detain. By failing to do so, Mr. Hawkins created the situation that led to his demise."

Rick blew out a breath, wondering if he should try harder to convince this witness of the flaws with his reasoning. With a grim understanding he wouldn't be able to shake the witness's testimony, he announced, "Nothing further."

As Rick took his seat, Arnie passed him a note. *"You made your point. The jury knows this guy is a hired gun."*

CHAPTER SIXTY

His ARM stiff and his hand pointed up to the ceiling, Michael McGarrity made taking the oath appear as solemn as giving last rites. Dressed in a black suit, crisp white shirt and a small red bow tie, he seated himself in the witness stand with his hands clasped together, ready to offer his story.

"My name is Michael McGarrity, but my friends call me Mick," he said as his six-foot-four frame consumed the witness box. His easy smile pulled in the jurors. Making people feel at ease was part of his nature and an asset in putting seats in the pews of his church every Sunday. He explained his role as pastor and the role the Lord had played in his life before Crotec had a chance to ask.

"Were you in the parking lot the afternoon Jerry Hawkins died?" Crotec asked.

"Yes. I was about to enter the store, when I heard a voice call out, 'Stop him. He's a thief.' I could immediately discern a few things: First, the man running through the lot had stolen something. Second, he appeared ready to cause more trouble, and third, the voice I heard came not just from the person yelling, but from the Lord telling me to intercede and help prevent further trouble."

Crotec's lips curled up at their edges. "What happened after that?"

The pastor sat up straighter, and gazed out towards the jurors, but over their heads, with a glossy sheen to his eyes.

"I turned to where I heard the voice and I saw a man running like something bad was chasing him. I saw the manager coming from a slightly different direction about to intersect with him when the man just turned and punched the manager, sending him flying. That's when I knew there was danger and I had to stop him and protect the people in the parking lot."

"So what did you do?"

His eyes widened even more. "I felt the Lord's strength run through me and I knew my obligation was to help." He threw his hands in the air. "I don't recall exactly what happened, but this man would not hurt anyone else. We stopped him and made sure he didn't move until the authorities arrived."

Crotec didn't really want any more information, but one more question might emphasize the mood he was trying to establish. "Anything else occurred while you waited for the police?"

McGarrity nodded four times before answering. "Yes. The man continued to struggle. I spoke to him in a calm voice asking him to relax, but he wouldn't. I felt the devil consuming his soul, so we all held on to make sure he did not prevail." He lowered his gaze to latch on to the eyes of the last juror. "And he did not prevail."

Crotec took a seat to signal he had no further questions.

With little idea how the jury was perceiving this witness, Arnie stood and stared at his notes. "Sir, did you ever watch the video of what happened in the parking lot?"

"I didn't. I remember what happened."

The video appeared again on the screen in the front of the courtroom starting at the point where Jerry left the store. Again, he runs towards the area where Byron Hucklesbee is shagging carts. Jerry runs directly at Hucklesbee who tries to get his arms around Jerry, but Jerry shoves him aside. Morgan Askew jumps on Jerry, followed by Deandra Bortz and then McGarrity.

"That doesn't quite jibe with your testimony, does it?" Arnie asked without too much of an accusatory tone.

McGarrity leaned back, rubbing his chin. "No, I believe it's completely in line with what I said." He turned and pointed to the screen. "We took him down and made sure he stayed down until the police arrived."

Arnie scoffed inwardly. "So we're clear, you agree now that the lot attendant made the first physical contact."

"That's not quite how I remember it, but I see it on the video."

"You agree your memory is not quite accurate. Do you also agree God did not call to you to get involved?"

"I believe God is behind everything we do."

"I'm sure you do. But you didn't answer my question. God didn't specifically call to you, did he?"

"Probably not."

"The manager Morgan Askew, not God, called to you and demanded you get involved."

"Yes."

"Mr. Askew was the person in charge and he directed everyone to hold down Mr. Hawkins before he died, correct?"

"Yes."

"Mr. Askew instructed that you should continue to hold down the victim until the police arrived."

"He never specifically said that."

"How about, he never told you to release your hold on Mr. Hawkins?"

"True."

"Even after Mr. Hawkins stopped moving and lay motionless with his face down towards the pavement?"

"I always felt like the man was a danger and could hurt people in the parking lot. I never believed the risk was gone until the police arrived."

"Do you agree that Mr. Askew never checked to make sure Mr. Hawkins was breathing or was in any way responsive?"

"I guess that's true. Like I said, we were more concerned with whether he would break loose and hurt someone."

"Even though he couldn't breathe?" Arnie said as he turned his back on the witness and headed towards his seat, waiting for the inevitable objection and knowing it would be sustained.

He said, "Nothing further," while seated at counsel table."

Spencer rose and turned his body partly towards the jurors. "Defendants have no more witnesses and rest their case."

Markum turned to the jury box. "You've heard all the evidence. Tomorrow morning you will hear the closing arguments, first for the defendants and then for the plaintiff. After which, I will tell you what the law is governing this case. At that point, you will retire for your deliberations."

He instructed his tipstaff to lead them out.

The jurors kept their eyes posted straight ahead and didn't glance a moment in the direction of the participants.

Still have no idea what you're thinking, Rick thought as the last member disappeared from the courtroom.

CHAPTER SIXTY-ONE

AT THE END of a trial day, after dueling with witnesses and stressing over how a jury is perceiving their case, no attorney likes to spend additional time in the presence of adversaries or the judge, and would rather return to the office to prepare for the next day's events. Most judges don't care about the desires of the attorneys and have the authority to make them respond to the court's requests no matter how backlogged a lawyer's schedule might be.

So, when Judge Markum told the lawyers he wanted to finalize the jury instructions and discuss any other necessary matters prior to jury deliberations, they nodded their heads, picked up their yellow pads and headed directly to his chambers.

In the courtroom, they are expected to joust with witnesses while advocating for their client. In chambers, the client still comes first, but the tone softens into a more civilized banter. The four attorneys sat on both sides of Markum's desk holding copies of the points for charge they each submitted to the court on the first day of trial.

Culled from standard jury instructions or pulled from written appellate opinions, each side wanted the judge to select their version of the law. The judge would readily include points in his jury charge which both sides requested. Others were nearly similar so that Markum would make minor alterations to the language creating a more balanced statement of the law, in between the language argued for by the two parties. Sometimes, the points differed drastically forcing the judge to pick one side's version, or to draft compromising language for what he said to the jury.

"Gentlemen," he began, "this was a difficult trial because emotions run high on both sides. I want to commend counsel on advocating strongly for your respective clients, while maintaining civility. You have both raised interesting arguments, and truth be told, I have no idea which way this jury might be leaning." He smiled, "I wouldn't tell you if I thought I knew. Are there any matters to discuss before we deal with my charge?"

Spencer leaned forward and said, "There is, Your Honor."

Markum nodded. "Proceed, counselor."

"Plaintiff has included in her claims against the defendants a claim for punitive damages. Plaintiff has failed to present sufficient evidence to proceed with this element of damages and defendants move for judgment on this portion of her claim."

He paused for a moment before continuing.

"Punitive damages are designed to punish a wrongdoer for evil intent or for the conscious disregard of the rights of others. Plaintiff has presented nothing along those lines during this trial. Taking the evidence in the light most favorable to her, plaintiff has only presented evidence the company may have failed to train its employees properly. Nothing more. The company has shown it knew of the prevalence of shoplifting, was aware of its rights under the statute to stop suspected

278

shoplifters and detain them until the police arrive. They allowed only managers to stop shoplifters. What happened here may have been tragic, but was not the result of a conscious disregard of any known and understood risk."

Markum looked to Emily's attorneys. Arnie cleared his throat to signal he would speak.

"Defendants acknowledged shoplifting occurred all of the time. They accepted their responsibility to detain shoplifters safely and admitted they knew someone accused of shoplifting could act out. In spite of this knowledge, they never trained their employees how to detain an accused shoplifter who didn't agree to be detained. They never trained their people not to get physical with people who try to flee. What happened to Jerry Hawkins was not only tragic, but abundantly foreseeable. He died as a direct result of their failure to properly train and they should be punished to make sure it doesn't happen again."

"I don't agree, Mr. McBride," Markum said. "If this were to happen again, without a change in their training, then there would be a strong argument of a conscious disregard of a known risk. But here, this was atypical and I don't believe the defendants are liable for anything other than, possibly, ordinary negligence."

Arnie scoffed. "C'mon judge. The guy died a horrible death while they sat on him."

"I understand your point, but his manner of death doesn't affect my analysis of whether you can claim punitive damages. Considering the arguments of both sides, I am granting defendants' motion to enter judgment on plaintiff's punitive damage claim. You can argue to the jury for compensatory damages based on negligence. You will not argue they should be punished."

Arnie slunk back in his chair.

Markum signaled to the court reporter to stop typing. "Off

the record. If the jury awards damages, I don't believe it will make any difference whether they also get to decide punitive damages. If you pissed them off enough, they will include them in their award, whether they're supposed to or not. Let's go back on the record and discuss the jury charge."

Markum held up both sets of submitted points of law and stated, "I have taken from both sides to include in my charge. Most of what you submitted isn't in dispute and is included. I think the primary issues are first, the standard stores must utilize in detaining shoplifters and, second, what damages the plaintiff can claim."

He handed out a bound set of papers. "This is my charge. Your objections are preserved, so you don't need to make them here. Look at page thirteen. That's where I discuss the standard of when a store can detain a shoplifter. I will tell the jury, 'A store has the right to detain a person suspected of shoplifting if the store reasonably believes the person attempted to take an item from the store without paying for it. The store can detain the suspected shoplifter to provide an opportunity for the police to arrive so long as the detention is done in a reasonable manner under the circumstances and for a reasonable period.'"

Markum peeked up from his papers, but wasn't looking for a discussion. "With respect to the damages the plaintiff can claim, I accepted the plaintiff's itemization of what potential damages are allowed. Plaintiff can, under her theories of the case, claim conscious pain and suffering, medical expenses, the decedent's past and prospective lost earnings, and Mrs. Hawkins' loss of the services and companionship of her husband. Of course, as I will tell the jury, they are only entitled to recover any damages if they prove the defendants are liable for the death of her husband."

The judge smiled. "As you know, the court remains neutral. Good luck with your closings."

Once outside, Rick whispered to Arnie. "We got some, but didn't get everything. In all honesty, I don't think the charge is a game changer with this jury."

Arnie nodded. "Agreed. Same question they faced at the beginning. Should someone die for stealing a loaf of bread?" He put an arm over Rick's shoulders. "I really hope these jurors cried during *Les Mis*."

CHAPTER SIXTY-TWO

THE MORNING HELD many hopes for Rick. He wanted to give a closing worthy of Emily's trust in him. He wanted them to come back from their deliberations and announce a substantial verdict in her favor. As he sat waiting for defendants' closing, he thought of many wishes, short term and longer.

Rick's wish that Crotec crap his pants while walking up to the jury went unfulfilled. *Hopefully, his teeth will fall out,* he thought. When that didn't happen either, Rick turned his attention to the clean sheet of paper on the top of his pad. During defendants' closing he would keep his head down and not let the jurors see any facial expressions. He would not write much substantive–he would be listening intently–but would utilize what he wrote more to calm his nerves, than to help him with his closing. His acerbic scribbles such as, "you're an ass," and "your hair looks like a Brillo pad," were not for public consumption.

The jurors stared at Crotec appearing eager to listen to counsel's reasoning why B & D's conduct was appropriate and how he would justify the death of Jerry Hawkins.

"Let's start where there is no disagreement," Crotec said with his arms spread and his yellow pad off to the side. He placed one hand in a fist mimicking the gesture they used in the opening. He held up one finger. "First there is no dispute that theft is a huge problem." He held up another finger. "There is no dispute, like all retailers, B & D has the authority to stop people who they suspect of shoplifting." He continued to lift fingers. "And, there is no dispute Jerry Hawkins stole that afternoon."

Crotec paused to turn and stare at Rick. "They tried to suggest Mr. Hawkins didn't steal and what we all found out was, not only did he steal, but he systematically came to the store and each time he walked the aisles, he stole. Even Mrs. Hawkins agreed he was a thief."

Crotec raised his fifth finger. "Finally, everyone agrees, if Jerry Hawkins stopped at any point he would still be alive. Whether it was before he stole, or when Morgan Askew approached him near the checkouts, or in the parking lot, if he stopped, he would be alive. He let the stop sign face the jury without uttering more.

Crotec paused as the video flickered to life on the screen. "Let's go through what happened at the store."

He pulled out a red laser pointer and directed it at the images.

"Jerry Hawkins stood in line and purposely didn't pay for the higher ticket items in his cart. Morgan Askew, consistent with his training and experience, detected what Hawkins did. At this point, Askew, entirely consistent with the rights granted to him under the law, moved in to detain Hawkins for shoplifting. There is no dispute Morgan Askew's actions were completely legit."

The jurors jotted notes on their pads, but for the most part, listened attentively to counsel's argument.

"What changed?" Crotec asked rhetorically. "Unlike each of the other times he came into the store to steal, this time Jerry Hawkins got caught. So instead of submitting to Askew's authority, Hawkins becomes a fugitive."

The video synced with Crotec's timeline showing Jerry smacking away Askew's hand and fleeing toward the front door. "Hawkins first escalates the situation by hitting Mr. Askew and then running away.

"Next, Hawkins gets to the parking lot, but is concerned about possible capture. Byron Hucklesbee is in the parking lot doing his job. After Askew yells to Hucklesbee to stop the shoplifter, Hucklesbee moves in front of Hawkins and Hawkins sucker punches him in the face. Yes, that's exactly what happened, Mr. Hawkins, the fleeing shoplifter, trying to avoid capture, punches an innocent young man in the face."

The video jumped to the depiction of the two store employees and two customers getting control of Jerry and sitting on top of him in the parking lot.

Crotec points at Rick. "They keep asking, 'why did this happen?' The video tells you exactly why. Jerry Hawkins couldn't accept that he got caught—so he smacked Mr. Askew and punched Mr. Hucklesbee in the face. Who knows what he would have done next if those four brave individuals didn't stop him. Who would have been hurt next? This all happened because Jerry Hawkins wouldn't stop until those four people stopped him.

"Obviously, Jerry Hawkins had no right to steal and no right to punch anyone. What Morgan Askew did, however, is completely acceptable under the law. He had the right to detain Jerry Hawkins for shoplifting and the obligation to protect the store's customers from the increasing violence of Jerry Hawkins in the parking lot."

"We completely agree with Mrs. Hawkins that no one should die for stealing–and Jerry Hawkins wouldn't have died if he just stopped. If he stopped before he fled the store and threw the first punch, he wouldn't have died. He would likely have been arrested for shoplifting and maybe the store would have found out how much he actually stole, but no, he wouldn't have died. The reason he died is that he escalated the situation and continued to escalate until it took four people to control him.

"Just like the expert witness, Mr. Copelman, said, 'The entire situation escalated solely because of what Mr. Hawkins decided to do.' The store only responded to Mr. Hawkins' decision to escalate.

"When you put it all together, the store and its employees acted with the authority of law–trying to detain a shoplifter. Mr. Hawkins had no legal backing for what he did. He stole and then tried to fight his way out, harming store employees and potentially harming customers of the store.

"The store employees acted completely reasonably and completely within their rights. Because of this, plaintiff has not proven her claim. It's tragic her husband died, but the store does not bear responsibility for his death. On behalf of my clients B & D Stores and Morgan Askew, I implore you to follow the evidence and return a verdict in favor of the defendants.

Crotec turned and grabbed a plastic glass of water to signal he was moving on to a new portion of his argument.

"Let me address one more point," he said after turning back to the jurors. "Damages. I laid out the reasons why I believe you should find no liability here, but you may see things differently than me. If you do, you will need to address what compensation she should receive. The court will instruct you that you should not be guided by sympathy or prejudice, but rather must award damages based on the evidence provided."

A list of potential damages then appeared on the screen. While acknowledging the inherent difficulty of losing a spouse, Crotec pointed out how there was little evidence of some of the itemized types of damages. For example, given how little Jerry said while on the ground, he believed plaintiff failed to present evidence of conscious pain and suffering. Other than the bills for the ambulance and emergency room, there was no other medical expenses incurred.

He then turned to Emily's claims that she lost significant money for jobs Jerry would hold in the future.

"Mr. Hawkins didn't work a real job for years. He received little training to get any job, let alone a high paying one in the future. Yet Mrs. Hawkins claims Jerry was well on his way to making lots of money, so you should pay her all the money Jerry might ever earn in the future. Unfortunately, the evidence is Jerry didn't have a lot of motivation and couldn't hold a job for any significant period. Her suggestion he was on the verge of high paying employment reeks of an attempt to garner sympathy from you when the evidence would lead you to award only a nominal amount for whatever work he might fall into in the future. It's your decision, but the evidence doesn't support what she is trying to sell to you.

"Ladies and gentlemen, Emily Hawkins suffered a significant loss and nothing I say to you can change that. The issue before you is, who bears responsibility for his death? I say that when you steal, you must be ready to suffer the consequences. When you get caught and try to fight your way out, you must accept the consequences. Here they were significant and cost Mr. Hawkins his life. He created the chain of events, and he exacerbated the situation every step along the way. As a result, his death is his responsibility. Review the evidence without undue sympathy. If you do, you will return a verdict in favor of the defendants."

With his closing complete, Crotec nodded and returned to his seat. Rick placed the folder with the materials for his closing in his hand, ready to argue to the jury why everything Crotec just said was garbage.

CHAPTER SIXTY-THREE

Standing before the jury, despite wearing a newly dry-cleaned suit and pressed shirt, Rick felt naked. The jurors stared at him, but he only sensed Emily's eyes boring in on him. She sat behind Arnie, yet he felt her need for vindication to prove her husband's death was not in vain. Her testimony was her only real input at trial. She relied on Rick and Arnie to argue her case and to convince the jury Jerry didn't deserve his tragic fate. Rick still believed in her, but the nagging doubts about the strength of her case which interrupted his sleep every night during trial, returned right as he was about to make her last appeal.

He gave his head an almost imperceptible shake to rid it of any negative thoughts and focused on the young woman juror in the back row who, demographically at least, aligned most closely with Emily.

"Here's what is not in dispute: Jerry Hawkins is dead, and the only reason he's dead is because B & D failed to train its employees how to detain a suspected shoplifter, even though they knew that a situation like this, where they tried to stop a scared and threatened individual, could and would escalate into a brawl. They knew if they gave untrained employees the responsibility to act like police officers, they needed to be trained on how to deal with any type of foreseeable situation to make sure they didn't kill anyone.

"Despite this knowledge, they never trained their employees, they ignored the risk, and they killed Jerry.

"Want to know something else that's not in dispute?" Rick asked before offering his answer. "This was all predictable. Every one of their witnesses came in here and told you about how bad shoplifting is. They made it seem like half the people in their stores came there to steal. The experts told you when people are stopped for shoplifting, the risk of them trying to escape is high. So it is completely expected that if someone steals, and their employees attempt to detain them without adequate training, someone will get hurt."

Rick moved a few steps to the other side of the jury box.

"Let's stop right there, because there is no reason to accept that the store employees needed to detain Jerry. They possessed enough information they could have gotten the police involved without physically detaining him. How? There was video of him–which is a decent start to identifying him. Moreover, Mr. Askew was in position to take down his vehicle information while in the parking lot. The video also captured his car and would have likely included his license. If Askew took down his information and went to the police, they could have dealt with it–because that's what they are trained to do–and Jerry would still be alive today.

"So rather than letting the police be the ones who deal with shoplifters, the company decides it wants its managers to be right in the middle of the action and make split-second decisions on capturing those they suspect of shoplifting. But even knowing those situations will often lead to violence, they provided no training on how to properly detain a suspected shoplifter, if the person resists being detained.

"The only policy they shared even tangentially related to this likely situation is the pet expression of their Loss Prevention Director, 'When they are out the door, chase no more.' Unfortunately, this policy was barely transmitted to any of the managers and if it was, they sure had no idea what it meant. Morgan Askew wasn't aware he shouldn't chase shoplifters in the parking lot. Bottom line, when Jerry Hawkins left the store, by both practicality and by policy, Morgan Askew should've dropped his pursuit and called the police to go find him.

"Instead, Mr. Askew let his emotions dictate his conduct. Whatever his training was, it didn't kick in and had no effect on his actions while chasing Jerry. He was uncontrolled running after Jerry, calling for help from a lot attendant and then demanding help from customers in the parking lot to pin Jerry to the ground." Rick scoffed and threw his hand forward. "What could go wrong under those circumstances?"

He locked eyes with a juror. "What could go wrong is exactly what went wrong. An accused shoplifter didn't want to stop when Morgan Askew demanded him to stop. Not much of a surprise. He's not a police officer and doesn't wear a uniform which would suggest he has any authority. So Jerry didn't want to stop when Askew demanded and then left the store. Had Askew followed the mandate of, 'If he's out the door, chase no more,' once again Jerry would still be alive–arrested by the police, probably an hour later.

"Morgan Askew wanted to be in charge, so didn't do anything to get the police involved."

Rick glared at Askew in the second row of seating. Askew turned his head away.

"No, he followed him into the parking lot, into the area with lots of traffic, customers and potential danger. Yet, Askew couldn't catch up to him. If he realized the danger to everyone he would have stopped and Jerry would still be alive.

"Instead, he yelled to Byron Hucklesbee, to do the work of the police and to stop him. Byron received no training in stopping shoplifters, even less than the minimal training Askew received. Hucklesbee, a physically intimidating young man, stepped in Jerry's path. The least surprising thing that happens is Jerry gets scared and hits Hucklesbee.

"You've seen the video enough. You know what happens. Askew gets mad and tackles Jerry, who is now cornered prey, fighting for his life. Ultimately, four people pin him to the ground.

"This is where B & D's lack of training becomes even more significant. Nobody at the store ever received training on how to detain a non-compliant person. They also didn't train anyone as to what the typical physiological response someone might undergo if they are strangled. That almost sounds funny, but if it's expected someone accused of shoplifting might not willingly accept the authority of a twenty-something assistant store manager and it is likely the physicality of the situation will escalate, then it is likely someone like Jerry will end up struggling on the ground and store personnel will resort to sitting on him to prevent him from moving."

Rick stopped to take a sip of water and then turned back to the jurors.

"Anything is foreseeable in these situations and that is why B & D needed to train it employees, because by allowing them to engage with shoplifters and failing to train them properly, people could get hurt. There is one, final way how the company could have prevented Jerry from dying. You heard Dr. Creft tell you about how a person reacts when they are being strangled. They struggle for air and their body convulses. This is typical.

"Unfortunately, Mr. Askew and three other people climbed on top of Jerry denying him air. He couldn't breathe, so he struggled mightily to get oxygen into his lungs. Morgan Askew mistook his efforts to satisfy this basic human need for an attempt to escape and hurt them. If Askew at any point received training that a person being strangled would convulse and it would feel like they are trying to escape, he might've told his posse to get off of him, instead of clamping down even harder–denying him the breath he so desperately needed.

"Had B & D trained its employees properly or had B & D allowed the police to do its job, Jerry would be alive, and we wouldn't be here. But they didn't. They decided they were the best people to enforce the law, and they didn't need anyone's help. Jerry's death proves how wrong they were and proves their culpability for his death. So when you get a chance to discuss what happened to Jerry, I am confident you will find B & D is at fault and Emily Hawkins is entitled to compensation as a result.

"So what's the appropriate compensation for Emily?"

Rick stopped, wanting the jury to take a moment to catch its breath and to ponder numbers large enough to adequately make up for the losses she suffered.

"Let's go through some areas of damages Emily would be entitled to receive if you find B & D wrongfully caused Jerry death.

Rick took a few minutes to discuss Jerry's conscious pain and suffering and how revolting and difficult it would be to struggle for breath while nearly a thousand pounds clamps down making it impossible to do what we all do naturally thousands of times each day. He went through the bills Emily incurred as a result of Jerry's death and then spoke of Emily's loss of companionship by having her husband taken away from her.

"They were a young couple who spent most of every day together discussing the dreams of having babies, and growing old. They relied on each other, providing comfort, support and care whenever needed. Now, Emily is alone, without the one person who could help her overcome this horrific loss, every morning waking up alone, with no one to talk to, figuring out a way just to make it to the end of the day."

Rick painted a picture of a young, vibrant couple looking eagerly to the future and able to lean into each other in difficult times. He informed them under Pennsylvania law he couldn't suggest a dollar number that would compensate her for this loss, but told them to put their heads together and use their collective judgment to figure out what amount of money would be appropriate to compensate Emily for this tragic loss.

"I know trying to put a dollar figure on a person's life is crass. Emily would have little interest in asking you to determine the value of Jerry's life, if only you could bring Jerry back."

He paused. "You can't—and you can't order B & D to go back in time and do better so Jerry won't die. He's dead. The only thing Emily can ask you to do is to award money and it's your responsibility to work together and do that."

Rick turned the jury's attention to Emily's last element of damages, Jerry's lost earnings, and explained how Emily was entitled to any earnings Jerry would have earned in the future and how it was their job to determine what those earnings would be.

"No, he hadn't worked much right before he died, but you heard Emily. They had plans to start a family and the plan included Jerry getting a solid job and supporting the family at least while the kids were young. She told you what type of jobs he wanted. It might take a little time, but the types of jobs he sought would pay him over one hundred thousand dollars per year once he got his feet on the ground. He would work at least thirty years.

"Once you do the math, you'll find Jerry and Emily lost a lot of future earnings because of what the store did."

He walked them through the calculations and the figure two and a half million dollars appeared on the screen.

"This is a reasonable estimate of what Jerry could've earned over his career and is fair compensation to Emily for Jerry's wage loss."

The jurors were fidgeting.

"You've been in your seats for a while. But obviously this is important. This is Emily's only time to be compensated for her losses. When this trial is over, you go back to your lives. She goes back to being alone. This is the only chance she will ever have to let people evaluate the conduct of the people at B & D. You heard the evidence and the sad truth is those people. . . ."

Rick turned and pointed to the B & D employees seated to his right.

". . . killed Jerry. They sat on him without remorse, smothering his life because no one taught them better."

He turned to his client.

"Emily sits in this courtroom alone and you are the only ones who can right this wrong. We thank you for your time and attention."

The courtroom stayed silent as Rick walked back to his seat.

CHAPTER SIXTY-FOUR

MARKUM ENJOYED HAVING every eyeball on him. He was the judge, and he sat higher than everyone else for a reason. The back and forth of litigation held his interest, but the winner of this, or any other, trial was not terribly important to him. More so, he fastidiously wanted to avoid any potential error which could give the appellate court a reason to reverse the jury's determination and force a new trial. He had no interest in hearing the same arguments, ruling on the same objections, or listening to the same witnesses again.

The jury charge was the most likely target on appeal. Juries needed to hear a proper recitation of the law. Subtle nuances in language could offer a toehold for an appeal, and he remained hell-bent to make sure neither side could leverage his instructions on appeal if they received an adverse verdict.

In this case, both sides agreed on the statute that governed the conduct of B & D's employees when they sought to stop a shoplifter. The Pennsylvania Retail Theft Act had been in existence for decades and provided shop owners with undeniable rights to detain suspected shoplifters. The gray area in the law was that the detention must be "for a reasonable time and in a reasonable manner."

He would provide the jury with certain guidelines of what "reasonable" meant under the law, but they were essentially platitudes. This jury would make its own determination of whether they condoned B & D's conduct.

The charge took a little more than twenty minutes for Markum to read to the jurors.

He prided himself on his ability to modify arcane standard jury instructions by substituting normal English for the more stilted legalese to provide the jury a concise, understandable statement of the rights and responsibilities of the parties. The jurors appeared to listen, but Markum knew they would bring their own interpretations of his instructions into their deliberations.

He told them if they needed to rehear any of his instructions again while they deliberated, he would bring them back and reread the relevant portion of the charge. If past was prologue, this would be the only time they heard his instructions.

Markum believed the jury charge ordinarily didn't affect the jurors' thinking much. In this case, he was convinced they would bring their own sense of right and wrong into their discussions, especially because in their determination of whether the store was culpable, their primary decision was whether the detention was reasonable.

There would likely be disagreement, and as he always did, he told the jurors, "Listen to the other jurors and hear their arguments. Consider them, but you do not need to accept them. This is a civil trial seeking monetary damages. Unlike a criminal case where a jury's verdict must be unanimous, here, once ten out of twelve of you agree on any issue, you have reached your verdict on that issue. You will mark it on the verdict slip."

The judge turned to the questions the jury needed to answer to complete its deliberations.

"The first question you will answer is: 'Were the defendants negligent in causing the death of Jerry Hawkins?'

"If you answer no, you will enter a verdict in favor of the defendants on the verdict slip. If you answer yes, you will next determine whether Jerry Hawkins' negligence also was a factor in his death."

Markum explained to the jurors the concept of comparative fault and how they would have to assess the relative culpability between the defendants and Jerry Hawkins.

"If you get to that point, you will answer the third question, 'What monetary damages do you award to plaintiff, Emily Hawkins?' There is only one line for the damages. If you award damages, you will add all the damages you award to plaintiff in a lump sum and enter it on the verdict slip."

Markum shuffled his papers and returned his attention to the jurors. "Your deliberations are a matter of significant importance to the parties. Please respect their interests and respect the feelings and thoughts of your fellow jurors. Once you reach a verdict, please inform my tipstaff. We will bring the parties back into the courtroom to read your verdict."

The only sound in the courtroom was the soft footsteps of the tipstaff as she moved to the edge of the jury box and signaled for the members to follow her. In single file, without uttering a word, they walked out the back door of the courtroom.

Once the jurors cleared the room, the lawyers stood and faced each other. Rick took a step towards Crotec and extended his hand. "Seb, you tried a strong case."

Crotec held Rick's gaze. "You both did an excellent job."

Spencer and Arnie clasped hands and offered token expressions of luck.

Arnie and Rick returned to their table to gather their papers.

"Damn, they tried a solid case," Arnie said, "but I still think they're assholes."

Rick nodded.

Emily Hawkins sat quietly in the seat behind them and a slight smile crossed her face when Rick approached. "What do you think?" she asked.

"I truly don't know. The jury understands what happened. It's all a matter of assessing blame."

Emily's head moved up and down. "I hope they understand what my situation is going to be like."

"I think you painted a compelling picture of what your life without Jerry will be. First, they will decide if the employees were justified in what they did. Hopefully, we'll wait a while until they tell us what they're thinking."

Emily followed Rick and Arnie out of the courtroom to head to the office. Rick offered a quick prayer it would be a long while before they heard anything.

CHAPTER SIXTY-FIVE

THE EMPTINESS of the office jolted Rick when he opened the door, however, upon quick reflection, it was no surprise. The jury had begun its deliberations just after noon, and they arrived at the office almost thirty minutes later. He had told Audrey she could take the afternoon off knowing he wouldn't want anyone bothering him while he waited for the verdict.

His goal was to sit in his office, return emails, and review the letters which had piled up since the trial started. He needed something to distract him as the minutes ticked by on the clock, so he wouldn't perseverate on what was happening in the jury room.

Emily waited in the small conference room with three magazines and a bottle of water, but Rick knew she would start to bounce off of the walls within a few minutes, the pressure of the unknown playing with her mind.

Right on schedule, less than ten minutes later, Emily appeared at the door to his office with the "I can't sleep" look of a five-year-old.

He waved her in, and she plopped into the chair in front of

his desk causing Rick to smile. "It's not easy," he said. "The jurors never said a word to you the whole trial and now they are locked in a secret meeting talking about you."

"Judging me," she interjected.

Rick nodded. "Call it what you want. They're making decisions now which will impact the rest of your life and there's nothing you can do to influence them."

Emily's eyes turned down. "I hope I did enough during trial."

He reached across the desk and grabbed her arm. "You did great. Whatever the jury decides, don't doubt yourself. You were everything a witness should be."

She leaned back and ran a hand through her hair causing the sleeve on her cream blouse to fall below her wrist. Dark colored lettering, part of a tattoo, peeked out.

Noticing the design, Rick asked, "What's that?"

Emily blushed and pulled the sleeve back down to her wrist. "It's some ink I got a long time ago. Not something I'm terribly proud of. Thought about getting it removed, but never did." She leaned forward and pulled her sleeve up to reveal Gothic letters made out of black and dark green. "In High School I went through a Metallica phase. We went to a concert and I came home with this. Mom wasn't happy. She didn't let me go to any more concerts that year."

Rick laughed. "Funny. I think you wore long sleeves every time we've gotten together. I never noticed it before."

"Not the image I want to project."

For the next twenty minutes they spoke, trying to kill time, knocking around stories of home, music and the weather. Although Rick wanted to do a bit of work, he also wanted to make sure Emily controlled her nerves. If exchanging stories until the jury came back was necessary, he was fine with it.

Before he could finish telling her about his first dog, his cell phone buzzed. He recognized the number. "It's the court," he whispered as he grabbed it.

"Rick Waterston."

"Hi Rick. It's Nicole, the tipstaff from Judge Markum's chambers. The jury has a question."

The air rushed out of him. Not a verdict yet. He thanked her and told her they would head back over to court immediately.

He looked up at Emily. "The jurors want to ask a question."

"Is that good?"

"We won't know anything until we hear it. We'll head back to court so the judge can read the question and get input from the lawyers about how to answer it."

"My blood pressure just shot up. I wish it was the verdict."

"Me, too, but we must deal with whatever it is they want. No reactions no matter what the question is."

"Gotcha."

They walked by Arnie's office and informed him they had to return to court without an impending verdict. Arnie's disappointed expression mirrored Emily's. They left the office in silence wondering if the question might reveal some aspect of the jury's thinking, but more wanting to hear its final decision.

CHAPTER SIXTY-SIX

THE VIEW from her seat was the same for Emily as it had been the entire trial. The jurors sat impassive to her right staring at the judge who held a slip of paper handed to him by his tipstaff. Emily understood the potential importance of the slip of paper. She offered a small prayer that the question signaled the jury's intent to find in her favor and asking only some ministerial question on how to end their deliberations.

Judge Markum signaled the four attorneys and court reporter to approach so they could confer out of the hearing of everybody else in the courtroom. They passed the piece of paper between them until the judge appeared to read the question into the record.

For the next five minutes, Arnie and Crotec exchanged vigorous argument marked by heavy gesticulation, but with an absence of discernible words.

Emily tapped her foot waiting for the caucus to end, so she could finally hear what the jury wanted to ask.

Markum scribbled notes on his pad. He nodded at the lawyers who stepped back and walked to their respective tables. Rick flashed Emily a grimace before he sat causing her to fidget more.

"The parties and the lawyers are assembled in the courtroom," the judge began. "The jury's been deliberating for over four hours and has a question. The attorneys and I reviewed the question. They offered suggestions for the response I should give. I will now read the question and my answer."

He turned to face the jurors. "Your jury foreperson signed the question and delivered it to my tipstaff. It is well within your rights to ask the Court a question to assist in your deliberations. It's my responsibility to answer your inquiry consistent with the law."

He unfolded the sheet of paper.

"You submitted the following question: 'Does a store have the right to detain a suspected shoplifter with significant force if the shoplifter refuses to submit to the demands of the store personnel to stop and wait for the police?'"

Markum took a breath and turned to the notes on his pad. "This is the court's response: 'Under Pennsylvania law, a merchant may detain a person suspected of shoplifting for a reasonable time and in a reasonable manner if it had a reasonable suspicion the person attempted to shoplift.' If you wish to ask any further questions, you must submit them in writing, and we will reconvene to provide you with an answer. Please resume your deliberations."

The tipstaff returned to the edge of the jury box and directed the jurors out of the courtroom and back to their deliberations.

Rick turned to Emily, her face a bright crimson. "What does that mean?" she wailed.

He shook his head. "Let's go outside, and we can hash it out."

CHAPTER SIXTY-SEVEN

RICK GRABBED Emily's arm and escorted her down the hallway to a secluded alcove. Upon stopping, she smacked his arm away. Tears formed in the corners of her eyes. Her head hung at an odd angle from her neck.

"They hate me. They don't trust me. They believe everything the store is saying."

Like watching her being attacked by a swarm of piranhas, Rick didn't know how to protect her. He put his hands on both of her shoulders and gave her a gentle shake. "You don't know any of that. You don't know why they asked that question or what they are thinking."

He took a deep breath which allowed Emily a chance to collect herself. A wave of desperation swirled in his gut, but he forced himself to maintain a false aura of control to rein in his client. There was nothing they could do now. Whatever the jury was thinking or saying, it was too late to rebut or challenge it.

He guided Emily over to a seat in the hallway. She slumped into it with a petulant smirk covering her face. "I don't care anymore. I said what I needed to say. They can do whatever they want."

He playfully kicked her in the leg causing her to yelp. He said, "I know you care. I know you care deeply. I want you to win almost as much as you do. Don't pretend otherwise. If the jury finds against us, try not to take it personally. I know you will and it will be very painful–but. . . ." Rick couldn't finish his sentence.

A semblance of a smile crossed her face. "I just want this to end. Not knowing sucks."

Rick nodded and let the quiet wash over him. It was late in the day and few voices could be heard as most courtrooms had emptied hours earlier. The mood was in stark contrast to the overwhelming stress which hung over the building during the day when litigants battled.

A light touch on his shoulder caused Rick to bolt upright.

Arnie stood over him with a blank expression on his face. "The jury is back. We have a verdict."

Rick adjusted his tie and Emily popped out her seat. "Let's go hear their decision," she said, leading the group down the hall towards the courtroom.

CHAPTER SIXTY-EIGHT

NOTHING COMPARES to the moments before the jury announces its decision. Rick had been in a courtroom for a few verdicts, with each indelibly etched in his memory.

Even in the most mundane of cases, a verdict will have ramifications for every participant in the trial. A decision in a party's favor provides validation that, simply speaking, the truth alone cannot. Conversely, losing at trial and having a jury denounce one's credibility in public is akin to a stabbing. It hurts when it happens and can leave scars which last a long time.

Lawyers are not immune to the effects of a jury determination. Egos grow proportionally with the size of a favorable verdict, while months of lost sleep often result from a jury finding for the other side. Every lawyer understands that they cannot control the facts of the case or the actions of a wayward witness, but most crave the validation only a jury can give.

Rick pushed every extraneous thought out of his head as the jurors streamed back into the courtroom and took their seats in the jury box without looking anywhere in the direction of the participants. Seated closest to the judge's bench, Juror One held a manila envelope with the verdict inside. The jurors all stared blankly ahead, unwilling to provide any clue as to which side prevailed, trying to keep their decision private for as long as possible.

Once everyone settled in their places, the tipstaff knocked on the wooden door to Markum's chambers who opened it and walked up to his seat. Turning his attention to the attorneys, he asked, "Any matters to be discussed before we hear from the jury?" He smiled.

Yes, let's talk about what you ate for lunch, you ass. Stop trying to be so cute. We all want to get to the verdict.

Rick was in no mood for games. "No, Your Honor," he said with a quick half-stand.

"Defendants have nothing to discuss at this point," Crotec added.

Markum swiveled his chair to face the jury. "Have you reached a verdict?" The court reporter pecked at her keys to transcribe the rendering of the jury's decision.

The first juror rose from her seat, unsure whether she should speak. "We have."

The tipstaff who was standing next to the first juror took the envelope, walked over to the judge and handed it to him.

The stress of still not knowing the result forced Rick to keep his eyes glued to his yellow pad as if looking at the verdict slip would jinx it into a bad result.

Emily leaned forward with her head resting on Arnie's shoulder.

The group of B & D employees and executives sat erect behind their attorneys, not moving any muscles, also transfixed.

The envelope was the nexus of everyone's attention. Markum opened it and removed the three pages of jury interrogatories. The papers held the fates of both sides, but other than the judge, nobody could see the responses. Markum flipped through the pages, but offered no clue of the results by his actions, despite the participants' best attempts to interpret any twitch or pause.

Finally, he turned his attention to the jurors and announced. "Members of the jury, I have reviewed your verdict and I will now read your answers to the questions. After each, I will ask if this is your verdict and will direct you to respond verbally whether it was. Understood?" The jurors nodded in unison.

"Question number one asks, 'Do you find that defendants B & D, Inc., and Morgan Askew were negligent in causing the death of Plaintiff's decedent, Jerry Hawkins?'"

It was difficult for Rick to draw in air. Emily squeezed his shoulder as they both knew that a "no" to this question would bring the trial to a swift and ignominious conclusion and Emily's return home empty-handed. A positive answer wouldn't be the end of the inquiry, but it was a necessary step to recover for what Emily had been forced to endure.

Markum continued. "Your answer to question one is, 'yes.' Is this your response?" Most of the jurors nodded, while a couple answered affirmatively out loud.

Rick's body slumped forward with his breath, and he felt Emily's weight on his back. Arnie grabbed their arms to avoid them toppling over and nodded his head in the direction of the B & D group that appeared like they'd been collectively hit with a sucker punch. Rick straightened up and readied himself for the next question.

"Do you find Jerry Hawkins' actions contributed to his death?" Markum said. "Answer, 'yes.' Is that your answer?"

Most of the jurors bobbed their heads.

Arnie gave an equivocal shake of his head. They knew the jury would be hard-pressed not to find that Jerry bore some responsibility for what happened in the parking lot. Now, the jury had to allocate the responsibility for Jerry's death between the defendants and Jerry with any verdict reduced by the percentage amount of Jerry's culpability. Also, if the jury found Jerry's negligence greater than the defendants', Emily would be precluded from any recovery.

The judge returned to reading the verdict slip. "If you found both plaintiff and defendants causally responsible, you were to allocate the negligence between them. The next question was, 'What percentage negligence do you find is attributable to the conduct of the plaintiff and what percentage to the defendants?'

"You wrote, 'Thirty percent for plaintiff and seventy percent for the defendants.' Is this your verdict?"

The jurors assented, allowing Markum to return to reading their decision.

"The next question is, 'How much in damages do you award plaintiff without identifying the line amounts for each element and providing a lump sum in your verdict?'

"You wrote, 'Five million, one hundred and sixty-six thousand dollars.' Is that your verdict?"

The wail escaping Emily surprised nearly every person in the courtroom. She put her hand over her mouth, but Rick grabbed her in a bear hug.

"They believe you. Congratulations," he said while lifting her off the ground.

Markum didn't wait for the jurors to acknowledge this was their decision before returning his attention to the litigants and their attorneys. "Is there anything from the parties before I mold the verdict?"

Spencer stood. "Defendants request the court poll the jury."

"Members of the jury," Markum said as he turned back to them, "I will now ask each of you individually if this was your decision. When it is your turn, please stand and acknowledge whether you agree with the verdict."

Rick tensed. As long as at least ten of the twelve jurors agreed, they would be done. If less than ten said they approved of the verdict, Markum would send them back out to deliberate more. Rick bowed his head hoping to avoid any unexpected surprises.

Each juror rose when requested. The first three signed off on the verdict and Markum quickly moved on to the next. Juror Four, a tall, angular woman, rose and indicated she did not agree with the verdict. Rick turned to Arnie, "Damn, let's get through this without two more dissenters."

When the judge got through Juror Eleven with all agreeing with the verdict, Rick knew the verdict remained safe. Even though Jury Twelve indicated he disagreed with the verdict, the game was over. Their only worry now was any rulings on appeal.

There was still some more work to do as Markum reminded the courtroom. "With the jury's finding on comparative fault, I must mold the verdict to reflect the relative culpability of the parties." Markum pulled out a calculator. "Given the amount of the verdict and the finding that plaintiff's decedent was thirty percent negligent, I will mold the verdict to $3,616,200.00."

Markum jotted notes on his pad, but nobody moved until he thanked the jurors for their service, reminding them they were necessary to allow the parties to resolve their disputes.

Often parties and the attorneys want to speak with the jurors after the court releases them from their service. The judge let them know this was permissible, "You are now free and can speak with whomever you wish."

The tipstaff handed envelopes out to each member. One juror opened hers and laughed. "With this amount, my husband and I can go get dinner—at McDonald's."

The rest of the jurors chuckled and started to regain their every-day personas which they had hidden under their juror facades since the first day of trial.

As Rick, Arnie, and Emily stood by counsel table hoping to interact with the jurors, Juror Number One, the jury foreperson, approached. She touched Rick on his sleeve and said, "Can we speak in the hallway? It would be helpful."

Without any inkling of her thoughts, Rick nodded. They followed the juror out into the hallway.

CHAPTER SIXTY-NINE

"Sweetie, let me tell you straight," the juror said as she pulled Emily further down the hallway. "You had us right from the start. I saw in your eyes the pain you are feeling." The juror put her arms around Emily and pulled her in close, patting her back.

Emily put her head on the juror's shoulder and let a sob escape. Through her tears, she whispered, "Thank you. You don't know what your words mean to me."

Rick and Arnie shuffled over not intending to interrupt, but also wanting to hear the conversation.

The juror continued whispering to Emily, "I can't imagine being in your shoes. Your beautiful husband murdered and you having to watch the video of it in a courtroom—over and over."

Emily stood back nodding her head. "So horrible. They made me watch him die so many times."

Rick stepped forward. "Can I ask you something about the trial?"

"Of course, Mr. Waterston. I would love to talk about what happened."

"Thanks," Rick looked up. "Let's start with your thoughts about Jerry and what he did."

"Oh, honey," the juror remarked as she grabbed Emily's hand. "That husband of yours certainly had some issues. I don't like stealing, not at all, but so what if Jerry stole some stuff. Big deal. Not for one moment did I think he should have died. Once the store decided to stop him, they had a responsibility to him, but they never trained anyone. This was a disaster waiting to happen."

The woman's words caused Rick to smile inwardly. Nothing's better than hearing a juror regurgitate your arguments.

He asked, "How did the jury deal with the issue of Jerry's comparative fault?"

She grimaced. "We agreed we would find some fault on Jerry's behalf. He started the whole situation–but again, that doesn't mean he should die for it. There were a couple who wanted to find Jerry more than fifty percent responsible, but most of us wouldn't hear it. We compromised a little at the end, but we felt the store bore responsibility for what happened."

"What about their claim Jerry ran and started the fight in the parking lot by throwing the first punch?"

"We didn't like that, to you the truth, but we also thought it was expected he would act like that. For the manager to ask the cart kid to detain him we just thought it was a poor decision, but one that came about because the company never trained their people to deal properly with these situations." The juror thought for a moment and continued. "Emily was a huge factor." She again grabbed Emily's hand. "Most of us loved her. She seemed so sincere and devastated by her situation. It may not have been all of us, but more than enough did."

Emily patted her hand. "Thank you for listening and understanding."

A pained expression crossed the juror's face. "I think I

should leave. One of the jurors who kept arguing with us is coming down the hall and I can't listen to him whine anymore."

Rick thanked the juror and caught sight of Juror Number Twelve, one of the two who dissented from the verdict, lumbering down the hallway towards them. Part of him wasn't sure if he wanted to speak with the hulking man, but he was curious of his reasons for dissenting. At this point, it didn't really matter what he said, the verdict was safe.

Tall, overweight, and dressed in blue jeans and a plaid flannel shirt, below even the reduced standards of dress currently followed by most jurors, the juror made a beeline towards Rick's group. No way could they avoid him now, even if they wanted to. His forced smile attempted to cover a simmering anger boiling not far from the surface.

The conversation started out civilly. "Good afternoon. My name is Tom, and I want to talk about the trial." He peered out under bushy, black eyebrows.

Rick nodded assent, but took a small step in between the beefy man and Emily. "Sure, what do you have to say?"

"I wanted to let you know I don't agree with the verdict. It's wrong."

No longer caring why he objected, Rick attempted to cut the conversation short. "I'm sorry to hear that. It sometimes happens that not everyone agrees."

Tom pushed on. "The other jurors wouldn't listen. They kept talking over me. I had a lot to say." He stopped for a moment, but then kept spewing. "This is wrong. Completely wrong—and I know why."

"Thank you, sir," Rick said, turning away.

"Don't you leave. Let me finish."

Rick halted, sensing this would be the best way to avoid any escalation.

"I never trusted her," Tom said, pointing a finger in Emily's direction. "She's all prim and proper, but I didn't buy it. Jerry was a thief, and he should have stopped when the store people told him to. He has no rights as a criminal. She and her husband were in this together, and she don't deserve anything even if he did die."

Emily stared at the man while gripping Rick's arm. Tears rolled down her cheeks.

What an asshole. This is about to get ugly. "We appreciate your insights," Rick said, turning on his heels and grabbing Emily. "Have a great life."

They sped-walked down the hall towards the elevator.

When they had put enough distance between themselves and Tom, Rick stopped. "Don't let him ruin your moment. It doesn't change anything. You won, and he is a bitter, angry person."

Emily wiped at her eyes. "I know. I just don't know where that comes from. I try not to listen to men like him. Never will."

After a few moments collecting herself, Emily turned to Rick and Arnie. "I'm okay. It's forgotten. You promised me a celebration if we won. Well, let's get to it."

CHAPTER SEVENTY

BILLY BLEVINS SWAGGERED into the office, and announced, "I'm here. Who's wants to talk?"

Rick peered out his office smiling. "My favorite client–or should I say my former favorite client?"

Billy grabbed at his chest. "What? I'm no longer number one?"

Rick sidled over to Billy and placed an arm around his shoulders. "I still love you, man, but you don't generate the biggest fees here anymore. Not by a mile."

"You win one big verdict and then you forget the friends who taught you how to be a lawyer. Just remember, I'm the same guy you'll be passing on your way down." He nudged Rick. "Plus, you told me on the phone last week there would be appeals and nothing is guaranteed until they're done, which could take years."

"That's true, but I haven't had a chance to tell you–I talked to defendants' counsel last week, and we reached a resolution."

"How can that be?" Billy asked, his voice jumping higher and his eyebrows scrunching together.

Rick walked over to the couch and took a seat. "It happens. They agreed to drop their appeal, and we agreed to waive any interest owing, which would be substantial. We shaved the verdict a bit."

"How much?"

"You know I can't tell you. I probably said too much already." He winked at Billy. "It wasn't much of a haircut and the client is very happy to get paid. In fact, after I get rid of you, I'm meeting with defense counsel who's bringing the check over. So, Billy Blevins, you are looking at one unstressed lawyer."

"Congrats man," Billy said. "I'm happy for you, but don't you want to know what's happening with me?"

"Not really, but I'm sure you're going to tell me anyway."

"I'll be quick. You probably won't give me much time anyway because you're now a superstar lawyer. Here's the quick rundown: First, we're opening a new park and I expect you will be at the opening. I'll get you a picture with our new star attraction, a Persian tiger we're importing next week. Second, things are going well with Frank. Really well. We're moving in together. We took the money we both saved from fighting each other and put it into the new park and bought a house together. So, thanks to you guys, I'm not stuck in litigation fighting everyone. My life is picking up."

"Billy, that's awesome. I couldn't be happier for you. It might be a problem for me with this new-found antipathy for suing people, but we'll figure out a way to get you to pay for some legal services." Rick laughed as he led Billy to the front door. "Thanks for stopping by. I'm really glad things are working out for you."

Billy waved. Rick turned back to his office to call Virgil Spencer and get Emily's check. Happy day, even if it meant spending a little time with Spencer who had informed Rick earlier he wanted to deliver it in person.

Twenty minutes later, Spencer appeared at the door, holding a manila envelope.

CHAPTER SEVENTY-ONE

THE CHAIR in the conference room squeaked when Spencer pulled it out. He pushed the envelope across the table to Rick who placed a hand on top.

"Before you open it," Spencer said, "I want to say something."

Rick raised his eyebrows.

"I know we had our differences. I treated your departure from our firm wrong and handled it like a schmuck. What can I say? We thought we were smarter than everyone else. We've learned a lot since then. I'm man enough to admit when I make a mistake. I did with you."

Rick tugged at his sleeve. "You and Crotec acted like asses and I carried a lot of anger with me as a result."

Spencer's lips slid out revealing a half-smile, half-grimace. "You and Arnie tried a great case. You've grown as a lawyer. You took that hick of a client and dressed her up. The jury thought she had suffered so much. It was some great lawyering."

"She had a compelling story to tell. I give her all the credit for standing up to your big company client."

Spencer shook his head. "No, I give you the praise. She couldn't have done it on her own." He paused to scratch his nose. "We thought we had the case won from the beginning. You were on the side of a thief and had to defend what he did. Once we got all of that video of him stealing, we assumed the jury would hate them. For some reason, they didn't. And like I said, you're the reason."

"That's nice of you to say, but. . ."

Spencer interrupted, "We watched you and realized you are much more cut out to be working on our side than on the one you're working now."

Rick turned his head and glanced sideways. "I don't think so. . . ."

"Absolutely," Spencer said waving his hand. "You are big firm material and your performance at trial proved it. We had a partners' meeting last night and I fought for you."

"You fought for me?" Rick eyes narrowed.

"Of course. I brought up the idea of bringing you back. This victory of yours is going to be quite marketable. I think with some assistance from our firm's resources, you could be a big rainmaker. They agreed, and wanted me to offer you a job with the firm."

Rick's eyebrows shot straight up. "You're kidding, right?"

"Nope. This is on the up-and-up."

Rick stood and walked to the window to look out at the parking lot. He turned around and said, "It's nice to hear that your view of me has changed after all you put me through. What about Arnie?"

"This isn't about him. We want you?"

"Seriously, you don't want him, too?"

"Let's talk terms. Here's the deal. . . ."

Spencer continued to talk, but Rick tuned him out. Those three words, *here's the deal,* sending his mind back to being walked out of the firm. The utter humiliation once again causing his stomach to churn. He then pictured the indignities they forced Arnie to suffer. This wasn't about the firm thinking he was a talented lawyer. Spencer and Crotec just wanted another opportunity to control him and make him dance. It didn't matter how much money they offered, he wasn't listening.

Rick held up a hand. "Stop embarrassing yourself. I'm not coming back to your firm, not on any terms you could offer. I thought maybe you and Crotec had changed, gained some maturity, perhaps learned to treat people with respect. You only want me back because we left and improved our positions. This may be a small firm, but this firm just kicked your well-heeled butt, pretty bad."

Spencer started to talk, but Rick wouldn't let him. "Let's end it here." He waved the envelop Spencer had brought. This will help this firm get additional clients and, hopefully, we'll get more chances to meet in court. I was thinking I might give a couple of lawyers in your firm a call, and see if I can poach anyone and convince them to move over here."

Rick walked over to the door to the conference room and opened it. "Virgil, it's been a real pleasure taking your client's money. Maybe next time you'll convince them to make a real offer before going to trial."

Spencer slid by Rick, not saying a word. He headed to the front door.

CHAPTER SEVENTY-TWO

RICK POKED his head into Arnie's office. "Billy Blevins just stopped by. He misses you, and wanted to say 'hi.'"

Arnie chuckled. "I miss that dude."

"After he left, guess what I got?"

Arnie shook his head and shrugged his shoulders.

"We got paid for Emily's case," Rick said waving the check in the air. "Spencer came here to drop it off personally."

"I thought I detected the scent of Lucifer."

"Funny. He actually wore just a hint of cologne and it smelled fine."

"How did it go? Hopefully, you got the check from him and sent him on his way."

Rick shook his head. "No, it was a little more involved. He had a lot to say about the trial and about when we worked at the firm."

The quizzical expression returned to Arnie's face. "What the hell did he say?"

"He was rather complimentary–of both of us. He apologized

for how he and Crotec handled our firings. Then, he told me how well we tried the case. All done without a hint of disdain or condescension. I know it's hard to believe, but he acted like a human."

Arnie shook his head. "I'm having trouble believing this. In some ways, it's easier looking at them in black and white. So until I get direct evidence to the contrary, I will still continue to think of them as the spawn of the devil."

"It's your prerogative to do whatever you want. We probably won't be seeing them for a while." Rick pulled out a chair and sat. "There's something else I wanted to talk about."

Arnie fiddled with a pen waiting.

"You came here at a rough time," Rick said. "The future didn't look so bright. You took a chance and I appreciate it."

"I didn't have a lot of choices. I needed you at least as much as you needed me."

"Don't sell yourself short. You're a talented lawyer. Luckily, we had Emily's case which left us with a ton of work to do. You stepped up and handled more than your share. I wanted to let you know, I appreciated it."

Arnie smiled. "Your appreciation is noted. I'll still be coming in to work on Monday."

"I think you're missing the point. I wanted to demonstrate that what I said when you came here was true. I hired you as a partner and I will treat you as one." Rick stepped forward and handed Arnie a white envelope.

"What's this?"

"Just open it."

Arnie tore at the edges of the envelope and pulled out a check.

Rick said, with a smile, "It's your share of the firm's cut of Emily's verdict. I hope it's sufficient."

Arnie's eyes widened as he took in the figure written on the check. "You've got to be kidding. I'm on salary. This is ridiculous."

"We're partners and you earned it. Enjoy."

Arnie kissed the check and held it up to the light. "This will be put to good use."

Rick left Arnie staring at his check and laughing. He returned to his desk and poked around until he found what hc needed for his last two stops. He skipped down the front steps of his building and considered doing a Magnum slide across the hood of the car. Avoiding any unnecessary embarrassment, he walked around the front, opened the door and settled into the front seat.

CHAPTER SEVENTY-THREE

THE SUN SAT above the horizon, spreading color on the tips of the clouds hovering over the town. The crisp air signaled fall's impending arrival. The music pulsated on the car radio with a strong beat while Rick tapped out the rhythm on the steering wheel. He sang with gusto, despite knowing fewer than half the lyrics. The final guitar riff of the second song faded as he pulled onto Emily's block, not knowing if anyone outside could actually hear the pulsing from his speakers.

He'd never been on this street before. The recognition he and Emily spoke so often in his office, yet never interacted at her residence, surprised him. He eased the car to the curb in front of the house matching the address. Sprawling, leafy weeds sprouted from the splits in the pavement. He got out and walked towards her front door. A small, warped hibachi grill sat against the water stained siding surrounded by a pile of cigarette butts.

The wooden screen door clanged against the frame as he knocked twice.

"We're out back," Emily's voice called out from behind the chipped, white privacy fence. "Come on in."

Rick's heart raced with excitement to give Emily her portion of the settlement.

Representing plaintiffs often meant losing cases, or at best, meager settlements where the client scoffed at the amount remaining after costs and Rick's cut. "'That's all I get?" was a common refrain his clients chirped when they finally understood they didn't get every last dollar of a settlement. Today, Rick was about to hand Emily just north of two million dollars. He had no concern she would offer any objection.

Rounding the corner to the backyard, Rick spied Emily on a beach chair, beer in hand, with empties resting in cardboard six packs at her side. To her right, a younger, muscular man lay on a towel collecting rays while glistening in oil, surrounded by his own set of empties.

Rick waved the envelope holding her check as he approached, causing Emily to run to him and consume him in a hug. She grabbed the envelope and ripped it open. "Ewww, this is so exciting,"

Rick spied Emily's backyard garb–tank top and shorts that barely covered her ass. A far cry from the demure outfits she wore to his office and in court. The most obvious difference, he noticed, was the multi-colored artwork adorning both arms running from her wrists to her shoulders and disappearing under her top. Snakes, lightning bolts, and a variety of devils were the first images Rick saw, but there was so much density to the artwork, such variation in color, Rick couldn't take it all in unless he grabbed her arm and examined each intricate design that coalesced into a jolting canvas on her skin.

Rick had no issues with body work having hung out with enough friends and family to know that tats were a form of personal expression. Emily, however, clearly did not want him, or anyone in the courtroom, to see her body art and made a significant effort to cover them during the trial.

"You going to introduce me to your lawyer?" the muscle man said, rolling towards Emily and then grabbing another beer.

"Sure, baby," Emily tapped his arm and lowered the sunglasses perched on her head.

"Rick, this is Trey. Trey, this is my lawyer Rick."

Rick leaned over to shake hands, overtaken by the sheer force Trey could muster. "Nice to meet you. Thanks for taking care of my little woman."

Your little woman? Who the hell are you? Rick's thoughts jumbled in his head, thrown off by the presence of Trey. "You also," Rick said under his breath and directed his attention back to Emily. He tried to say something, but couldn't convey anything coherent.

Emily detected his hesitation and pointed to the kitchen door. "Let me put the check inside. Why don't you come in? I'll get you something to drink."

Rick dutifully followed her into the house.

Inside, she motioned to a chair and gave him a glass of water once he sat. She put the check up to the light. "This is awesome. This is a shit-load of money."

"It is," Rick mumbled, but his mind still focused on the oily mass of muscle out back. "Who the hell is Trey?"

Emily smiled and ran her fingers through her hair. "Trey and I have been seeing each other."

"I gathered. How come I never heard of him?"

"I didn't think you needed to know."

"I didn't need to know?" Rick stammered. "I had to know every detail of your life, so I could present it to the jury."

Emily shook her head. "No, I didn't think it was relevant."

Rick stood and started pacing the kitchen. "How long have you been seeing him?"

"For a while."

"How long?" Rick said, nearly shouting.

Emily paused. "You don't want to know."

"Tell me."

Emily put a hand on Rick's arm. "Rick, I'm happy to tell you, but I just want to confirm that you are still my attorney."

"Of course I am. It's why I'm here."

"Like you told me at our first meeting, our conversations are only between us, 'privileged' was the term you used. You can't tell anyone what we talk about, can you?"

"That's the nature of our relationship." His head spun, so he sat back in the chair.

"Honey, I'm about to tell you some things because you probably deserve to know them. You won't like them. I don't think I did anything wrong, but you should hear them."

Emily took the check from the table and put it in a drawer near the window.

She turned back to Rick. "To answer your question, Trey and I've been seeing each for a long time–since before Jerry died."

"Shit," he said, looking down at the table.

"Jerry wasn't a bad guy, but we just weren't happy together. He was relatively simple and it didn't appear like he was going places. We argued a lot. Not like most couples, but intense, nasty fights. I usually started them because the dude never did anything. He didn't work. He didn't want to work. He was a lazy ass to the core."

Rick shook his head. "So when did Trey come into the picture?"

"Probably about a year before Jerry died. Sex with Jerry was rather routine. Trey taught me there's more than one way to skin an onion." She took a swig of beer. "Once you drink the fine wine, you don't go back to tap water."

"So I heard," he said, without intending for Emily to hear.

"Anyway, Trey was a distraction before Jerry died. Since then, well, we're much closer."

Emily waved out the window at Trey. "This has nothing to do with Trey. Jerry and I had little going on, and he wouldn't listen to what I wanted him to do."

"What do you mean?"

"I wanted him to get a job. Build a career. That's what he promised me when we first met. But he never would. He just wanted to hang around the house. So we changed our plans."

"How so?"

"Jerry found out he possessed one exceptional skill. He had a talent for stealing. He liked doing it and looked forward to it. Finally, we found some way to get him out of the house, which helped Trey and me find a little more time together. Anyway, he'd be gone for a couple of hours and when he came back he usually had a bunch of food to stock the refrigerator or some stuff for our closets. If you look around the house, much of what you see are things he got for us."

"Without paying for them?"

"Yes, Rick, without paying for them."

"And you knew about him doing it?"

"I did. I was kind of proud of him. It made him happy to finally contribute to the household."

Emily's revelations proved difficult for Rick to handle. Her small kitchen felt like it was about to collapse on him. He placed his hand on his head. "This is nothing like what you told the jury."

"I felt like I was in the ballpark of the truth. He promised he would always take care of me. What I said to the jury was my way of helping him keep his word."

"He was never going to have any career, was he? This whole picture of marital bliss, was it just an act?"

Emily walked over to Rick, who turned his back on her. "We talked about telling the truth so many times. You told me that truth is graded on a curve. You helped me hone my story so it was perfect for the jury. They ate it up and I thank you for helping me create the story of our lives together. It's so much better than the way it was."

During those many hours alone in the conference room practicing, Rick wanted to believe her and knew the better her story sounded, the more likely it would resonate with the jury and the more likely she would get a bigger award. Nothing had proven more accurate. She manipulated him the whole time, so he would help her and believe in her.

He thought for a moment before asking, "Did you have anything to do with him dying?"

"No, of course not. I could never do that." She contemplated what to say. "I was quite sad after he died. I never like watching some person or animal die, but then I realized how unfair it all was. Jerry didn't deserve to die and I certainly didn't deserve to lose any possibility of a future. So after a couple of days, I did some research and I found you. You were perfect. Young, good-looking, trying to build up your practice. I knew you would give my case the attention it deserved."

"Wow, Emily. You're a fine actress." Rick started a slow, rhythmic clap.

Emily's face reddened. "Don't be an ass. You made out quite well yourself. Got a huge check. Probably gonna get lots of new clients after marketing your victory over the bad corporation. C'mon, Rick, you knew I was too good to be true."

He examined her up and down like it was the first time he had ever seen her. The nagging feeling she knew and understood him better than he did gnawed at him. Inside, he felt like he was bleeding. "Congratulations, Emily. I hope you and Trey enjoy a great life together."

The screen door slammed behind him, and he sucked in a huge gulp of air. He wiped his hands on his pants, and jumped in his car. He was glad he planned to make one last stop.

CHAPTER SEVENTY-FOUR

RICK'S HEAD still spun as he again got out of his car. He touched the final envelope in his pocket, which offered him a mild amount of reassurance as he walked up the pathway.

Emily's revelations stung. He wanted to go home and pull the covers over his head. Did it matter if she'd concocted her version of her life out of thin air? To him, absolutely. He understood that truth was relative, but complete deception shouldn't ever be rewarded–and he had been a participant in her lies. Perhaps unknowingly, but at this point even he couldn't be sure how unwilling he'd been.

He would likely not deal with Emily Hawkins again, and she was now free to spend her new-found wealth in any manner she chose. The issues for him would be whether he could rationalize his role in the deceit and how he would reconstruct his practice going forward. One concept already crystalized in his head–in the future he would better vet his clients and not let the potential of a significant payoff dazzle him.

He rapped on the door and moments later his ex opened it displaying a blank expression.

"Hey, Rick, you know this isn't your weekend with Sam."

He nodded. "I know. I wanted to talk."

Her eyebrows scrunched together. "I thought something might be wrong. You look like you just got hit by a train."

A sardonic smile etched across Rick's face. "In some ways that's accurate, but it's not why I'm here. I need to set the record straight."

"What record is that?" Molly's face eased into an expression of compassion and concern. "You don't need to say anything. I assume it's water under the bridge."

"No. I got a lot to say and there's no better time than now." Rick pointed at the porch swing. Molly acquiesced. They sat on it with the springs offering a slight squeak. Two birds flew onto a branch in a nearby tree rustling some leaves and then offered the neighborhood a song. Rick and Molly sat silently, both staring straight ahead.

A minute passed without either saying anything, until Molly offered, "What's on your mind, Rick?

Rick sighed. "I want to apologize and make due on my promises." When he didn't get any pushback, he said, "I don't need to rehash our breakup, but I want to make sure you realize I accept responsibility for the mistakes I made. I doubt if I accepted blame sooner we would still be married, but I want you to understand it kills me knowing how poorly I performed while we were together.

Rick put a hand on Molly's arm. "I hope I expressed this before, but why I'm here has more to do with the future than our past. We share a daughter who will bind us together forever. I thought because we broke up, I broke up with Sam as well. I didn't understand that whatever happened to us is separate from my relationship with her. I understand better now."

He stopped to take a breath and Molly waited without injecting any of her thoughts. "I realize," he continued, "I messed up with Sam. She needed me. You needed me to be there for her and I haven't been there. I'm consumed with guilt."

"You shouldn't beat yourself up," Molly interrupted.

Rick scoffed. "Yes, I should. I've said it before. I need to be around her more and I will. Here's the thing I think I'm most embarrassed about—I owe you money for her care. I mean, I'm in violation of a court order. I shouldn't need a judge to tell me to take care of my daughter and I shouldn't have to rely upon your positive nature to avoid getting in trouble for failing to keep up with my obligations."

Molly nodded.

"So, I want to make it right." Rick reached for his last envelope and handed it over.

Molly ripped it open and gasped when she read the check.

"You got to be kidding," she exclaimed. This is a lot more than you owe. Six hundred and thirty-two thousand dollars. C'mon, Rick, even with a lot of interest, this would cover what you owe past the time Sammie's grandchildren got married. You're joking, right?

"No, Moll. It's yours. I want you and Sam to use it. I want her to get everything she ever wanted and I want you never to worry about her health or welfare."

"This is too much. Way too much. Isn't this everything you got from your case?"

"It's the exact right amount. I don't want it for me. It's not quite my entire fee. I saved two hundred dollars for me. I'm going to eat an enormous steak dinner tonight thanks to Emily Hawkins."

Molly examined the check. "This is really going to help."

"I hope so. I know you never told Sam I wasn't keeping up my end of the deal. Please don't tell her about this either."

"I won't."

The birds continued to warble. "I want to spend more time with her. I hope that'll be okay."

"Absolutely, it would be a positive for all of us."

"Wonderful. I'll call you. Hopefully, I can take her out this week. Right now, I'm going to stuff myself with a juicy fillet."

Rick stood and walked to his car. Molly called out, "Thanks Rick. You're not such a bad guy."

He acted like he didn't hear the compliment and jumped into his car. He sped away, revving the engine as he headed down the road.

If you enjoyed this book, please consider leaving a review on Goodreads and Amazon.

ABOUT THE AUTHOR

James Rosenberg is a 3rd generation trial attorney with plenty of stories to tell. Inspired not only by the courtroom stories his father and grandfather used to tell him when he was a child, but also by the wild adventures he's encountered through his own experience as a lawyer. James is fascinated by the intricate, interpersonal dynamics of every trial he's endured. Whether it's the raw emotion on display in court, the tension in the air that builds until someone wins, or the impact that a case's decision has on the parties involved, James is always paying attention and keeping tabs on what's happening.

A native of Pittsburgh and a graduate of Taylor Allderdice High School and the University of Pittsburgh School of Law, James has been a trial attorney in Pittsburgh for almost 30 years. He started writing legal thrillers as a stress reducer and finds this creative outlet to be a fun and meaningful diversion from his day job.

When he's not trying cases, he's either dreaming up his next book idea, spending time with his wife and three kids, or both.

Check out his website: www.JamesRosenbergAuthor.com or follow him on social media:

ALSO BY JAMES ROSENBERG

Legal Reserves

The Jersey: A Story of Loss and Redemption

Made in the USA
Middletown, DE
29 December 2023

46965912R00205